T0305035

City Distribution and Urban Freight Transport

NECTAR SERIES ON TRANSPORTATION AND COMMUNICATIONS NETWORKS RESEARCH

Series Editor: Aura Reggiani, *Professor of Economic Policy, University of Bologna, Italy*

NECTAR (Network on European Communications and Transport Activities Research) is an international scientific, interdisciplinary association with a network culture. Its primary objective is to foster research collaboration and the exchange of information between experts in the fields of transport, communication and mobility.

NECTAR members study the behaviour of individuals, groups and governments within a spatial framework. They bring a wide variety of perspectives to analyse the challenges facing transport and communication, and the impact these challenges have on society at all levels of spatial aggregation.

This series acts as a companion to, and an expansion of, activities of NECTAR. The volumes in the series are broad in their scope with the intention of disseminating some of the work of the association. The contributions come from all parts of the world and the range of topics covered is extensive, reflecting the breadth and continuously changing nature of issues that confront researchers and practitioners involved in spatial and transport analysis.

Titles in the series include:

Transportation and Economic Development Challenges
Edited by Kenneth Button and Aura Reggiani

City Distribution and Urban Freight Transport
Multiple Perspectives
Edited by Cathy Macharis and Sandra Melo

City Distribution and Urban Freight Transport

Multiple Perspectives

Edited by

Cathy Macharis

Vrije Universiteit Brussel-Research group MOBI, dep. MOSI-Transport and Logistics, Belgium

Sandra Melo

Faculdade de Engenharia de Universidade do Porto (FEUP) and the Institute of Mechanical Engineering (IDMEC) – Instituto Superior Técnico de Lisboa, Portugal

NECTAR SERIES ON TRANSPORTATION AND COMMUNICATIONS NETWORKS RESEARCH

Edward Elgar
Cheltenham, UK • Northampton, MA, USA

Published by
Edward Elgar Publishing Limited
The Lypiatts
15 Lansdown Road
Cheltenham
Glos GL50 2JA
UK

Edward Elgar Publishing, Inc.
William Pratt House
9 Dewey Court
Northampton
Massachusetts 01060
USA

A catalogue record for this book
is available from the British Library

Library of Congress Control Number: 2011925763

ISBN 978 0 85793 274 7

Typeset by Servis Filmsetting Ltd, Stockport, Cheshire
Printed and bound by MPG Books Group, UK

Contents

Contributors

Antonio Comi is Assistant Professor of Transport and Environment at 'Tor Vergata' University of Rome. His research activity is mainly focused on developing and applying models and methods for the analysis and design of passenger and freight transport systems at the urban and extra-urban scale.

Álvaro Costa is Professor of Transport at FEUP (Faculdade de Engenharia da Universidade do Porto), Coordinator of the Transport Planning and Logistics Group at the Research Centre on Territory, Transports and Environment, FEUP and CEO of TRENMO (Transportes, Engharia e Modelação). He holds a Ph.D. in Transport Economics, and has broad experience as project manager on R&D projects on city logistics, transport networks, urban mobility and transport organization and management.

Laetitia Dablanc is a senior researcher at the French Institute of Science and Technology for Transport, Development and Networks (IFSTTAR) in the research unit SPLOTT (Productive Systems, Logistics, Transport Organization, Work). Her areas of research are freight transport, freight and environment, sustainable transport, urban logistics, rail freight, and freight transport policies. She is a member of the steering committee of the World Conference on Transport Research and a member of the Urban Freight Committee of the Transportation Research Board (USA).

Laetitia was a visiting scholar at the Georgia Institute of Technology during academic year 2010–11.

Wanda Debauche As a transport economist, Wanda worked for several years in a consultant agency specialized in this field. After a spell at the management of the National Railway Company of Belgium (SNCB) as an adviser at the office of one of the administrators/directors, she is now head of the Mobility Division of the Belgian Road Research Centre (BRRC) and also a member of the Executive Committee. Her main professional occupations within BRRC are research, training and expertise in the field of mobility, as well as team management. She is a member of several national and international working groups.

Valerio Gatta is a lecturer in Advanced Marketing at the Department of Statistics, University of Rome 'La Sapienza'. He obtained a Ph.D. in Economic Statistics and an M.Sc. in Econometrics and Management Science at Erasmus University of Rotterdam. His research interests include discrete choice modelling of airport choice and quality in local public transport.

Roel Gevaers obtained his Master's degree as a transport economist at the Faculty of Applied Economics (University of Antwerp) in 2007. Since July of that year he has been working as a scientific Ph.D. student at the Department of Transport and Regional Economics (Faculty of Applied Economics, University of Antwerp). His research focuses on innovations in last-mile, reverse, waste and green logistics.

Paul Hebes is a geographer and has been studying commercial transport since 2009. As a doctoral candidate at the German Aerospace Center, Institute of Transport Research, Berlin, he studies city logistics. His special concern is electro-mobility, and how it is implemented in commercial urban transport.

Cathy Macharis is a professor at the Vrije Universiteit Brussel. She teaches courses in operations and logistics management, as well as in transport and sustainable mobility. Her research group MOSI – Transport and Logistics focuses on establishing links between advanced operations research methodologies and impact assessment. She has been involved in several national and European research projects dealing with topics such as the location of intermodal terminals, assessment of policy measures in the field of logistics and sustainable mobility.

Jochen Maes obtained his Master's degree as a transport economist at the Faculty of Applied Economics (University of Antwerp, Belgium) in 2008. Since August 2008 he has been working as a scientific Ph.D. student at the Policy Research Centre on Commodity Flows (Steunpunt Goederenstromen) of the Department of Transport and Regional Economics (Faculty of Applied Economics, University of Antwerp). His research focuses on solutions for improved logistics capacity utilization on two levels: a micro and a macro level. The micro-level scale concerns the search for innovative city distribution techniques. The macro level consists of bundling logistics flows in order to set up smart complex logistics concepts. His main focus here is on supply chains using rail transport.

Edoardo Marcucci is Associate Professor of Applied Economics at the 'Roma Tre' University of Rome, as well as Director of CREI (Centre for Research on Institutional Economics) and General Secretary of SIET

(Italian Society of Transport Economists). His research focuses on modelling of travelling, freight agent and household behaviour, by means of discrete-choice methods.

Sandra Melo is Associate Professor at Instituto Superior de Engenharia do Porto (ISEP), Post-Doc Researcher at Instituto Superior Tecnico in Lisbon and Senior Researcher of the Transport Planning and Logistics Group at the Research Centre on Territory Transports and Environment, FEUP. She holds a Ph.D. in City Distribution, and has broad experience of R&D projects and consultancy on city logistics, urban mobility and micro simulation.

Julius Menge has been working on the topic of commercial transport since 2004 (from 2004 to 2009 in research). He became a member of Berlin's Senate Department for Urban Development in 2010 and is now responsible for all transport-planning-related aspects of commercial transport in Berlin.

Agostino Nuzzolo is Full Professor of Transportation Planning at the Faculty of Engineering of 'Tor Vergata' University of Rome. He is currently the president of the Italian Academic Society of Transport (SIDT). His research involves the theory of transportation systems and its application in transportation analysis, modelling and planning.

Marco Percoco is Assistant Professor of Urban and Regional Economics at Bocconi University in Milan. He teaches, among other courses, policy evaluation and macroeconomics. His research interests include path dependence of local development, local development policy evaluation and local political economics. He is also affiliated to CERTeT (Center for Research on Regional Economics Transport and Tourism).

H.J. (Hans) Quak has been working as a logistics adviser at TNO Mobility (since 2007) and as Assistant Professor at the Delft University of Technology (in the Transport Policy and Logistics Organization section). He focuses on urban freight transport, collaboration and sustainability in logistics. Hans successfully defended his Ph.D. thesis 'Sustainability of urban freight transport' in March 2008 at the Rotterdam School of Management, Erasmus University.

Amanda Stathopoulos is a Ph.D. student at Trieste University. Her research activity centres on survey methodologies and statistical modelling of behaviour in passenger and freight transport with specific reference to information processing and individual versus joint decision-making.

Carlo Vaghi is a project manager and researcher in the field of applied economics for Gruppo CLAS and CERTeT–Bocconi University in Milan (Italy). He is Adjunct Professor in the Master Course 'MEMIT' (Economics and Management of Transport, Logistics and Infrastructure) at Bocconi University in Milan. Urban logistics is one of his main specialization topics within the broader field of transport economics.

Eva Valeri is a Ph.D. student at Trieste University. Her thesis deals with intra- and inter-mode choice in the Rome–Milan route and her research interest involve competition strategies of airports/airlines and analysis of freight agent behaviour in a multi-agent setting.

Eddy Van de Voorde is Full Professor at the University of Antwerp, Faculty of Applied Economics. His interests are in maritime economics, port economics, air transport and logistics. He is also a professor at the University of Ghent and at the Technical University of Delft, and he is visiting professor at different foreign universities, such as Lisbon, Bari, London and MIT (Cambridge, Boston). In Genoa in 2005, he was awarded a prestigious international prize, the Premio Internationale delle Communicazioni 'Cristoforo Colombo', for his scientific research in the field of maritime economics.

Thierry Vanelslander graduated as a doctor in Applied Economics at the University of Antwerp in 2005. He is currently holder of the BNP Paribas Fortis chair on transport, logistics and ports. Before that, he was Scientific Director of the Flemish Research Centre on Commodity Flows, hosted by the University of Antwerp. His Ph.D. dealt with cooperation and competition in sea-port container handling.

Ellen Van Hoeck is a research associate in the research group MOSI – Transport and Logistics (Vrije Universiteit Brussel) led by Prof. Dr Cathy Macharis. Her Ph.D. work focuses on city distribution.

Tom van Lier is a research associate in the research group MOSI – Transport and Logistics (Vrije Universiteit Brussel) led by Prof. Dr Cathy Macharis. His Ph.D. work focuses on sustainable logistics and calculations of external costs of transport. He is currently also a teaching assistant for courses in sustainable logistics and mobility, operations research and operations management.

Sara Verlinde is a research assistant at the Geography Department of Ghent University. She holds a Master of Engineering degree in Architecture and a Master of Complementary Studies in Business Economics. She is doing Ph.D. research on possible solutions for urban freight distribution problems in Belgian cities.

Frank Witlox holds a Ph.D. in Urban Planning (Eindhoven University of Technology), a Master's degree in Applied Economics and a Master's degree in Maritime Sciences (both University of Antwerp). Currently, he is Professor of Economic Geography at the Department of Geography of Ghent University. He is also a visiting professor at ITMMA (Institute of Transport and Maritime Management Antwerp), where he teaches warehouse and hinterland distribution management, and an associate director of GaWC (Globalization and World Cities, Loughborough University). Since 2010 he has been Director of the Doctoral School of Natural Sciences (UGent). His research focuses on transport economics and geography, economic geography, spatial modelling techniques, (city) logistics, and world cities and globalization.

Introduction – city distribution: challenges for cities and researchers

Cathy Macharis and Sandra Melo

BACKGROUND AND RATIONALE OF THE STUDY

Urban goods distribution (UGD) plays an important role in the sustainable development of cities. It helps to support urban lifestyles, to serve and retain industrial and trading activities, and contributes to the competitiveness of industry in the region concerned (Anderson et al., 2005). Despite the relevant role of this activity, goods distribution also conflicts with other urban functions and thus generates negative (economic, environmental and social) impacts on the economic power, accessibility, quality of life and attractiveness of urban areas. The most common examples of such impacts at the three dimensions of sustainability are: air pollution (environmental sustainability); fatalities, noise disturbance, local traffic safety (social sustainability); and journey unreliability and delivery delays (economic sustainability). Furthermore, goods traffic reduces the accessibility of passenger transport in urban areas, and the efficiency of the UGD process itself can be affected by congestion, in this way also affecting mobility in the area. To give some quantitative examples, freight traffic operated by heavy goods vehicles (HGVs) contributes to approximately 30 per cent of transport-related energy consumption, which accounts for about 20 per cent of all energy consumption in advanced economies (OECD, 2003) and goods movements in urban areas represent between 20 and 30 per cent of vehicle-kilometres (Dablanc, 2007), so there is no doubt that dealing with logistics and freight distribution is imperative.

Despite the critical significance of logistics and freight distribution, neither urban studies nor transport research has paid any particular attention to this subject until recently. Spatial studies still lack a full understanding of logistics organization and freight distribution, which particularly applies to the role that cities and urban development play in this respect (Hesse and Rodrigue, 2004). In turn, the relationships between logistics and spatial or urban development are usually neglected by industry stakeholders.

1

In such a context, and even though they were aware of the negative side of UGD, to some extent cities tried to live with those problems. Each city has tried to find and implement its own solution, resulting in initiatives that were usually less than optimal from a societal, environmental or economic point of view. However, society is now becoming more demanding than it was in the past, and cities are facing a difficult challenge that must be met without further delay. Cities need to maintain and promote their sustainability, mobility and quality of life, while ensuring that UGD systems efficiently serve their needs. To meet this challenge, cities mainly have to face the difficult task of promoting UGD systems that are environmentally friendly and at the same time efficient enough to satisfy both society and distribution companies. Second, cities need to overcome the lack of awareness and knowledge about UGD among governments and city planners that results in policy-making mainly from the passenger transport perspective, without adequate consideration of the actors involved in goods movement and its complex characteristics (Melo, 2010).

Various measures and initiatives have been aimed at improving goods distribution performance and reducing the environmental and socio-economic negative effects of urban freight transport. These include zero-emission zones, restrictions on vehicle dimensions and design, time windows for deliveries, consolidation strategies, use of city distribution centres, use of electric cars, use of freight trams, mobility management and night distribution. Results and experiences have, however, shown that unintended side-effects might occur when implementing many of these actions. As an example, investments in urban freight consolidation centres have certainly been a failure in many cities (Zunder and Ibanez, 2004; Marcucci and Danielis, 2008). This is partly due to the fact that not all stakeholders were taken into account when pre-assessing the actions and due to difficulties in cooperating with such different perspectives. Moreover, there is a lack of evaluation and systematic assessment of the effects of different measures, which may lead to the promotion and implementation of solutions unsuitable to the local context. In urban distribution several actors are involved: the receivers of the goods; the transport companies; sometimes a city distribution centre manager; the citizens and the government. Failing to take the aims of these different stakeholders into account leads to problems in the implementation phase. A measure might seem a good action from the city council perspective, but if the receivers or the logistic service providers do not support it (or if the measure does not reflect their interests), it will be very difficult to implement it. It is therefore necessary to design new measures that overcome the shortcomings of previously developed measures and to take the aims of the stakeholders explicitly into account.

Research into freight transport and distribution presented throughout this book provides information about the changes and consequences imposed by the integration of stakeholder perceptions of policy measures and allows us to identify issues that should be studied further: (a) it presents initiatives that in specific contexts were considered 'best practices' in terms of their contribution to an increasing sustainability and quality of life; (b) it analyses the impacts on society and on several types of stakeholders along the logistics chain by adopting methodologies that reflect their interests; and (c) it gives recommendations on the inclusion of stakeholder perspectives and expectations on the simulated scenarios, providing a transparent and objective support for decision-making.

STRUCTURE AND OUTLINE OF THE BOOK

The starting point of the book is an overview of the main fields of research and the related questions that have been investigated. The book brings together knowledge of the problem situation and its different possible solutions (Part I), looks at possible methodologies to tackle its multi-dimensional aspects (Part II) and examines several cases in different European cities (Part III).

The first part starts with a chapter by Laetitia Dablanc that discusses recent advances in urban freight research, as well as the diversity of urban freight activities in different world regions. As a result, it identifies urban freight transport issues that are shared by cities in both the developed and developing world and provides recommendations for cities seeking to promote a more efficient and environmentally friendly freight system. The underlying principle of those recommendations is that freight transport must serve the local economy and the environment. The author argues convincingly that although it is not easy to create an urban freight system that benefits the urban economy and the environment, there are possibilities for progress at low cost and with great benefits.

H.J. Quak enumerates no less than 106 measures that can be used in urban freight transport. He distinguishes three main solution directions to be considered and geared to one another in order to improve sustainability of city distribution: logistical solutions; policy solutions; and technological solutions. His chapter discusses the evaluation of these initiatives structured as 12 different types: road pricing; licensing and regulation; parking and unloading; carrier cooperation; vehicle routing improvement; technological vehicle innovation; consolidation centres; underground logistics systems; road infrastructure development; standardization of load units; transport action; and intermodal transport. The author emphasizes the existence of a limited interaction between the different actors, local authorities and carriers that prevents the stakeholders from obtaining insights into each other's problems and thus getting a complete picture of the different urban freight transport issues. To develop more sustainable urban freight transport, the author suggests increased interaction between different stakeholders and their actions.

Roel Gevaers, Eddy Van de Voorde and Thierry Vanelslander tackle the problem of the last mile – the direct-to-consumer deliveries mostly created by e-commerce activities. Two main problems create a cost-ineffective operation: the not-at-home problem and a lack of critical mass. A last-mile typology is put forward based on the value of the goods shipped. Several factors play a role in the cost-effectiveness of last-mile delivery: consumer service level (the larger the time window, the better the routes can be optimized); security and delivery type (whether a signature is necessary or not); the geographical region and market penetration or density (the more dense, the more efficiently routes can be combined); the vehicle fleet and technology (e.g. use of electric vehicles); and the environment. This last factor is mostly in contradiction with the others as consumers are not willing to pay more or wait longer for their delivery, especially not in the case of a low-value product.

In terms of methodology, the challenge for researchers lies in finding ways to assess the manifold effects and incorporating the points of view of the different stakeholders. To overcome that challenge, three different approaches are presented in Part II of the book.

Amanda Stathopoulos and her co-authors examine the problem structure as identified by three main stakeholder types (freight carriers, local policy-makers and retailers) in the discussion surrounding the hypothetical introduction of new policy measures to improve the current scheme of managing freight distribution in Rome's Limited Traffic Zone (LTZ). The identification of the points of consensus and discord from the perspective of three main types of stakeholder is achieved through a number of in-depth stated-preference interviews in the Roman city logistics sector. The main point of this chapter is that, to be able to define a comprehensive framework for planning and developing efficient freight distribution systems in urban areas, a broad spectrum of actors needs to be involved, ranging from government policy-makers, transport operators, freight forwarders, retailers and residents.

Cathy Macharis and her co-authors propose a multi-actor multi-criteria analysis (MAMCA) to incorporate the points of view of the different stakeholders. The MAMCA makes it possible to compare different options (in this case different options for night distribution) in light of what the stakeholders find important. For city distribution, these actors are the receivers, the transport sector, society as a whole and the employees. The evaluation of the different options for night distribution shows to what extent the aims and objectives are attained for each of these stakeholders. This information is crucial in defining possible implementation paths for innovative city distribution concepts.

Sandra Melo and Álvaro Costa suggest the use of quantitative tools such as the definition of a set of indicators to predict stakeholders' opinions and concerns about (operational) mobility and sustainability. The main idea (as also argued by Hans Quak in Chapter 2) is that the more each partner knows about the other's expectations, the easier it will be to achieve win–win solutions. The defined set aims not only to be an instrument of comparative evaluation and evolution, but also an accessory tool to be used by assessment tools such as simulation, surveys or empirical-data collections. With the support of a case study carried out in Porto (Portugal) and a survey to scrutinize the suggested set, the chapter presents a methodology that may serve as a framework for the assessment of the performance of goods distribution initiatives, as well as for the analysis and comparison of policy scenarios/strategies to mitigate negative impacts that originate from goods transport and distribution activities.

A GUIDED TOUR THROUGH THE CASES

As stated above, several actors are involved in city distribution and a good understanding of what the drivers are for these stakeholders determines what innovative concepts are implemented. The cases presented in the book, coming from different geographical origins and looking at different concepts, were selected to show different angles from which city distribution can be seen. They all differ in terms of type of transportation mode, geographical location and, most important, from which stakeholder point of view they are presented.

The chapter by Carlo Vaghi and Marco Percoco highlights the point of view of the policy-makers and its interaction with other actors in the definition of the 'city logistics system'. The authors present a comparative analysis of the main city logistics systems in Italian cities and an in-depth cost–benefit analysis of the case of Padua (CityPorto Padova). The case study of Padua consists of a city logistics system based on a formal agreement between public and private stakeholders on regulations and reciprocal supply of specific assets. The analysis, made through a cost–benefit analysis approach, assesses the environmental and social effectiveness of this business model, measured in terms of social benefits versus costs. The outcome is very promising concerning the environmental effectiveness of the implementation of such city logistics scheme in medium-sized cities.

The chapter by Tom van Lier and Cathy Macharis takes the point of view of an inland port. Inland ports, in this case the port of Brussels, can play an important role in sustainable city distribution. The logistic functions of city ports are however under pressure in several countries as residential lofts with a view on the canal are bringing in more money for real-estate developers and the building sector. The authors show how to measure the avoided external costs of avoided truck transport thanks to the use of the inland waterways. This allows incorporating sustainability indicators in policy measures and investment decisions in the port, and can help to counteract the actual pressure on inland ports.

The chapter by Julius Menge and Paul Hebbes focuses on the CEP (courier, express and parcel) services. Their case is situated in Berlin and gives the point of view of drivers. The case study examines a research and implementation project 'SmartTruck' implemented by DHL Express's depot in Berlin. SmartTruck is a combination of real-time route planning (which allows operators to insert last-minute requests and information on accidents and construction sites) and consignments monitored by RFID (radio-frequency identification). In CEP services, several actors are involved, namely the drivers (often freelancers), the planners and the customers. Often it is difficult to take into account ecological aims in the optimization of CEP services as customers expect high-quality standards from a higher-priced express service. What is also important is to see if ICT devices are accepted by the drivers. To test this, no quantitative or even qualitative survey method is really suited, and so a participating surveillance method was used. All in all, the SmartTruck device helped to identify more compact routes, characterized by significantly fewer kilometres per tour while even increasing the use of the vehicle's capacity. This leads logically to a decrease in fuel consumption and therefore also in greenhouse-gas emissions.

Jochen Maes and Thierry Vanelslander look at the possibility of rail for urban transport. Rail transport is known for its potential for longer distances and its usefulness in the intermodal chain. For urban transport, the case of Monoprix, a large retailer in France, shows very clearly the possibilities for rail transport on shorter distances. In order to avoid congestion in the Paris area, Monoprix ships large volumes of freight from a so-called smart logistics centre to a downtown logistics centre, a distance of only 30 km. From there on, goods are distributed by natural-gas-powered vehicles. In Paris, as in other cities, different actors are involved with quite different perspectives, namely the citizens, the transport company and the shipper. In order to come to a common understanding, a charter was signed by the different partners, leading to more sustainable deliveries.

Sandra Melo finally brings together the different points of view. Her chapter evaluates 'good practices' in city distribution through the use of a quantitative methodology considering both public and private stakeholders' perspectives and the local intrinsic characteristics of implementation. The quantification is carried out through a systemic model specifically developed for the city of Porto (Portugal) and using the microscopic traffic simulator AIMSUN. This software calculates each of the output indicators adopted to measure mobility and sustainability under public and private objectives of three scenarios; cooperative systems; collaborative systems; and enforcement. The author argues that if the effects of an initiative can be estimated, stakeholders will be conscious of the benefits available from a specific measure, which can easily lead to an integrated strategy. The challenge is to find that common level of acceptance by all stakeholders involved in the negotiation. That level will not be the best level each group would individually aspire to, but it is the one that maximizes the consideration of all the interests involved.

RESEARCH AGENDA

City distribution has a minor role in transport planning procedures in most cities, although freight transport operations represent a substantial proportion of negative effects on the functionality of spatial activities. The case studies described throughout the book show that knowledge and awareness in the area of urban freight transport is low, which also contributes to a low level of interest in the subject and makes it hard to predict outcomes of certain actions. This is in line with the conclusions of the European project BUSTRIP, which found that for Swedish cities only 1 per cent had a full-time employee working on freight transport issues, and that people working on transport planning showed very little interest in city distribution (Lindholm, 2010). The implication for local authorities is that the issue of urban freight transport should have higher priority on the agenda. Knowledge in this area should be improved. We hope that this book helps to improve awareness and raises interesting possibilities in this area.

For the analysis of UGD, results are highly dependent on the framework conditions and, thus, selected initiatives are described looking at a specific transport chain, and considering spatial constraints and commercial activities located in the respective area. This disables the transferability of results usually associated with the term 'best practices'. This does not mean that existing practices, which have been designed for one particular context, cannot serve as sources of inspiration in the design of another context's response to its own challenges. Nevertheless, depending on the city, not all the tools may be equally suitable, nor may they be uniformly applicable.

There is probably no perfect solution for sustainable city distribution. Even a perfect combination of measures is difficult to find. What we are trying to show with this book is that measures should be evaluated according to the typical situation of the city, but, even more important, that the different stakeholders should be taken into account. Indeed, recognizing and understanding the concerns of different stakeholders and their recognition of the problem with respect to urban freight is a key factor in successfully introducing urban freight policies. The main challenge for researchers lies in developing methodologies that facilitate communication and cooperation between the different actors. This can be done, for example, by defining a common evaluation framework with quantitative indicators or an evaluation framework where the points of view are explicitly modelled.

Altogether, the chapters presented here underline the need for the development of an integrated agent-based approach to the evaluation of the performance of initiatives on UGD. The book describes some work that has already been done in that direction. More information on the aims of the different actors should be collected in order to assess them accordingly.

ACKNOWLEDGEMENTS

The editors would like to thank the NECTAR organization for the support they gave for the cluster meeting in Porto. This brought together these contributions. We would also like to thank all the authors. Special thanks also to Annalia Bernardini for her help in organizing the contributions. During the editing of this book, Sandra made another delivery, which is why we dedicate this book to Matilde.

REFERENCES

Anderson, S., J. Allen, and M. Browne (2005), 'Urban logistics – how can it meet policy makers' sustainability objectives?', *Journal of Transport Geography*, **13**, 71–81.
Dablanc, L. (2007), 'Goods transport in large European cities: difficult to organize, difficult to modernize', *Transportation Research Part A: Policy and Practice*, **41**(3), 280–85.
Hesse, M. and J. Rodrigue (2004), 'The transport geography of logistics and freight distribution', *Journal of Transport Geography*, **12**, 171–84.

Lindholm, Maria (2010), 'A sustainable perspective on urban freight transport: factors affecting local authorities in the planning procedures', *Procedia – Social and Behavioral Sciences*, **2** (3), 6205–16.

Marcucci, E. and R. Danielis (2008), 'The potential demand for an urban freight consolidation centre', *Transportation*, **35** (2), 269–84.

Melo, S. (2010), 'Evaluation of urban goods distribution initiatives towards mobility and sustainability: indicators, stakeholders and assessment tools', Ph.D. thesis, Faculty of Engineering, University of Porto.

OECD (2003), *Delivering the Goods – 21st Century Challenges to Urban Goods Transport*, Paris: OECD.

Zunder, T.H. and J.N. Ibanez (2004), 'Urban freight logistics in the European Union', *European Transport*, **28**, 77–84.

PART I

The Problem Situation and Possible Solutions

1. City distribution, a key element of the urban economy: guidelines for practitioners

Laetitia Dablanc

INTRODUCTION

Cities need freight, but they tend to ignore this particular kind of urban transport. Freight transport, despite providing thousands of jobs and much-needed services to the urban economy, has been neglected by transport surveys and models, transport strategies and regional master planning. In the meantime, freight operators have carried on with their business, providing the goods required by shops, companies and households at the right place and the right time. They usually succeed, but sometimes at an environmental or social cost. In large cities, one fourth of CO_2, one third of nitrate oxides, and half of the particulates that come from transport are generated by trucks and vans (LET et al., 2006). Today, municipalities must make freight transport one of their priorities if it is to become more efficient and sustainable.

For the purpose of this chapter, the definition of urban freight includes all goods movements generated by the economic needs of local businesses, that is, all deliveries and collections of supplies, materials, parts, consumables, mail and refuse that businesses require to operate. It also includes home deliveries by means of commercial transactions. We consider neither private transport undertaken by individuals to acquire goods for themselves (shopping trips), nor through traffic (trucks passing through a city en route to another destination without serving any business or household in the city). These two kinds of transport generate a large number of vehicle-kilometers (LET et al., 2006) and are legitimate policy targets, but a city's priority is the accommodation and improved management of freight transport and logistics activities directly serving the local economy.

This is all the more important since urban economies are evolving rapidly. Major changes have taken place in cities in developed countries. The size of store inventories has shrunk, and businesses are increasingly supplied on a just-in-time (JIT) basis. The number of different products sold has increased considerably, and collections change several times a year. With the rise of the service economy, the demand for express transport and courier services is soaring. These factors have made urban economies more dependent on transportation systems, with more frequent and customized deliveries (Dablanc, 2007). Developing countries have experienced similar changes (though not always at the same pace), along with additional transformations such as growth in very small manufacturing operations in homes or small high-tech parks. This generates new transport services in residential areas that did not previously need freight services.

Urban freight is notable for its phenomenal diversity. In a single city, vehicles, delivery times and the size of shipments may differ for each business or customer. When comparing cities worldwide, the diversity of urban freight is even more evident. How can one compare a Yamato employee in a small hybrid multi-temperature truck delivering to homes in Tokyo residential districts with a farmer transporting homegrown vegetables in a little pushcart to be sold on a street market in La Paz? Nevertheless, both of them contribute to the urban economy and the well-being of residents and businesses. And they actually have many issues in common. A shared feature of all urban freight activities around the world is their difficulty. A recent survey of 1650 Mexico City truck drivers (Lozano, 2006) reveals the challenges of urban freight operations that are common to all large cities: congestion, lack of loading and unloading space, complex legislation, police corruption, risk of theft and lack of safety are among the drivers' greatest concerns.

In this chapter, we provide guidelines and recommendations for urban freight transport practitioners in cities around the world, including those in developing countries. In the first section, we discuss recent advances in urban freight research, as well as the diversity of urban freight activity in different world regions. In the second section, we present data on urban freight and discuss its impact on local communities. Finally, policy recommendations are presented for cities that hope to create a more efficient and environmentally friendly freight system.

INFORMATION IS SCARCE – BUT THE SITUATION IS IMPROVING

Data and sources of information regarding urban goods movements were quite abundant in the 1960s and 1970s, especially in the USA and Australia, as well as in some European and Latin American cities

(Dablanc, 1998; Transportation Research Board, 1981). At that time, major metropolitan transport studies were quite popular, including those on truck traffic management. Later, interest in data collection and modeling for urban freight declined (Dablanc, 1998; Transportation Research Board, 1981). In 1992, Ken Ogden published the first comprehensive book on urban freight (Ogden, 1992). In this book, which is still a key resource for transport practitioners today, he notes that urban passenger transport is much better monitored than urban freight.

Fortunately, important steps to remedy this situation have been taken over the last few years in different parts of the world. In Europe, urban freight has been the subject of major programs, providing statistics and impact assessments. In the USA and Japan, reliable data exist. For developing countries, the data are more fragmented, and are usually collected on a case-by-case basis. Still, many large cities have carried out freight and logistics surveys.[1] In many countries, though, comparisons are still confounded by differing local survey methodologies, and surveys are also conducted differently over time, making historical analyses and projections difficult.

Recent Advances in Urban Freight Surveys and Methods

In the USA, the annual National Urban Freight Conference monitors advances in data collection and modeling methods. Ambitious freight studies have been done in large cities such as Dallas/Fort Worth, Chicago, Portland, and Vancouver in Canada. The Urban Freight Committee of the Transportation Research Board promotes advances in urban freight transport. The International Conference on City Logistics brings together academic researchers from around the world to discuss recent findings (Taniguchi and Thompson, 2008). At the World Conference on Transport Research, a Special Interest Group on Urban Goods Movement promotes sessions on urban freight.

Surveys are most developed in Europe, with experimental programs and networking activities supported by the European Union, as well as national urban freight programs. BESTUFS (BEST Urban Freight Solutions) harmonized freight data and published a *Good Practice Guide on Urban Freight* in 17 European languages (BESTUFS, 2007). Other European programs focus on urban logistics experiments. All of these projects have helped disseminate practices and methods. At the French national level, the 'goods in cities' program has sponsored large-scale urban freight surveys (LET, 2000). The UK government has promoted 'freight quality partnerships' in all large British cities. The Dutch administration has established the PIEK program on urban truck noise emissions and supports the national public/

private 'Committee for Urban Distribution' (Dablanc, 2007). In Padua, Italy, an annual city logistics fair brings together Italian municipalities, transport practitioners and logistics providers in the interest of improving the urban environment.

The Diversity of Urban Freight in Different World Regions

Cities throughout the world are different – and so are their freight transport and logistics activities. Freight strategies have depended on local economic, geographic and cultural characteristics. For example, Chicago has been preoccupied with maintaining its role as a rail hub for North America, and is thus concerned with rail freight movements between the numerous rail terminals located within the city: Chicago wants to 'develop a transformation system that enhances the region's eminence in the national and global freight economy' (Chicago Metropolitan Agency for Planning, 2008). Los Angeles is primarily concerned with air pollution, and thus targets urban trucking associated with the ports of Long Beach and Los Angeles.[2] Shanghai is becoming the largest cargo port in the world: port throughput was 443 million tons in 2005, out of a total of 678 million going through the city. The fact that, in 2005, 13 percent of Shanghai's GDP was value added by logistics underscores the city's vocation as a transport hub.

Cities in developing countries are even more diverse, but have some common characteristics that imply specific urban freight issues. In poorer countries, rural flight and population growth have led to very rapid urbanization, while the public supply of infrastructure and transport services has lagged behind. A significant proportion of roads are unpaved and poorly maintained (Gutierrez, 2009). Air pollution has decreased with the gradual phasing out of leaded gasoline and the introduction of regulations on cleaner fuels in many countries, such as India and Mexico. However, diesel trucks remain a major source of particulate matter and NO_x. Traffic congestion is a significant operational problem for the urban freight system. A major culprit in this congestion is the mixing of transport modes, with slow non-motorized vehicles (including hand- or animal-pulled carts) merging into faster motorized traffic.

Other features of cities in developing countries include a greater use of manual labor for transport and handling. Warehouses and logistic processes are less mechanized than in more developed economies. Also, the recycling of used goods, packaging and cardboard takes specific forms: in developing countries, cities essentially leave a significant share of the recycling of goods to the informal sector. Rag-pickers and scavengers are an important feature of city life. The volumes and financial flows generated by informal waste recycling may actually be more important to these urban economies than they are in European or North American cities. Urban scenes in developing regions also include street vending. In the poorest cities of Africa or Asia, street vendors literally take over the streets, selling everything from fresh fruit to electronic goods. Slums are also part of the city landscape in many developing countries, and have specific characteristics and supply needs. In general, the share of urban freight depending on the informal sector is hard to evaluate, as are economic, environmental and social indicators for these underground activities. Finally, in some countries (China, Egypt, Morocco, for example) the deregulation of what was previously a tightly controlled truck market has had wide-reaching effects on urban operations. Cooperatives and small private firms are largely replacing state-controlled trucking companies, expanding freight capacity in cities.

However, it is important to note that in most cities in developing countries, part of the economy is fully integrated into global economic networks. What best characterizes the cities of the developing world is their economic dualism: the informal sector operates alongside very advanced industries and services that have logistics behaviors and concerns similar to those in developed countries. Today, the demand for modern logistics services is as strong in São Paulo or Istanbul as in Athens or Sydney.

MAJOR FEATURES OF URBAN FREIGHT TRANSPORT AND POLICIES

Urban freight transport is complex and heterogeneous. There is a reason for this: urban freight is determined by the urban economy, and there is a great number of different economic sectors in a city, from industry to services, private and public, from major conglomerates to informal retail and manufacturing. This diversity is what makes cities so unique and valuable, a place where thousands of activities converge – but in a limited and constrained environment.

One Supply Chain for Each Economic Sector

Urban freight transport is the result of logistic decisions, which seek to move goods efficiently within a production and distribution system. These logistic decisions are based on the demands of economic agents and are not greatly influenced by the specific patterns of a particular city (Dablanc, 2007).

A city is provisioned by hundreds of supply chains (at least 150 were observed in European cities (LET, 2000)), one for each economic sector. All these supply chains are the result of logistic decisions, which are in turn based on the demands of the production and distribution sectors, themselves dependent on the behavior of economic agents such as households and firms. Each activity (commercial, service, industrial, administrative etc.) taking place in an urban environment can be associated with a specific freight generation profile, which is constant from one city to another. From a logistic point of view, a drugstore (or a bakery or a bank) operates in much the same way whether it is located at the center of a large metropolis or on the outskirts of a medium-sized city (LET, 2000). Whereas passenger transport can be roughly broken down into a handful of categories (usually by mode or trip purpose), freight transport is extremely fragmented by transport mode, operator type and goods origin (i.e. long-distance supply chain or very local transactions). Vehicles are also very diverse: trucks and vans of all sizes and weights (and various names, such as tuk-tuks or sudakos, a sort of minibus also used for freight in Indonesia), passenger cars, motorbikes and bicycles, three-wheelers and rickshaws, pedestrian pushcarts, animal-powered carriages, rail and waterborne transport. Genuine urban delivery systems unique to one city can also develop, such as the famous 'dabbawallas' in Mumbai, India: 200,000 lunch boxes made at home are delivered every day to businessmen in their workplace through a collection/sorting/delivery system using bicycles, trains and pedestrian modes of transport (Rai, 2007). Freight can be handled as private carriage (also called 'own account', where transport is carried out by manufacturers with their own employees and fleet, or by an independent retailer with his or her own vehicle to supply the store) or by a common carrier (on 'third account', i.e. by a professional carrier). In a typical European city, both categories make an equal amount of deliveries. In developing countries, private carriage is more dominant, and includes transport serving the informal sector. In Medan, Indonesia, 90 percent of local companies surveyed in 2004 owned their own delivery trucks (Kato and Sato, 2006).

Common indicators
Although collected for specific regions and specific situations (LET et al., 2006; Ogden, 1992; LET, 2000; BESTUFS, 2006; Figliozzi, 2007), some data on urban freight do converge. They are quite representative of urban freight supply and demand in developed countries. A city generates about:

- 1 delivery or pick-up per job per week
- 300 to 400 truck trips per 1000 people per day
- 30 to 50 tons of goods per person per year.

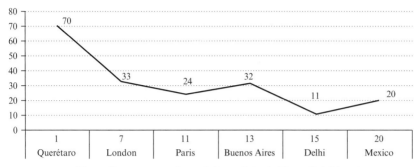

Metropolitan areas according to their population (millions of inhabitants)

Source: the author, from various sources (Betanz and Navarrete, 2009; Lozano, 2006; Transport for London, 2007b; Universidad Tecnologica Nacional, 2005).

Figure 1.1   Number of registered freight vehicles by city size

Urban freight represents 10–15 percent of vehicle equivalent miles traveled on city streets and 2–5 percent of the employed urban workforce (LET, 2000). A total of 3–5 percent of urban land is devoted to freight transport and logistics. A city not only receives goods, but also ships them: 20–25 percent of truck-km in urban areas are outgoing freight, 40–50 percent are incoming freight, and the rest both originates from and is delivered within the city (LET, 2000).

Transport companies providing urban freight services are generally very small. In Europe, 85 percent of short-distance truck companies have fewer than five employees. In Italy, the 'padroncini' (small individual entrepreneurs, usually owning one truck) carry 80 percent of all consignments delivered in urban areas. This is also true on other continents: in Mexico City, 80 percent of private carriers with a fleet of 100 vehicles or fewer have fewer than five vehicles (Lozano, 2006). A total of 70 percent of these companies' vehicles are light commercial vehicles (less than 3.5 tons) (Lozano, 2006).

Trucks and vans are the most visible (and best-monitored) modes of transport. Some interesting indicators have emerged from the literature (Betanzo and Navarrete, 2009), such as the number of freight vehicles for 1000 urban residents (see Figure 1.1). All vehicles are included: trailers, trucks and vans. Although registration methods may differ from one country to another, it seems that this ratio decreases as city size increases. This supports the idea that very large cities are more efficient in terms of urban freight delivery. In 2003, Phnom Penh, Cambodia had 27 830 registered trucks, an increase of 240 percent since 1992 (Ripert, 2006).

Registered trucks may not be representative of all trucks, and other modes of transport may account for a very large share of urban freight. In Medan, Indonesia, a cordon survey showed that motorbikes carried 20 percent of freight at the morning peak hour (Sato and Kato, 2006).

Principal urban logistics chains

Some large categories of urban logistics chains exist for which common freight transport characteristics can be identified.

- *Independent retailing, including the informal sector and local conven-ience stores.* These sectors together may represent 30–40 percent of all daily deliveries in a city. These local stores are supplied three to ten times a week. Suppliers are diverse, with a predominant use of own-account vans (or bikes and carriages in poorer countries).
- *Chain retailing and commercial centers.* In European cities, large retailing brands with subsidiaries or franchises are increasing their share of urban space at the expense of independent local stores (this transition has already occurred in the USA). This changes the way goods are supplied to stores, with less frequent deliveries, a larger share of consolidated shipments, and larger and better-loaded vehicles.
- *Food markets*, particularly important in developing countries, have extremely diverse supply modes, including bicycles and hand- or animal-driven carts. Few data exist on the actual volume of freight flows generated. A survey of 300 market vendors in Phnom Penh, Cambodia showed that 87 percent of market deliveries were made by the vendors themselves, and 13 percent by transport providers (Ripert, 2006).
- *Parcel transport (less than a full truck-load) and express services* are one of the fastest-growing urban transport businesses. This industry uses large vans or small to medium-sized trucks, and is based on consolidated delivery tours departing from cross-dock terminals in inner suburban areas. Vehicles from the leading express trans-port companies (UPS, DHL, TNT, FedEx) now operate in most of the world's cities, with some geographic specialization (DHL in European cities, UPS in US cities). This industry, undergoing con-stant restructuring, is hit by the current crisis, as customers down-grade their demand from express to cheaper services.
- A subsector of the parcel transport business is *home deliveries*. The home-shopping market represents €80 billion (5 percent of all retailing) in Europe today. Large postal operators dominate these markets, but new players are emerging. Japanese *takkyubins*, or

parcel transport companies that specialize in home deliveries, are a unique feature of Japanese urban logistics (Dablanc, 2009b).

• *Building sites* are a key segment because of the tonnage they generate (up to 30 percent of tonnage carried in cities). Vehicles are generally heavy trucks that do damage to roads. Building sites supply is notoriously inefficient. Multiple suppliers and poorly planned delivery schedules lead to a high number of deliveries, queuing and general disorder on the sites. Some cities, such as London and Stockholm in Europe, have launched consolidation schemes. The London Construction Consolidation Centre was implemented in 2006 with funds from Transport for London and private investors. A 2007 assessment showed that the scheme achieved a 68 percent reduction in the number of vehicles and a 75 percent reduction in CO_2 emissions (Transport for London, 2007a).[3]

Environmental impact

Urban freight is more polluting than long-distance freight transport because vehicles are older on average and there are a large number of stops and short trips. Freight transport is responsible for a third of transport-related NO_x and half of transport-related particulate matter (LET et al., 2006). In the metropolitan area of Mexico, 71 percent of the 3500 tons of $PM_{2.5}$ generated in 2002 by mobile sources was from freight vehicles (Lozano, 2006). Greenhouse-gas emissions and noise pollution are also among the most severe environmental effects of urban freight transport. In Dijon, France, freight transport consumes 26 percent of the total road-traffic-related TOE (tons of oil equivalent, the amount of energy released by burning one ton of crude oil). It has been calculated that during the morning rush hour in Bordeaux, France, freight transport traffic added five decibels (dB(A)) to the noise from the circulation of private cars (LET et al., 2006).

Urban freight vehicles can be quite old. In Dublin in 2004, a fourth of all vehicles were manufactured in or before 1994. Only 15 percent of vehicles were new (one year or less). In the Milan region, 40 percent of circulating trucks are more than ten years old. The renewal of the freight fleet is generally slower than for non-urban road freight traffic because urban freight involves numerous competing small operators that cut costs as much as possible. Another important issue is road safety. Trucks participate in a small share of the accidents in cities, but the accidents involving them are serious. On London's roads in 2005, about 14 percent of all collisions involving goods vehicles result in serious or fatal injuries, which is higher than the figure for other road users (BESTUFS, 2006).

The conciliation of truck traffic with bicycle use has been a recent policy target in Paris and London following fatal collisions that received a lot of media attention.

MAIN RECOMMENDATIONS FOR PRACTITIONERS

When faced with the challenges of an inefficient and unsustainable freight system, cities must take action. There are tools for policy-makers to better organize urban freight, although the task is not easy: even in countries with strong local political entities, policy leverage is weak regarding urban freight. Possibilities for progress do exist and realistic governance of urban freight transport can be defined around a few principles and the adoption of best practices.

For the most part, policy recommendations identified in the following sections can be implemented in the short term, and can have short- to medium-term effects. Best practices illustrate each of the recommended policies and measures.

Assessing the Needs of the Economy

Cities must act knowledgeably. They should make informed decisions on urban freight by collecting data at regular intervals. Data collection methods are many (Ogden, 1992; Figliozzi, 2007; OECD, 2003). To minimize costs and provide a comprehensive overview of goods flows in a city, surveys should target local businesses and assess their freight demand patterns. These surveys give more relevant information about the transport needs of the various economic sectors than simple vehicle cordon surveys (Ambrosini and Routhier, 2004).

No successful urban freight policy is possible without prior consultation with freight companies and their organizations, local business groups and residents. A permanent urban freight forum should be set up with all target groups and meet on a regular basis. In June 2006, the city of Paris and the largest carriers' and shippers' associations signed an urban freight transport 'charter' in which they commit to certain points favorable to the environment, working conditions and the productivity of urban delivery activities. It is very important that all stakeholders be included. Representatives of small transport operators should be identified (which is not an easy task) and invited. If they do not participate in the forum, some companies in this category should be interviewed on a regular basis. Also, shopkeepers' associations must be persuaded to attend. These local organizations are generally not interested in freight and delivery issues, although they may greatly benefit from better services and enhanced street attractiveness.

An essential feature of good communication with operators and other stakeholders is a city-sponsored, dedicated website providing information on traffic, truck access and delivery regulations, the provision of loading/unloading bays, and any other subjects related to urban freight.

Serving Urban Growth and Providing Value-added Logistics Services

Except in unusual circumstances (wars, natural disasters, or rationing in state-controlled economies), very few cities in the world experience ruptures in goods supplies. Goods always find a way to reach urban businesses and consumers. However, enhancing the *quality* and *added value* of goods distribution, in the formal as well as the informal sectors, is a very important objective for policy-makers.

A priority: promoting and organizing local initiatives

In the first section, we pointed out the important role of the informal urban freight sector in cities in poor countries, particularly in poor neighborhoods or in specific supply chains (street markets, waste recycling). Acknowledging these situations, cities should promote individual initiatives, however modest, that could result in more efficient goods transport. This may be the promotion of microcredit programs for waste-pickers to buy bicycles or for peasants going to the city market every week to organize a collective transport service, with a small truck replacing individual carriages, or for more coordinated (consolidated) deliveries of building materials to neighborhoods.

Programs that support grass-roots or private initiatives are already well developed, and are obviously not specific to freight or transport. However, urban freight may have been a neglected target so far, and specifically promoting entrepreneurship in the informal urban goods distribution market may have significant economic and social benefits for local communities.

Setting up logistics training programs

All cities, including those in poor or medium-income countries, should work on improving freight and logistics training. Together with bodies such as chambers of commerce, municipalities should promote campaigns and educational programs for logistics employees, from warehouse workers to managers. In 2006, Vilnius, Lithuania, experienced a shortage of logistics managers. The logistics professional organization, together with the municipality and the chamber of commerce, cooperated with other countries to recruit trained staff. Another option is to discuss with local universities new training programs (including Master's programs) in logistics and supply chain management. Georgia Tech, in Atlanta, USA, has implemented a training program on the premises of Savannah's major Logistics Park.

A step further: providing logistics parks

Higher-quality goods distribution is closely related to logistics service provision. Making logistics services available means organizing business opportunities, providing space at affordable prices, and promoting logistics job training. An interesting global solution is the development of logistics parks, partly through public investment. These parks include common services for all companies located on the site, such as surveillance, catering, fueling, cleaning stations for trucks, overnight truck parking and night accommodation for drivers. These parks must be accessible by public transport over extended hours, as logistics jobs require unconventional working hours. Environmental standards set or promoted by the municipality should enhance the quality of the buildings and mitigate local opposition (low-noise road surface, solar panels on roofs, protection from earthquake exposure).

Former industrial areas can be used when developing specialized logistics areas. However, necessary remediation efforts (e.g. for the removal of polluted soil) should not be too extensive, as programs for logistics spaces cannot tolerate high land costs.

Space is scarce, and must be used in the best possible way. Some municipalities accept the development of multi-activity buildings, with logistics at street level and other activities on upper levels. Some also develop multi-story warehouses. The US-based logistics developer ProLogis has built seven- to nine-story logistics terminals in Tokyo. These terminals are also common in Hong Kong. The acceptance of such projects is increasingly dependent on environmental criteria and careful integration of the buildings into the neighborhood.

Developing urban logistics spaces

Ideally, public authorities can promote the development of 'urban logistics spaces' in central areas, that is, terminals located in dense urban areas providing logistics services to neighborhood businesses and residents. These logistics spaces (of about 500 to 2000 m²) can be expensive to set up. Experiments may begin in the most commercial and/or touristic parts of cities, with the cooperation of retailers' associations. Motomachi in Japan (see below) is an interesting example. Such facilities can be provided directly by public authorities in the spaces they control, such as underground parking spaces. A request for proposal can be organized so that

---

BOX 1.1   MOTOMACHI UCC IN YOKOHAMA, JAPAN

The Urban Consolidation Center (UCC) of Motomachi, an area of upscale pedestrian shopping streets in the city of Yokohama, processes 85 percent of flows delivered to the neighborhood's shops. The remaining 15 percent are fresh products, furniture, and goods for retail chains that manage their own logistics. Three CNG trucks make delivery tours from the UCC, located a few hundred meters away from the retail area.

The truck companies that use the UCC pay ¥150 (€1.25) per parcel delivered. Motomachi UCC was difficult to implement – it took seven years for the local retailers' association to work out a sound business plan and efficient logistics organization. Today, the scheme provides very good delivery service to shopkeepers, at a low environmental cost to the community.

Source: Dablanc (2009b).

---

operators demonstrating best practice with regard to environmental, social and economic objectives become users of the facilities at low rental cost.

Urban logistics spaces may provide services such as receiving parcels destined for local businesses and residents. They may also provide final deliveries to clients, collection and sorting of pallets and cardboard from shops, short- or medium-term storage space, packaging and order processing for local manufacturing firms, and the provision of technologies that may not be affordable to individual firms (including basic services such as Internet access).

Urban consolidation centers (UCC) specifically provide a bundled and coordinated delivery service. A UCC is a logistics facility located close to the city center from which consolidated deliveries are carried out; it provides a range of other value-added logistics services (BESTUFS, 2007). Up to 200 such terminals existed in European cities in the 1990s and early 2000s. Due to operating costs, most of them closed down when municipalities could not subsidize them. Today, a few UCCs still operate, mostly in medium-sized cities: Bristol in the UK, Modena, Padua and other Italian cities, and La Rochelle in France. These consolidation centers are expensive, and it is difficult to cover operating costs.

An interesting recent trend in US metropolitan areas is to take freight into account in planning strategies. The Dallas/Fort Worth region has set up 'freight-oriented developments'. The greater Toronto area has defined 'freight-supportive land-use guidelines'. The Southern California Association of Governments (SCAG, Los Angeles) has recently identified 'freight-supportive design strategies' in its regional transportation plan.

Making Cities more Livable

There are three main goals a city should target with regard to a more sustainable urban freight distribution: reduce CO_2 emissions, reduce NO_x and particulate matter, and reduce noise. These objectives can be reached through a combination of the following policies.

Planning to prevent logistics sprawl

Logistics sprawl is the spatial deconcentration of logistics facilities in metropolitan areas. There is no longer enough space for logistics activities in central areas, so they are spreading through suburban areas, which generates a great deal of additional truck-km for deliveries. A recent study (Dablanc and Rakotonarivo, 2009) estimates that the relocation of cross-dock facilities serving the Paris region has increased CO_2 emissions by 500 000 tons over the last 35 years.

Metropolitan planning of logistics facilities is one of the key strategies for reducing truck vehicle-kilometers. The final choice for the location of logistics terminals results from a bilateral relationship between a developer (logistic real-estate companies, logistic providers) and a local community. Small municipalities may get requests for building permits from large companies such as ProLogis, a firm managing 51 million m^2 of logistics space worldwide. These cities sometimes find it hard to negotiate with these companies on equal terms. Some cities systematically oppose logistic spaces. This has been the case in Saint-Mard near the Charles de Gaulle airport in the Paris region. For the last 20 years, Saint-Mard's local government has opposed the development of a multimodal freight terminal on its territory, despite a general regional and nationwide consensus on the economic and environmental benefits of building such a terminal there. This is why a metropolitan or regional master plan must include logistics land-use provisions that can orient local decisions. The recently adopted master plan for the Paris region (2008) identifies 25 specific areas where logistic terminals will be given priority for development or redevelopment to improve access.

Maintaining or reintroducing non-motorized and cleaner modes of transportation

In many cities, specifically in developing countries, existing non-motorized vehicles (such as bicycles and animal-powered carts) must be better taken into account and promoted by providing privileged access to street space, such as reserved lanes on urban boulevards. A policy promoting bicycle use can have significant effects on freight transport. In Paris, protected bus lanes have been widened to five meters, allowing mixed use by bikes and buses, with buses passing slower vehicles when necessary and at minimal risk. Additionally, 272 kilometers of bicycle lanes have been created, making it possible for new delivery vehicles such as the Petite Reine, an electrically assisted three-wheeled delivery bike, to enhance the productivity of their delivery operations.

Despite many experiments, CNG (compressed natural gas) or electric vans and trucks are not yet satisfactory for urban deliveries because of high prices, difficult maintenance, a small second-hand market, and an insufficient number of refueling facilities. Cities should not commit themselves to actively developing these specific markets, as it is risky to spend a considerable amount of time and money for such limited positive effects. However, if major players (shippers, truck operators) demand it, cities should encourage the development of refueling facilities such as compressed-gas stations and access to plugs for electric vehicles in off-street parking facilities. One of the priorities of the London Freight Plan (Transport for London, 2007b) is to make detailed information about the use of alternative fuels and low-carbon vehicles accessible to all operators through a freight information portal. It may actually be most realistic for urban areas to accommodate hybrid vans and trucks. They are already quite common in Japanese cities.

Adopting environmental criteria for freight vehicle access
Cities should adopt delivery access regulations based on a simple combination of the size and the age of delivery vehicles. The following points must be taken into account to ensure simple and coordinated access control rules.

- A ban on very large trucks such as semi- or double trailers is relevant on most city streets, as these trucks pose safety problems, damage streets, block traffic and have difficulty maneuvering. However, the size limit should not be too strict. Vehicle weight limits from 3.5 up to 10 or 15 tons are too low; that is, only low-capacity vehicles could access the city. Strict weight regulations lead to a higher number of commercial vehicles in urban areas. According to studies quoted in Castro and Kuse (2005), access restrictions on trucks over 4.5 tons in Manila have reduced truck productivity by 50–60 percent. A simple size limit based on the number of axles is a good alternative to regulations based on tonnage or truck size. Two-axle trucks

*Table 1.1   Effects of truck environmental regulations in Gothenburg,
              Sweden (trucks more than 7 years old prohibited)*

	PM_{10} (kg/year)
Trucks < 16 tons with regulation	187
Trucks < 16 tons without regulation	566
Trucks > 16 tons with regulation	3312
Trucks > 16 tons without regulation	4531

Source: Data from City of Gothenburg, May 2006, after four years of implementation.

are in the range of 17 to 20 tons and 25 to 30 m², depending on the
manufacturer and national regulations. A ban on trucks with three
or more axles has the important advantage of being easy to enforce.

- A ban on the oldest commercial vehicles. Because of regulatory
  standards and technical progress, today's trucks and vans consume
  less fuel and pollute much less than older ones. This is particularly true for NO_x and PM_{10}. For CO_2 emissions, progress is more
  recent. A European Union initiative may soon impose a 120g
  CO_2/km limit on cars and light-duty trucks sold in Europe. Some
  Swedish cities are preparing to include CO_2 emissions criteria in
  their truck access regulations. In any case, access rules based on
  age or equivalent pollution category yield rapid results as truck
  operators replace old vehicles with more recent and cleaner ones
  (Table 1.1). In London, the Low Emission Zone set up in 2008
  prohibits trucks older than the Euro 3 standard from entering the
  metropolitan area (totaling 1580 km²). Another important impact
  of age-based truck regulations is that they require small operators
  to organize their activities differently. Local authorities can help
  operators comply with the new rules by providing subsidies to buy
  newer vehicles.

- Harmonized rules on truck access and deliveries at the metropolitan level. One of the most important policies on urban freight
  is to provide a coherent set of regulations concerning delivery time
  windows and vehicle characteristics (tonnage, size, age) in all of the
  metropolitan area's municipalities. Truck drivers should be given
  clear and simple rules. Harmonized rules also provide a more stable
  framework for vehicle manufacturers to develop products catering
  to the specific needs of urban delivery.

- The reduction of noise generated by deliveries and the promotion
  of night deliveries. Some cities ban trucks during the day. In Seoul,

trucks have been banned from central areas during working hours since 1979 (Castro and Kuse, 2005). According to a survey in New York City, the businesses most likely to switch to off-peak deliveries are shippers doing their own transport (own account) and receivers open during extended hours such as restaurants (Holguín-Veras et al., 2005). To increase the potential target group for the promotion of night deliveries, cities should have a strong policy combining the promotion of silent equipment and some regulations. In 25 pilot cities in the Netherlands, the national government provides financial help to operators investing in silent vehicles and handling equipment (generating noise emissions below 65 dB). Tests have shown that companies delivering to supermarkets at night save 30 percent in delivery costs and 25 percent in diesel consumption (BESTUFS, 2006). This program has been duplicated in other European cities.

Making access to ports more efficient
Measures can be taken to alleviate congestion to and from port areas. Many European cities have redeveloped modern port areas outside of the historical harbor with better connections to highway or rail networks. Obviously, this is not always an option when there is a lack of available land. Many port authorities have developed rail and waterway connections to and from port facilities to alleviate road congestion in their vicinity. More than 35 percent of containers leave the Port of Rotterdam in the Netherlands by barge, and a new railway line, the Betuwe Route, has recently increased the share of rail in the port's modal split. The Alameda corridor in Los Angeles is a 20-mile rail connection from the ports of Long Beach and Los Angeles to rail terminals in east downtown Los Angeles. It has considerably reduced congestion on the freeways it parallels.

These policies involve major investments that are not always possible for port authorities and cities. An easier and cheaper way of dealing with truck congestion in and around port areas is to manage the timing of truck arrivals and departures more efficiently. This can be achieved through better coordination and extended terminal opening hours. A good example is the ports of Los Angeles and Long Beach (Giuliano and O'Brien, 2008). A recent state regulation requires appointments or extended hours at terminal gates, and the 'Off-peak extended gate hours program' (2005) created night and Saturday shifts at both ports. The program far exceeded expectations, as an average of more than 60 000 truck movements per week have been diverted to the off-peak shifts. It has had a notable effect on truck traffic congestion at the terminal gates.

Promoting sustainable practices among truck operators

A municipality can create a certification scheme that identifies the best urban freight operators. Certification confers privileges on an operator, such as extended delivery hours or the use of designated loading/unloading facilities. It may also provide operators with a competitive advantage when bidding for contracts, as clients are increasingly committed to selecting bidders that offer the best environmental guarantees. A recent example of such an initiative is the FORS (Freight Operator Recognition Scheme) in London. FORS provides a performance benchmark for the trucking industry (Transport for London, 2007b) by certifying operators that comply with a list of efficiency, safety and environmental impact criteria at bronze, silver and gold levels.

Another way to make urban freight more sustainable is to facilitate the transition from individual shopping to home deliveries. Among the best policies a city can make regarding urban freight is to help freight carriers implement pick-up point networks. These local depots make it unnecessary to deliver all the way to customers' homes, reducing vehicle-kilometers and costs (Augereau and Dablanc, 2008). German municipalities have agreed to let the Deutsche Post implement its network of automated parcel delivery points ('packstations') on city streets and in other public places, contributing to the overall success of the scheme.

Changing public procurement to promote sustainable urban freight

Like a large company, a municipality receives all sorts of goods: letters and documents, office items, furniture and so on. It also controls contractual markets for public services, such as food supplies and furniture for schools or hospitals. Purchasers often do not consider how goods are supplied, and transport matters are usually the shipper's responsibility. However, cities can influence transport patterns by including energy-efficient and sustainable transport among their suppliers' contractual obligations. The municipality of Gothenburg, Sweden has established such requirements for some of its transport providers, such as taxi services and parcel transport companies.

Facilitating Deliveries and Providing Better Labor Conditions for Delivery Personnel

Delivery personnel are often given little thought in the trucking industry, which leads to poor working conditions and high turnover. Local and national governments can take decisive action to improve labor conditions and skills in the urban freight sector.

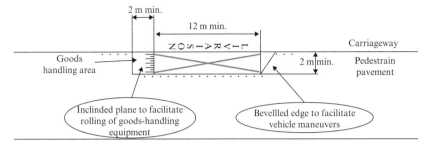

Note: LIVRAISON = DELIVERY.

Source: City of Paris (2005).

Figure 1.2   Proposed design of an unloading/loading bay

Promoting skills and fair competition
In many countries, trucking companies are subject to specific professional regulations. Although less common, specific regulations for the light transport market can have significant benefits for the urban freight sector. In France, all third-party freight providers using vans and bikes have to be registered in a 'light transport register' that requires proof of professional skills, proof of financial capacity (the company must detain €900 per vehicle as deposit) and proof of honorability (their police record must be free of contain certain offenses). Fair competition must be guaranteed through improved enforcement of transport regulations.

Local authorities and local chambers of commerce can set up or propose training programs for urban trucking employees, professional organizations and unions. These programs may include information about safe driving, eco-driving, the use of new technologies (positioning systems), city traffic and delivery regulations, and basic commercial transport legislation.

Better design of delivery areas
Delivery personnel must have appropriate collection and delivery points with good access. In busy urban areas and city centers, this means that adequate on-street loading and unloading bays must be identified. A minimal length of ten meters is necessary so that opening the rear doors of the vehicle and handling the goods is possible with ease. Figure 1.2 shows one specific delivery bay design that uses part of the sidewalk. This design has had good results in Paris. Alternative designs exist, such as loading bays positioned at an angle to the curb. Attention must be paid to removing obstacles around the loading bay, such as humps and posts. Obstacles often prevent drivers from operating on-board handling equipment, which

makes for more difficult manual work. A sufficient number of loading bays must be provided. A good ratio is one delivery area for 10 to 12 businesses at street level. Other interesting layouts include dedicating entire sections of a parking lane to deliveries during certain time windows. In Koriyama City in Japan, one lane of the roadway has been converted into loading space. In Kashiwa City, a joint parking space for delivery trucks is managed collectively by retailers (Futamata, 2009).

Time-sharing is a good way to improve the road network and parking capacity. In Seoul's four 'freight districts', different time windows have been allocated to trucks and passenger cars in on-street parking areas. In Barcelona, the main boulevards devote the two lateral lanes to traffic during peak hours, deliveries during off-peak hours, and residential parking during the night.

Many cities require new commercial or industrial developments to include off-street delivery areas. The 2002 Tokyo off-street parking ordinance requires all department stores, offices and warehouses to provide loading/unloading facilities if they have a floor area of more than 2000 m². European cities' regulations are generally stricter, as buildings of 400–1000 m² are subject to off-street loading zone requirements. Barcelona is very unusual in that it regulates the use of interior space by private businesses: since the municipal building code of 1998, all new bars and restaurants are asked to build a storage area of at least 5 m². The rationale behind this rule is that restaurants do not need daily deliveries of bottles and beverages if they can store sufficient volumes.

Some cities should also be careful to avoid inadequate regulations in their building codes. For example, access to underground parking can be very difficult for commercial vehicles because of height and size limits. The Chicago Downtown Freight Study (O'Laughlin et al., 2008) revealed that this was one of truck drivers' greatest problems.

Stricter enforcement, less corruption

Freight transport operations must be among the top enforcement targets for local police. This means enforcing any existing regulations on emissions, age and size of vehicles, as well as delivery time windows. It also means more operator checks to verify compliance with labor and professional rules. It is essential to ensure that law-abiding operators, especially small ones, do not face unfair competition from other companies that are unregistered or operate non-compliant vehicles.

Theft and corruption are also important issues for urban freight operators. Many urban freight operators worldwide face corruption among street police or customs employees in port areas. Delivery workers also encounter theft while delivering. Some local regulations actually make the problem worse: in some cities, leaving truck doors open is the only way of proving that a vehicle is being loaded or unloaded in the absence of the driver. In Paris, the problem was solved very simply by distributing a delivery parking disk to all operators. The time when unloading operations begin is marked on the disk, and the vehicle is allowed to remain in a delivery bay for 30 minutes without being fined. Doors can be locked during operations, so goods are more secure.

There are more sophisticated enforcement systems, such as cameras and automated license plate readers, but these come at a high operating cost to the city. In London, the cost is £30000 per camera, including installation and maintenance. In Barcelona, a special 'freight brigade' of 50 police officers on motorbikes has been created. These police are dedicated to enforcing freight traffic and delivery regulations in the city center, with a high benefit–cost ratio as additional fines compensate for additional salaries.

CONCLUSION

In this chapter, we have identified urban freight transport issues that are shared by cities in both the developed and developing world. We have provided four recommendations for cities seeking to promote a more efficient and environmentally friendly freight system. Their underlying principle is that freight transport must serve the local economy.

1. Cities must assess the needs and challenges of their specific economy by conducting surveys and establishing a freight forum to negotiate with private stakeholders. These can be low-cost actions with significant benefits to businesses.
2. Serving urban growth by improving the quality and added value of goods distribution is an important objective for policy-makers. Key priorities include promoting local initiatives and providing modern logistics facilities and training programs.
3. Land-use and planning policies should include logistics activities. Cleaner and quieter modes of transport should be (re)introduced on city streets. Truck access regulations based on environmental standards contribute to reducing pollutant emissions.
4. Governments can take decisive action to improve working conditions and skills in the urban freight sector, often the most neglected in the trucking industry. Fair competition must be guaranteed through improved enforcement of transport regulations. Well-designed on-street and off-street delivery areas must be provided to make urban deliveries faster and easier.

It is not easy to create an urban freight system that benefits the urban economy and the environment. Even in countries with strong local political entities, policy leverage is weak regarding urban freight. But in a complex urban environment where environmental, social and economic issues compete and difficult trade-offs are involved, there are possibilities for progress at low cost and with great benefits.

ACKNOWLEDGMENTS

This chapter is based on work done for the World Bank as part of the 'Freight Transport for Development' initiative, which aims to examine how freight transport operations contribute to development (Dablanc, 2009a). We thank J. Dubow, G. Gauthier, J. Hine and P. O'Neill for the opportunity to present some of this project's results in this book, as well as at the Transportation Research Board meeting of January 2010.

NOTES

1. Municipal services, consultants or academic groups have produced recent data on freight transport in cities such as Mexico City, São Paulo, Buenos Aires, Shanghai and Manila. The most ambitious of these surveys is the one for Mexico City (see Lozano, 2006).
2. See the San Pedro Bay Ports Clean Air Action Plan (CAAP) downloadable from www. portoflosangeles.org/environment/caap.asp (last accessed 10 August 2009).
3. See also www.tfl.gov.uk/microsites/freight/documents/publications/LCCC-interim-report-may-07.pdf (last accessed 10 August 2009).

REFERENCES

Ambrosini, C. and J.L. Routhier (2004), 'Objectives, methods and results of surveys carried out in the field of urban freight transport: an international comparison', *Transport Reviews*, **24** (1), 57–77.

Augereau, V. and L. Dablanc (2008), 'An evaluation of recent pick-up point experiments in European cities: the rise of two competing models?', in E. Taniguchi and R. Thompson (eds), *City Logistics V, Proceedings of the 5th International Conference on City Logistics*, New York: Nova Science Publisher, Inc., pp. 303–20.

BESTUFS (2006), *Quantification of Urban Freight Transport Effects I*, www. bestufs.net, 10 October.

BESTUFS (2007), *Good Practice Guide on Urban Freight*, downloadable from www.bestufs.net/download/BESTUFS_II/good_practice/English_BESTUFS_ Guide.pdf (last accessed 10 August 2009).

Betanzo Quezada, E. and J.A. Romero Navarrete (2009), 'Sustainable urban freight transportation in medium-sized cities in Mexico', submitted, courtesy of the authors.

Castro, J.T. and H. Kuse (2005), 'Impacts of large truck restrictions in freight carrier operations in metro Manila', *Journal of the Eastern Asia Society for Transportation Studies*, **6**, 2947–62.

Chicago Metropolitan Agency for Planning (2008), 'Updated 2030 Regional Transportation Plan for Northeastern Illinois', October, www.cmap.illinois. gov/2030-regional-transportation-plan, last accessed 21 January 2011.

City of Paris (2005), *Technical Guide to Delivery Areas for the City of Paris*, Paris. Available in English from Paris City Roads & Transport Department, Agence de la Mobilité.

Dablanc, L. (1998), *Entre police et service : l'action publique sur le transport de marchandises en ville, le cas des métropoles de Paris et New York*, Ph.D. dissertation, Ecole nationale des Ponts et Chaussées & Université de Paris-Est.

Dablanc, L. (2007), 'Goods transport in large European cities: difficult to organize, difficult to modernize', *Transportation Research Part A*, **41**, 280–85.

Dablanc, L. (2009a), 'Freight transport, a key for the new urban economy', Report for the World Bank as part of the initiative 'Freight Transport for Development: a Policy Toolkit'.

Dablanc, L. (2009b), 'Le territoire urbain des konbini et des takkyubin au Japon', *Flux*, October–December, 68–70.

Dablanc, L. and D. Rakotonarivo (2009), 'The impacts of logistic sprawl: how does the location of parcel transport terminals affect the energy efficiency of goods' movements in Paris and what can we do about it?', *Procedia – Social and Behavioral Sciences*, The Sixth International Conference on City Logistics, E. Tanguchi and R.G. Thompson (eds), **2** (3), 6087–96.

Figliozzi, M.A. (2007), 'Analysis of the efficiency of urban commercial vehicle tours: data collection, methodology, and policy implication', *Transportation Research Part B*, **41**, 1014–32.

Futamata, Y. (2009), 'City logistics from road policy aspect', Japanese–French seminar on Urban Freight Transport, 20 January, Japan Society of Civil Engineers, Tokyo.

Giuliano, G. and T. O'Brien (2008), 'Responding to increasing port-related freight volumes: lessons from Los Angeles/Long Beach and other US ports and hinterlands', OECD International Transport Forum, Discussion Paper 2008/12.

Gutierrez, A. (2009), 'Accessibilité, transport et mobilité au regard de l'inclusion sociale : réflexions théorico-pratiques, le cas de la métropole de Buenos Aires', communication at the seminar 'Mobilité au défi des inégalités', University Paris-Est, Marne la Vallée, 18 May.

Holguin-Veras, J. et al. (2005), 'Off-peak freight deliveries, challenges and stakeholders' perceptions', *Transportation Research Record: Journal of the Transportation Research Board*, **1906**, 42–8.

Kato, H. and J. Sato (2006), 'Urban freight transportation analysis in developing countries: case study in Medan, Indonesia', unpublished.

LET (2000), *Diagnostic du transport de marchandises dans une agglomération*, Paris: DRAST/Ministère des Transports.

LET et al. (2006), *Méthodologie pour un bilan environnemental physique du transport de marchandises en ville*, Paris: ADEME/Ministère des Transports.

Lozano Cuevas, A. (principal investigator) (2006), *Estudio integral metropolitano de transporte de carga y medio ambiente para el Valle de México (EIMTC–MAVM)*, Final Report, Universidad Autonoma de México, Comision Ambiental Metropolitana, September.

O'Laughlin, R., D. Thomas and M. Rinnan (2008), 'Chicago downtown freight study', Transportation Research Board Annual Meeting 2008, Paper #08-2465.

OECD (2003), *Delivering the Goods: 21st Century Challenges to Urban Goods Transport*, Paris: OECD.

Ogden, K. (1992), *Urban Goods Movement: A Guide to Policy and Planning*, Brookfield, VT: Ashgate Publishing.

Rai, S. (2007), 'In India, Grandma cooks, they deliver', *New York Times*, 29 May.

Ripert, C. (2006), 'Approvisionner, desservir, transiter', technical report, Municipalité de Phnom Penh Mairie de Paris, APUR, Phnom Penh Centre, APUR Publishing, Paris.

Taniguchi, E. and R. Thompson (eds) (2008), *City Logistics V, Proceedings of the 5th International Conference on City Logistics*, New York: Nova Science Publisher, Inc.

Transportation Research Board, Urban Goods Movement, *Transportation Research Record*, **496**.

Transport for London (2007a), *London Construction Consolidation Centre* Interim Report, May, www.tfl.gov.uk/microsites/freight/documents/publications/LCCC-interim-report-may-07.pdf (last accessed 10 August 2009).

Transport for London (2007b), *London Freight Plan – Sustainable Freight Distribution: A Plan for London*, Mayor of London, Transport for London, October. Also downloadable from www.tfl.gov.uk/microsites/freight/documents/publications/London-Freight-Plan-Executive-Summary.pdf (last accessed 10 August 2009).

Universidad Tecnologica Nacional (2005), *El Transporte Automotor de Cargas en la Argentina*, downloaded from www.edutecne.utn.edu.ar/transporte/capitulos.htm (last accessed 10 August 2009).

2. Urban freight transport: the challenge of sustainability

H.J. (Hans) Quak

INTRODUCTION

Sustainability of Urban Freight Transport

Urban freight transport is frequently censured for its unsustainable impacts. Although our current urbanized civilization requires an efficient freight transport system in order to sustain it, the common perception is that urban freight transport has negative impacts on all sustainability issues: social, economic and environmental (also known as the triple P: people, profit and planet). Urban freight transport, or urban goods movement, is identified as having the following unsustainable effects on:

- people, such as the consequences of traffic accidents, noise nuisance, visual intrusion, smell, vibration and the consequences of (local) emissions, such as NO_x and PM_{10}, on public health;
- profit, such as inefficiencies (especially for carriers) due to regulations and restrictions, congestion and reduced city accessibility;
- the planet, such as the contribution of transport to global pollutant emissions (CO_2) and the consequences for global warming.

Many different actors are involved in or with urban freight transport; they often have their own, sometimes conflicting, stakes in it. This makes it difficult to develop sustainable solutions for the issues raised. In what way urban freight transport is experienced as unsustainable depends on the actor in question, resulting in a wide variety of problem perceptions in the field. Accordingly, such problems are complex and compound, since a solution for one actor often forms the base of a new problem for another actor (Browne and Allen, 1999). We distinguish four main actor groups in urban freight transport (Quak, 2008):

1. The local authorities' main interest is to develop or maintain a liveable city. To reach this objective, local authorities aim at reducing truck traffic and nuisance and at improving air quality in cities by using regulations, such as time windows, vehicle restrictions and low-emission zones.

2. Carriers' main interest is to organize urban freight transport as efficiently as possible. Currently this is frustrated by local regulations, such as time windows that force carriers to make their deliveries during a limited time period, resulting in far from optimal round-trip planning. Time windows also oblige carriers to travel during the (morning) peak periods. Local regulations (seldom harmonized between cities) result in vehicle utilization problems, inefficient transport operations (and therefore extra emissions), and a serious cost increase for the carriers (see Quak and De Koster, 2007, 2009).

3. Receivers (e.g. shop owners) are not usually involved in urban freight transport, but their orders actually initiate the urban freight transport operations.

4. Receivers like an attractive shopping climate, with minimum nuisance from supplying trucks. Furthermore, they want a reliable distribution system in which deliveries are made in time.

Residents' main interest is a pleasant living environment. Local authorities tend to look after the interests of their 'voters'. Residents want clean air (as few local pollutant emissions as possible), no noise nuisance or other nuisance caused by supplying, loading or unloading trucks.

Other actors also have a stake in urban freight transport issues, but are often not directly involved. The national government, for example, aims at reducing congestion and global pollution. Shippers are interested in an urban freight transport system in which deliveries are made in time at low cost. Finally, the shopping public wants a pleasant shopping environment in the city centre.

Outline of this Chapter

In this chapter we discuss urban freight transport sustainability initiatives from the past. The next section discusses the three main solution directions to improve the sustainability of urban freight transport, and then we introduce a framework for evaluating urban freight transport initiatives and discuss the selection of urban freight transport sustainability initiatives. A further section presents 12 different types. The chapter concludes with final remarks. The majority of this contribution is based on Quak (2008) and more specifically on chapter 2, 'A framework and classification for urban

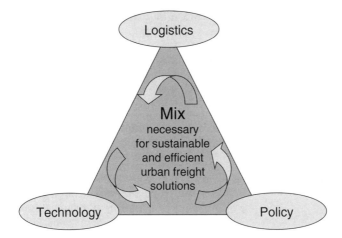

Figure 2.1   The mix of three solution directions for sustainable urban freight transport

freight transport sustainability initiatives' and chapter 3, 'Improving sustainability: a review of initiatives' of the Ph.D. thesis 'Sustainability of Urban Freight Transport'.

Three Solution Directions for Sustainable Urban Freight Transport

We distinguish three main solution directions to improve the sustainability of urban freight transport: logistical solutions; policy solutions; and technological solutions (see Figure 2.1). Very often these solution directions are brought into practice separately. However, to make urban freight transport more sustainable, all three directions should be considered and geared to one another. In this way, cities can use standardized initiatives from all three directions and make a mix that best fits the city in question. Thus the different cities can use standard initiatives to deal with the relevant issues for that specific city. In the following sections we discuss many different standard initiatives that often do not consider all solution directions and all actors' stakes. Therefore these initiatives have frequently failed to improve sustainability in practice.

One of the examples of where a good mix of all three solution directions led to an improvement in sustainability comes from the Netherlands; it is called in Dutch 'dagranddistributie', which means distribution at the margins of the day. Technological solutions made it possible to develop quiet equipment, such as trucks, trailers and roll containers. Policy solutions made it possible to deliver during the early morning outside the time windows (and before the morning peak congestion hours). Due to this change in policy, carriers were willing to invest in the innovative quiet equipment. If the policy had not been changed, there would be no reason to invest, although the nuisance would decrease, since these investments would not result in any (monetary) gains for the carriers. And finally logistical solutions made it possible to rearrange transport activities to take place in the early morning (e.g. drivers now have keys of stores, warehouse activities are at different times to prepare the truck loads earlier, etc.). By combining the three solution directions, the FTL (full truckload) deliveries of supermarket chains in the Netherlands became more sustainable in all respects: improved traffic safety (since fewer people are around when the truck unloads); fewer emissions (no congestion); no increase in nuisance (quiet equipment); and less logistics cost.

METHODOLOGY FOR REVIEWING URBAN FREIGHT TRANSPORT SUSTAINABILITY (UFTS) INITIATIVES

Framework for Evaluating UFTS Initiatives

Quak (2008) and Quak et al. (2008) develop a framework for evaluating UFTS initiatives (see Figure 2.2). These initiatives are defined as 'the actions, including both projects and studies, that aim at improving urban freight transport sustainability by making changes in the urban freight transport operations or the urban freight transport context' (Quak, 2008, p. 20). The framework starts with the design phase, which has four dimensions: 'what initiative (description)', 'why (objective)', 'who (actors involved)', and 'why (reasons for involvement)'. The next phase, the execution phase, contains two dimensions: 'where (geographical elements)' and 'what (transport characteristics)'. The evaluation phase forms the final phase in the framework, containing two dimensions: 'how (evaluation)' and 'what results'. Figure 2.2 shows how the dimensions relate and the classes examined per dimension. Quak (2008) also introduces elements to describe the classes (not shown in this chapter.

Selection of UFTS Initiatives

Over the last few decades several UFTS initiatives have been initiated. This contribution considers only initiatives that meet the following selection criteria:

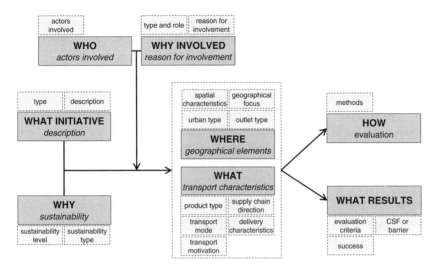

Note: CSF = critical success factor.

Figure 2.2 Framework for evaluating urban freight transport sustainability (UFTS) initiatives

- The initiative should aim at improving sustainability in an urban area by making a change or several changes in the context or the operations of urban freight transport.
- A reviewed journal or book reports the initiative or an (academic) expert in the urban freight transport field has pointed out the initiative as an important UFTS initiative.
- The initiative is reported in English and the description is profound; that is, the objective should be clear and should inform the results.

Based on these criteria, the UFTS initiative search used the following three directions:

- A keyword search in electronic databases; several databases were searched using different keywords to find published articles in academic journals between 1995 and 2006.
- Consultation of (academic) experts in the field: 35 experts from 19 countries received an e-mail that asked 'What are the most important UFTS initiatives in your country?'
- The proceedings of scientific conferences focusing on urban freight transport.

This search for initiatives resulted in 106 unique UFTS initiatives, under-taken between 1998 and 2006. This implies that more recent initiatives, although they show interesting results, are not included in this review (see, e.g., the City Logistics conferences of 2007 and 2009, but also other published initiatives). This chapter presents the lessons that can be learned from the selected initiatives. The selection is exhaustive within the pre-sented criteria. However, the more recent initiatives, in which some of the lessons presented are put into practice, are not part of this review. Many of the selected initiatives are policy direction solutions, since sustainability is especially a governmental objective (Taniguchi et al., 2004), but logisti-cal and technological solutions are also included in the selected initiatives.

URBAN FREIGHT TRANSPORT SUSTAINABILITY (UFTS) INITIATIVES

Structuring the UFTS Initiatives

It is possible to classify (see Table 2.1) the 106 UFTS initiatives based on the design phase dimensions of the framework (see Figure 2.2). We distin-guish two classes of initiatives:

A. Initiatives that aim at improving sustainability within the existing urban freight transport context.
B. Initiatives that aim at improving sustainability by changing the exist-ing urban freight transport context.

Class A initiatives aim at a better utilization of the available infrastruc-ture; think about scarce road capacity, unloading places in cities and vehicle capacity. Within this class there are two different initiative catego-ries: initiatives that are initiated by (local) authorities and those that are initiated by non-governmental actors, such as carriers, shippers, receivers and manufacturers. This distinction corresponds to that of other authors (e.g. Allen et al., 2000; Ambrosini and Routhier, 2004) and results in two categories in class A initiatives: policy initiatives (A1) and company-driven initiatives (A2). The initiatives in class B are more radical than those in class A: usually more actors are involved, and more solution directions are combined (or should have been combined). Class B initia-tives can usually also be characterized as more expensive, more difficult and more complex than class A initiatives. For the class B initiatives we also distinguish two categories: physical infrastructure initiatives (B1) and transport-reorganizing initiatives (B2). Table 2.1 shows the 12 initiative

Table 2.1   A structure for urban freight transport initiatives

Class	Category	Initiative type	Number of initiatives
Class A	*Category A1*	Road pricing	7
Improvements	*Policy initiatives*	Licensing and regulation	21
within the		Parking and unloading	8
context	*Category A2*	Carrier cooperation	12
	Company-driven	Vehicle routing	14
	initiatives	improvement	
		Technological vehicle	5
		innovation	
Class B	*Category B1*	Consolidation centre	15
Improvements	*Physical infrastructure*	Underground logistics	5
by changing	*initiatives*	system	
the context		Road infrastructure	4
		development	
		Standardization of load	4
		units	
	Category B2	Transport auction	15
	Transport-reorganizing	Intermodal	8
	initiatives	transport	

types that we distinguish as well as the number of initiatives that we found for the different types. In the following sections we explain the different types and discuss the main results of the different UFTS initiatives per type. Because of lack of space here, I refer to Quak (2008) for detailed information on the individual initiatives. In this contribution the 12 initiative types are presented on an aggregated level. Sometimes an individual initiative is presented as an illustration of the initiative type. However, the review and the aggregated results are based on more initiatives than the presented example.

Policy Initiatives

Road-pricing initiatives
The reason for road-pricing initiatives is to make the scarce road capacity subject to market functioning with the aim of better spreading traffic volume over time in order to reduce congestion as well as traffic-related emissions. Well-known road-pricing examples can be found in London (congestion charge) and Stockholm. Road pricing usually aims at all traffic participants and not only at urban freight transport (in contrast to all

other initiatives discussed in this chapter). Road pricing might discriminate between urban passenger and freight transport, but it usually does not. The increase in city accessibility that is reported in some initiatives is mainly due to the decrease in passenger transport, since urban freight transport seems quite indifferent to road price. In most cases carriers do not change their behaviour, because of customer/delivery requirements or the fact that they can charge the receiver the increased cost due to road pricing (see, e.g., Holguín-Veras et al., 2006 and Quak and Van Duin, 2010).

The road-pricing initiatives have especially positive effects on the accessibility of cities (due to the decrease in passenger transport), although most of the evaluated initiatives are not put into practice. Enforcement that does not hinder traffic and societal support adds to the likelihood of success. For the areas where congestion is caused mainly by urban freight transport, this policy initiative is probably not the best initiative to counter it, since it offers no alternatives. One of the reviewed road-pricing initiatives does provide an alternative: the introduction of truck-only toll lanes. These lanes have a higher toll than the free lanes (open to all traffic), but the speed is usually higher (Meyer, 2006).

Licensing and regulation
In licensing and regulation initiatives, local authorities aim at changing carriers' operations in order to become more sustainable (or at least to cause less nuisance) by complying with legislation. We distinguish several different licensing and regulation initiatives, usually with varying sustainability objectives: vehicle restrictions, vehicle load-factor controls, low-emission zones, time-access windows and dedicated infrastructure. These initiatives are not normally used in isolation, but to make other solution directions work (e.g. a low-emission zone forces carriers to use cleaner vehicles). Licensing and regulation initiatives are quite common in European countries (see OECD, 2003).

Local authorities use vehicle restrictions to improve traffic safety, reduce traffic problems, and protect buildings and infrastructure from damage. Besides, these restrictions are implemented to reduce nuisance caused by large trucks and so to improve quality of life in cities (e.g. reduction in visual nuisance and improvement in (perceived) traffic safety). As a result of vehicle restrictions, carriers have to use more small trucks. Therefore many vehicle restrictions result in a negative impact on the accessibility of cities, on the environment, and on logistical costs. Relaxing vehicle restrictions influences transport efficiency positively.

The main objective of vehicle load-factor controls is to reduce the number of vehicles entering the city due to stimulating consolidation outside the city centre in order to increase the vehicle load factor. The governmental objective corresponding to this type of initiative is improving city accessibility and liveability. Although the results are positive, vehicle load-factor controls are extremely hard to enforce. In the initiatives that were put into practice, it was easy to make an exception for carriers, which obviously undermined the effects of the policy measure.

Local authorities use low-emission zones (or environmental zones) to improve local air quality in cities by excluding pollutant trucks, that is, local pollutants such as PM and NO_x, from entering city centres. Only trucks that fulfil engine requirements (e.g. motor type Euro 4 and newer) are allowed in the low-emission zone. Obviously, this initiative type results in a decrease of local pollutants emitted, which by the way does not automatically improve air quality (i.e. the concentration of these pollutants in the air), since there are many other sources for PM and NO_x in cities (see, e.g., Van Rooijen and Quak, 2010). Low-emission zones might increase costs for carriers, depending on the number of zones and the vehicle replacement cycle. This initiative type is usually supported by society and industry where air quality problems in a city (or street) are obvious.

Time windows restrict trucks from entering areas, usually the city centre, during certain periods of the day. They usually allow vehicles only during hours in which residents are not bothered (so this excludes nights) and in which the shopping public is not hindered (so this excludes afternoons). Time windows reduce nuisance by trucks to periods that only few people notice; so they might improve the attractiveness of a city centre and traffic safety; these improvements are at the expense of the logistical costs and the environment (in pollutant emissions). These regulations are the opposite of practices in other European cities, where trucks are expected to work during the nights to alleviate congestion. Local authorities use dedicated infrastructure to oblige large vehicles to use only specific streets. The idea of forcing vehicles to use specific routes is to increase traffic safety and quality of life in an urban area (i.e. in the rest of the network) and to preserve infrastructure that was not designed for heavy vehicles. These initiatives can either originate from an attempt to ban or restrict urban freight operations or they could make urban freight transport more efficient. Especially the initiatives from the last case show positive results for accessibility and transport efficiency.

Finally, all licensing and regulation initiatives have in common that enforcement of these policy initiatives is necessary to make them successful in practice. If the initiatives are not enforced, carriers may not always oblige. Next, although many of these licensing and regulation initiatives are very local, a form of harmonization between these local regulations in cities shows better results for carriers (i.e. fewer logistical costs and better transport efficiency) without compromising environmental or social objectives.

Parking and unloading

Parking and unloading initiatives are used to solve two types of problem: those caused by the scarcity of available loading areas in crowded city centres; and those caused by unloading vehicles; for example, double-parked vehicles that are unloading result in traffic problems. Most parking and unloading initiatives focus on creation (e.g. using bus bays) or reservation of dedicated unloading areas. This is relatively easy and not expensive. Many of these initiatives are implemented in practice. Enforcement of the proper use of unloading areas is the key success factor. The sustainability impacts of these very local initiatives are limited. Only those cities that face serious problems due to vehicles that are unloading (e.g. illegal parking, congestion due to on-street unloading of vehicles, travelling extra kilometres because a truck driver can't find a suitable unloading area) should consider these initiatives.

Company-driven Initiatives

Carrier cooperation

The main aim of carrier cooperation initiatives, which require competitors to cooperate, is to improve the efficiency of urban freight deliveries. This is an example of a logistics-driven solution direction. As secondary objectives for carrier cooperation we find improving city accessibility, reducing city congestion, and reducing pollutant emissions. However, the main focus for private companies is to increase the efficiency of their operations. Carriers can cooperate in different ways, for example by consolidating goods at a specific premises or by using a neutral carrier (perhaps using shared participation) in order to prevent two half-filled vehicles from visiting one street. Most of the carrier cooperation initiatives found in this review were initiated by researchers from Japan, but the majority were not implemented (especially operational research propositions from academics). Those that were implemented suffer from a lack of participants. This can be explained by the fact that in most of the reviewed initiatives the logistical costs increase, whereas the carriers are supposed to join the initiative on a voluntary basis. A real incentive for carriers, except for the company's social and environmental reputation, seems to be lacking. Sustainability is becoming an increasingly real incentive for companies, however. Carrier cooperation initiatives in last-mile deliveries prove successful in theory (i.e. positive impacts on city accessibility, the environment and transport efficiency). However, in practice there are usually major barriers to its success; the (real) willingness to cooperate with a competitor or to share valuable information is lacking. Next, the driver and the truck are often considered the salesman or the signboard of the company. Successful implementation of carrier cooperation initiatives depends on: making sure that a company does not lose its identity; including social costs in the initiative; gaining support from the public sector; making all gains clearly visible and as transparent as possible; and appealing to an organization's social and environmental reputation.

Vehicle-routing improvements

Vehicle-routing improvements are an example of technological solutions based on IT. Many academic authors have focused on vehicle-routing problem-related issues. The vehicle-routing improvement initiatives in this review usually differ from those of the mainstream VRP authors, since city logistics-related objectives, such as sustainability in urban areas, are included. Typical city problems, for example congestion, result in infeasible vehicle planning. The main idea of vehicle-routing improvement initiatives is to better incorporate real-life problems and so to reduce the number of vehicle-kilometres travelled and the penalty cost. Therefore these initiatives show positive results on carriers' costs and on the environment. Most of the reviewed initiatives are not tested in practice, but only by simulation. It is obvious that infeasibilities are costly in terms of late arrivals and penalty costs. Some initiatives do not try to improve planning, but use real-time information to find the best possible solution after an event or congestion actually occurs; extra kilometres add to the congestion and also increase pollutant emissions as well as nuisance in cities.

Technological vehicle innovations

There are many examples of technological vehicle innovations; however, only a few of these initiatives were actually reported by academics and therefore meet the selection criteria of this review. Most technological vehicle innovations reduce some of the nuisance caused by vehicles, such as noise, emissions and even safety. These industrial solutions make trucks cleaner, and regulations stimulate cleaner technologies; for example Euro regulations on motor and permitted (local) pollutants have a huge impact on the amount of local pollutants emitted. Electric trucks, hybrid propulsion and compressed-natural-gas trucks are experimented with in urban areas. Many initiatives could be reported under this initiative type, but most of these innovations seem to be put into practice rather than described in the urban freight transport literature. Other initiatives, which focus on designing special trucks for urban operations, for example low floors to speed up loading and unloading, freight buses and so on, are usually initiated by manufacturers and therefore not readily found in the academic literature.

The technological vehicle innovation initiatives that were found show positive environmental results. The advantage is that this type of initiative does not usually require serious changes in urban freight operations; however, the investment cost are high for carriers. Therefore there could be an active role for governments in stimulating investments by subsidies or other advantages for clean trucks.

Physical Infrastructure Initiatives

Consolidation centres

City consolidation centre (CCC) initiatives are typical city logistics initiatives (see, e.g., Taniguchi and Van der Heijden, 2000) and are sometimes even used as a synonym for city logistics. The rationale for consolidation centre initiatives is to divide the freight transport into two parts: the part inside the city and the part outside the city. This distinction makes it possible to design both types of transport to fit the specific characteristics best; that is, use large vehicles for long-haul transportation outside the city on highways, without having disadvantages such as difficult manoeuvrability, visual intrusion and traffic safety issues in the city. Smaller trucks are used for distribution activities inside the city from the consolidation centre. A consolidation centre is especially interesting as a starting point for electric vehicles; in this way most nuisance from urban freight transport is countered (e.g. noise and pollution). Because the vehicle makes small round-trips from the consolidation centre, the electric vehicle's limited action radius is not a problem. In the consolidation centre cargo has to be transhipped from the large vehicles to the city distribution vehicles. This extra handling activity adds to the cost, which implies that there should be savings somewhere else in the supply chain. The business model for these city distribution centres is examined in more detail in Quak and Tavasszy (forthcoming 2011). Although this type of initiative seems very appealing, there are almost no examples of city consolidation centres that are running a successful business without financial support from governments. For example, Browne et al. (2005) find that of the approximately 200 planned or realized CCC schemes in Germany in the 1990s, at most five were actually operating in 2005. In many studies, carrier participation is estimated higher than it turned out to be in practice. This implies less bundling of goods and fewer scale advantages than planned for the participating carriers. Usually, carriers are not willing to cooperate in a consolidation centre initiative, since they often consider the operator that delivers goods from the consolidation centre to the outlets as a competitor. Browne et al. (2005, p. 3) state in their review that 'some urban consolidation centre trials have been based on intuition rather than a quantified assessment and as a consequence are never likely to be viable'. From the various reviewed consolidation centre initiatives we learn that many carriers consider supporting policy measures as a way for local authorities to keep the non-viable centre alive, instead of the consolidation centre as a means of dealing with (usually restricting) policy measures, such as time windows. A CCC provides a carrier with the opportunity to deliver all day and not only during the time window. If electric vehicles are used, these should not hinder other traffic (e.g. slow it down), because then public opinion will turn against the CCC. A CCC is not a solution for all deliveries to the city. For example, if an FTL (full truckload) delivery has to be delivered via a CCC, this would result in two smaller vehicles in the city. These two vehicles emit more pollutants and pressurize the congestion in the city centre more than the FTL delivery in one large vehicle. Besides, it adds to the total transport costs. So, already-efficient deliveries should not use the CCC. From a logistical point of view, the major potential beneficiaries of a CCC are independent and small retailers as well as operators making small multi-drop deliveries, especially in areas where there are constraints on delivery conditions (e.g. restricting regulations or congestion). Offering extra services, for example pick-up points or storage, could also add to a viable business model for a CCC. An example of an operating CCC can be found in Van Rooijen and Quak (2010). Finally, the decision on the location(s) can determine success or failure; many CCCs experience high land or rental prices. Currently, (huge) subsidies are necessary to operate CCCs. So there should be enough societal gains (e.g. less pollution) to justify the subsidies. These gains are not always clear. Overall, consolidation centres seem to be most feasible, if feasible at all, for historical cities that have restrictive and inhibitive conditions for urban freight transportation anyway, as well as potential governmental restrictions. Carriers, currently responsible for making deliveries in urban areas, are accustomed to do so without a consolidation centre. Besides, small (local) transport operators usually ask very low prices as subcontractors for urban deliveries because of the serious competition due to overcapacity in the market.

Underground logistics systems
One of the most radical initiatives to improve the sustainability of urban freight transport is the development of an underground logistics system. These initiatives are currently only theoretical. The studies were not put into practice. The main idea is that these initiatives eliminate all negative impacts without compromising the positive impacts of urban freight transport. This way of delivering goods to city centres was examined as early as 1860 for the London city centre (a pneumatic capsule system). In later studies, goods are transported underground by AGVs (automatic guided vehicles). In the studies all underground logistics

systems show great benefits in the form of reduced (or eliminated) nega-tive environmental and societal impacts. However, these positive results come at very high initial (investment) costs, whereas the actual mainte-nance costs are unknown. Other issues remain uncertain as well: how to involve different stakeholders and who will be responsible for operating the system and the transport underground. Obviously, these systems could only be developed with huge financial governmental support. From a cost–benefit point of view these enormous investments make sense only if all gains are considered (also social and environmental gains, although these gains do not currently have a monetary value) over the lifespan of such a system. Next, there are great risks in developing an underground system in a city – for example collapsing or damag-ing historical buildings in the city centre. On the other hand, this type of initiative shows enormous positive sustainability impacts as well as positive logistics effects, for example space for extra storage and 24-hour delivery possibilities.

Road infrastructure development
This type of initiative focuses on development of new infrastructure in the city. Many sustainability problems are related to the use of road infrastructure, so the development of road infrastructure might seem out of place as a UFTS initiative. However, for cities where the need for available road infrastructure is urgent and where congestion causes the majority of the sustainability issues, development of extra road infra-structure results in improvement of transport efficiency. As a result, city accessibility increases and there are fewer pollutant emissions. In histori-cal cities this type of initiative might simply not be possible, since it is difficult to develop road infrastructure in a dense area. For cities that suffer less from spatial scarcity, this type might work, for example cities in Australia.

Standardization of Load Units
The idea for this initiative type, a standard load unit for city distribu-tion, is based on the success of the sea container. Standardized load-unit initiatives are mainly enablers for the success of other initiative types that depend on the efficient transfer of goods (see, e.g., consolidation centre initiatives). Innovative distribution concepts, such as shuttle concepts, rail-bound systems, the combination of freight and passenger transport, or waterborne concepts (see also the section on intermodal transport) would be more likely to be put into practice if there were a widely accepted and used standard inland container. The development of a load unit, a city (or inland) container, is not difficult in itself; however,

it is hard to create a standard that is accepted and used by many actors. Large-scale utilization of standard load units could have positive impacts – for example, increase in city accessibility, fewer pollutant emissions, increase in transport efficiency and a decrease in logistics costs. Such a load unit makes transhipment easier, which makes it possible to develop a distribution system that suits different specific urban characteristics – for example, long-haul transport on large trucks with five load units and city distribution on small trucks with two load units (see also TNO, 2003). The main problem is to implement such a system; many actors have to make initial investments to profit from the advantages of a standardized load unit. If standardization is not achieved, the situation is similar to current distribution systems, where different actors use the load units that fit them best.

Transport-reorganizing Initiatives

Transport auction

A transport auction can be characterized as an IT solution. The main idea is to make the transport system more efficient by reducing the number of empty kilometres travelled and so reduce the number of truck-kilometres in urban areas as well as the corresponding emissions. This initiative type also takes into account the collections that have to be made in urban areas. A freight market, for example an Internet-based auction (or exchange) of collections and deliveries in urban areas, would increase transparency in transport supply and demand so that it becomes easier to find cargo for vehicles that would otherwise return empty from an urban area. The maximum efficiency gains are constrained by the available transport volume in the back-haul direction. So a reduction in (empty) kilometres is possible, but elimination is not. The gains are also limited by carriers' unwillingness to share information with competitors, lack of critical mass, the fact that carriers share only non-profitable cargo, and trust in the action system. Theoretically this initiative type shows large potential to reduce the total amount of vehicle-kilometres.

Intermodal transport

Intermodal urban freight transport initiatives try to reorganize transport by using non-road modes that produce fewer pollutant emissions. This initiative type especially appeals to policy-makers' imagination, since it shows concretely the change in transport and proves that (polluting) trucks are replaced. However, in most cities, rail or water networks are usually not dense enough to deliver a considerable part of the urban freight volume (apart from the obvious exceptions such as Venice). Some studies combine passenger and freight transport (e.g. trains, trams and metros), but these systems are not put into practice.

Some small-scale applications of intermodal transport exist, such as waterborne or rail concepts in city distribution:

- Parcel services (DHL boat) in Amsterdam: specific circumstances here are poor road accessibility and extensive canal network.
- Beer and beverage deliveries in Utrecht (the beer boat): many pubs and restaurants are located at a canal quay located lower than the road. Because of this, these premises are hard to access by truck, since a driver has to carry all beverages one level lower by stairs. The water is at the same level as the premises, which makes waterborne distribution ideal.
- The Monoprix example in France. Monoprix (a large supermarket company) delivers its dry products, non-alcoholic beverages and general products (specific volume) in Paris using regional rail services and urban deliveries by compressed-natural-gas trucks (see Dablanc and Rakotonarivo, 2010).
- The cargotram in Dresden: this is a dedicated freight tram between the logistics centre of Volkswagen and the Volkswagen factory. So there is only one customer (i.e. Volkswagen) and full tramloads are transported through the city centre to prevent over 200 truck movements per day.
- Other cargotram initiatives exist: in one initiative the tram is used as the collection point for bulky waste (Zurich); in another initiative for internal goods transport of the public transport company (Vienna).

Intermodal urban freight transport is feasible only in specific circumstances and for a limited part of the total urban freight transport volume. This initiative type is not a generic solution for urban freight transport issues. For specific cases and under specific circumstances, this initiative type shows improvements in both environmental effects and city-accessibility performance. There might be opportunities for transferring goods from other modes in an intermodal urban distribution centre from rail or road (for long-haul transport to the city) on trucks for city distribution (see also the consolidation centres and the Monoprix examples). Other success factors for using non-road modes in urban freight transport are the availability of rail or water infrastructural networks and the requirement not to hinder passenger transport (e.g. on the tram-rail network). Standardized load units (inland containers) would also make the use of other modalities more likely (see section on load units).

FINAL REMARKS

Based on the 106 UFTS initiatives that were reviewed and the identified 12 initiative types, we can come to some conclusions. First, many initiatives to improve sustainability in urban freight transport have been undertaken over recent years; however, great breakthroughs have not been made. In many initiatives the right mix between logistical, technological and policy solution directions is lacking. This implies that not all interests of all different actors were taken in account. From the initiatives we can learn that local authorities' knowledge of carriers' logistical operations appears to be inadequate, whereas most carriers know only very little about local authorities' sustainability issues. Even though the carbon footprint and the aim of reducing global pollution is becoming more common in companies (and also among carriers), the local sustainability issues (e.g. air quality and nuisance) that are very relevant for urban freight transport are not so well known. Carriers are usually active at a regional or national scale, whereas local authorities focus on a limited geographical scale – the city. Besides, national or economic factors make urban freight issues difficult to solve; for example, transport prices are in some European countries very low due to overcapacity in the market and the high number of (very) small transport companies. Next, the interaction between different actors, and that between local authorities and carriers in particular, is limited. This prevents the actors from obtaining insights into each other's problems and thus getting a complete picture of the different urban freight transport issues. An initiative is doomed to fail if the initiator is unable to realize what the implications of this initiative are outside its own (often narrow-bounded) interest field. For many UFTS initiatives, the active involvement of different actors shows whether there is a real incentive for the actor to change its behaviour. If those actors that are supposed to change their behaviour are not really involved in the initiative, the initiative usually fails.

Carriers are responsible for executing urban freight transport operations; but these actors seem to lack either the power or the willingness (since the margins in the transport world are often very narrow) to change their operations and make urban freight transport more sustainable. The lack of real stimuli (for carriers) to change results in a strong emphasis on legislation (and subsequently enforcement) of many initiatives. To change actors' behaviour, an initiative could target an actor who is able to increase the interaction between different actors and their actions, for example the receivers or the higher government, neither of whom is really involved in the reviewed UFTS initiatives. Receivers are not usually capable of linking local authorities and carriers, since they act locally and have contact with carriers only at the moment of delivery. Receivers, especially small private store-owners, often do not realize that they are (partly) responsible for the current unsustainable organization of urban freight transport (by ordering small quantities from many different suppliers). Currently many higher governments consider urban freight transport to be a local issue, and therefore not their business.

Finally, many initiatives fail to distinguish between different types of transport, such as parcel deliveries, LTL (less-than-truck load) and FTL (full truck load) deliveries. An initiative might be a good solution for LTL deliveries (e.g. the use of a consolidation centre), but if this solution is used for FTL deliveries, it results in an increase of the negative effects. This might result in the failure of the initiative, whereas the solution works well for parts of urban freight transport. Overall, a great many solutions have been considered and tested. Although many of these initiatives failed, it might be possible to use the standard solutions in a tailor-made mix of different solutions that considers different objectives and interests. In an appropriate mix, the city-specific circumstances are considered and those initiatives are combined that best fulfil local demands. This makes it possible to develop more sustainable urban freight transport without having to reinvent the wheel.

REFERENCES

Allen, J., S. Anderson, M. Browne and P. Jones (2000), 'A framework for considering policies to encourage sustainable urban freight traffic and goods/ service flows', Transport Studies Group, University of Westminster, London.

Ambrosini, C. and J.L. Routhier (2004), 'Objectives, methods and results of surveys carried out in the field of urban freight transport: an international comparison', *Transport Reviews*, **24** (1), 57–77.

Browne, M. and J. Allen (1999), 'The impact of sustainability policies on urban freight transport and logistics systems', in H. Meermans, E. Van de Voorde and W. Winkelmans (eds), *8th World Conference on Transport Research (WCTR), Volume 1 Transport Modes and Systems*, Antwerp: Elsevier, pp. 505–18.

Browne, M., M. Sweet, A. Woodburn and J. Allen (2005), 'Urban freight consolidation centres – final report', Transport Studies Group, University of Westminster, London.

Dablanc, L. and D. Rakotonarivo (2010), 'The impacts of logistic sprawl: how does the location of parcel transport terminals affect the energy efficiency of goods' movement in Paris and what can we do about it?', in E. Taniguchi and R.G. Thompson (eds), *City Logistics VI, Procedia – Social and Behavioral Sciences*, **2** (3), 6087–96.

Holguín-Veras, J., Q. Wang, N. Xu, K. Ozbay, M. Cetin and J. Polimeni (2006), 'The impacts of time of day pricing on the behavior of freight carriers in a congested urban area: implications to road pricing', *Transportation Research Part A: Policy and Practice*, **40** (9), 744–66.

Meyer, M.D. (2006), 'Feasibility of a metropolitan truck-only toll lane network: the case of Atlanta, Georgia', Metrans National Urban Freight Conference', Long Beach, CA, USA.

OECD (2003), *Delivering the Goods: 21st Century Challenges to Urban Goods Transport*, Paris: OECD.

Quak, H.J. (2008), 'Sustainability of urban freight transport – retail distribution and local regulations in cities', Ph.D. thesis (ERIM Ph.D. Series Research in Management 124, TRAIL Thesis Series T2008/5), ERIM, Rotterdam.

Quak, H.J. and M.B.M. De Koster (2007), 'Exploring retailers' sensitivity to local sustainability policies', *Journal of Operations Management*, **25** (6), 1103–22.

Quak, H.J. and M.B.M. De Koster (2009), 'Delivering in urban areas – how to deal with urban policy restrictions and the environment', *Transportation Science*, **43** (2), 211–27.

Quak, H.J. and L.A. Tavasszy (forthcoming 2011), 'Customized solutions for sustainable city logistics', in J. van Nunen, P. Rietveld and P. Huijbregts (eds), Transitions towards Sustainable Mobility, Berlin: Springer.

Quak, H.J. and J.H.R. Van Duin (2010), 'The influence of road pricing on physical distribution in urban areas', in E. Taniguchi and R.G. Thompson (eds), *City Logistics VI, Procedia – Social and Behavioral Sciences*, **2** (3), 6141–53.

Quak, H.J., J.H.R. Van Duin and J. Visser (2008), 'City logistics over the years. . . lessons learned, research directions and interests', in E. Taniguchi and R.G. Thompson (eds), *Innovations in City Logistics*, New York: Nova Science Publisher, pp. 37–54.

Taniguchi, E. and R.E.C.M. Van der Heijden (2000), 'An evaluation methodology for city logistics', *Transport Reviews*, **20** (1), 65–90.

Taniguchi, E., R.G. Thompson and T. Yamada (2004), 'Visions for city logistics', in E. Taniguchi and R.G. Thompson (eds), *Logistics Systems for Sustainable Cities*, Amsterdam: Elsevier, pp. 1–16.

TNO (2003), 'De economische haalbaarheid van de stadsbox in stedelijke distributie', TNO Inro, Delft.

Van Rooijen, T. and H.J. Quak (2010), 'Local impacts of a new urban consolidation centre – the case of Binnenstadservice', in E. Taniguchi and R.G. Thompson (eds), *City Logistics VI, Procedia – Social and Behavioral Sciences*, **2** (3), 5967–79.

3. Characteristics and typology of last-mile logistics from an innovation perspective in an urban context

Roel Gevaers, Eddy Van de Voorde and Thierry Vanelslander

INTRODUCTION

In the past decade, the e-commerce market for products ranging from high-value durable goods to low-value consumer goods has experienced strong growth as well as sweeping change. The expansion of the market has coincided with an upsurge in direct-to-consumer deliveries. While this type of service is not new (as evidenced by the mail-order firms of the 1980s and 1990s), the e-commerce boom has certainly stimulated its further development. Concurrently, this evolution has drawn attention to certain issues in the final part of the supply chain. These are referred to collectively as the last-mile problem.

The last mile is currently regarded as one of the more expensive, least efficient and most polluting sections of the entire logistics chain. This is due to a number of inherent factors. In home deliveries, for example, there is the security aspect and the associated not-at-home problem to consider, especially as the recipient may have to sign a reception confirmation. This results in high delivery failure and empty trip[1] rates, which substantially affect cost, efficiency and environmental performance (cf. emissions). Another potential problem is lack of critical mass in certain areas or regions, which will likewise affect cost. The fact that a substantial proportion of home deliveries are performed by van is also regarded as a drawback, as this translates into higher emissions per parcel as compared to delivery by truck.

Hitherto, relatively little attention has been paid in the academic literature to the specificities of last-mile logistics and their relevance to innovation in this crucial part of the supply chain. The present contribution therefore aims to identify characteristics and determinants that are instrumental to the efficiency and cost effects of innovative concepts in a last-mile context[2] in urban areas. The research question under consideration is as follows: which specific and demonstrable characteristics of the last mile offer scope for innovation that will substantially and significantly affect efficiency, cost and environmental performance? In other words, which aspects must companies and the public authorities take into account when implementing innovative concepts in last-mile logistics in order that efficiency gains, cost reductions and environmental improvements can be optimized?

This chapter is organized as follows. First, the notion of the 'last mile' is defined. Subsequently, the focus shifts to an assessment of a last-mile typology proposed in the literature. Finally, we offer a detailed analysis – from an innovation perspective – of the last-mile problem, whereby the issue is broken down into flow-dependent characteristics and ways of measuring them.

THE CONCEPT OF LAST MILE

Defining the Last Mile

The last mile may be defined as the final leg in a business-to-consumer delivery service whereby the consignment is delivered to the recipient, either at the recipient's home or at a collection point.

In this chapter, we restrict ourselves to the very last section of the supply chain, starting from the moment that the goods or parcels leave the warehouse of the supplier or logistics provider. Thus the aspect of order-picking is left aside for our present purpose. Figure 3.1 is a schematic representation of the last mile in a supply chain.

A standard logistics chain may be organized as follows. Raw materials are supplied to the processing industry, from where finished

Source: Own design, based on De Smedt and Gevaers (2009).

Figure 3.1   Basic structure of a supply chain

product is (possibly via a number of intermediate steps) shipped to the storage facilities (i.e. warehouses or distribution centres) of the logistics provider. From this point onwards, there are two distribution options: either through traditional outlets such as stores or supermarkets, or through direct sales to consumers. The term 'last mile' refers specifically to the final leg in a system involving direct-to-consumer deliveries.

As a result of the ongoing growth in e-commerce, the direct-sales market is presently experiencing substantial expansion. This has important implications for the last mile in the supply chain, not least in terms of capacity.

A Typology of Last-mile Deliveries

In order to be able to adequately analyse and interpret the typical characteristics of the last-mile concept, we need to differentiate between various types of last-mile deliveries.

The typology proposed by Boyer et al. (2005) is arguably the most advanced and commonly applied model. It distinguishes between four subtypes, corresponding to four kinds of supply chain: the semi-extended supply chain, the decoupled supply chain, the fully extended supply chain and the centralized extended supply chain.

The model uses a matrix based on the variables warehousing and/or distribution point on the one hand and delivery type on the other (see Figure 3.2).

The semi-extended supply chain uses shops and supermarkets (lower fixed capital investments – but lower efficiency) as locations for order-picking, and it relies on distribution methods whereby the deliveries are outsourced to a third party. The fully extended supply chain likewise uses stores as order-picking locations, but keeps the (home) deliveries internal (not outsourced).

The decoupled supply chain relies on distribution centres and uses outsourced delivery methods. Finally, the centralized extended supply chain similarly makes use of distribution centres, but does not outsource the deliveries.

The typology proposed by Boyer et al. (2005) does have a serious drawback, however. As it is based on a rather crude distinction, it does not adequately reflect the specific characteristics of the last mile and its associated problems.

However, if we consider the various types of delivery, we arrive at the overview shown in Figure 3.3.

The principal last-mile problems will be discussed on the basis of the

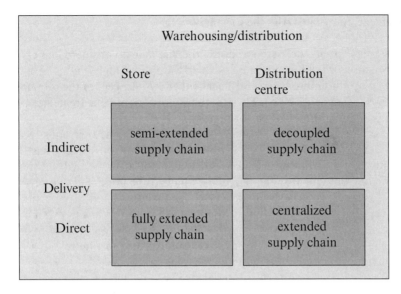

Source: Boyer et al. (2005).

Figure 3.2   A last-mile typology

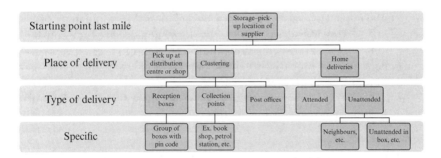

Sources: based on Gevaers et al. (2008, 2009a,b), Leavit (2008), Madlberger (2005), Murphy (2006), Punakivi et al. (2001), Van Oosterhout (2004) and Weltevreden (2008).

Figure 3.3   Various delivery methods in the last mile

above overview of delivery methods. In this context, the term 'charac-teristic' should be understood to mean a typical aspect with a potentially important and significant impact on efficiency and cost in relation to the last mile of a supply chain.

Problems Associated with the Last Mile

Due to its specific delivery structure, the last mile is considered an expensive section, if not the most expensive, in the entire supply chain. Last-mile costs may amount to between 13 per cent and 75 per cent of the total logistics cost[3] (Onghena, 2008). These high proportions are due to inefficiencies and poor environmental performance.

The most substantial last-mile issues occur in home deliveries requiring a signature for reception. If no specific window of delivery has been arranged, the failure rate due to 'customer not at home' will inevitably be high. Consequently, the parcel may have to be presented two or three times before it is successfully delivered. On the other hand, a pre-arranged delivery window will inevitably compromise routing efficiency. After all, limited delivery windows imply that a courier needs to cover more miles for the same number of deliveries, as demonstrated in Figure 3.4, a phenomenon commonly referred to as the 'ping-pong effect'.[4]

A second frequently encountered problem is lack of critical mass in a given region, due to inadequate market density or penetration. If, by consequence, a courier needs to travel over 30 miles in order to deliver a single parcel, efficiency will be strongly reduced and cost greatly increased.

Furthermore, consumers are becoming increasingly aware of the environmental impact of logistics and transport choices. More and more often, they demand from logistics providers that they should strive for a constant reduction of their carbon emissions footprint. Yet, more often than not, consumers are not prepared to either pay more or wait longer for their goods in return for a greener service.

In what follows, we sum up and analyse the most significant last-mile characteristics in an innovation context.

LAST-MILE CHARACTERISTICS FROM AN INNOVATION PERSPECTIVE

The nature of the last mile is determined largely by five fundamental aspects: the level of consumer service; security and delivery type; the geographical area; the degree of market penetration and density; the vehicle fleet and technology employed; and the environmental impact. Each of these elements will be elucidated and analysed in detail. Subsequently, we shall assess their relevance to the different last-mile subflows in order to identify suitable areas for innovation.

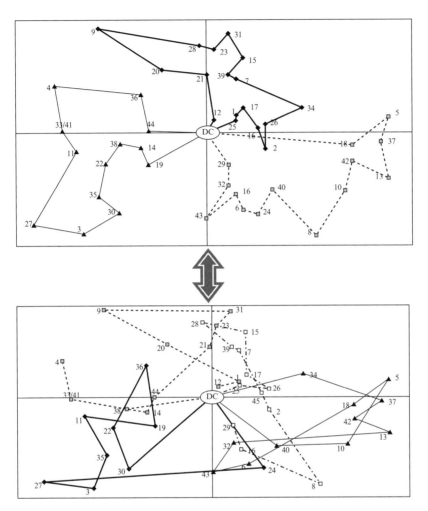

Note: DC = distribution centre.

Source: Boyer et al. (2005).

Figure 3.4 *Simulation of a delivery route with (bottom) and without (top) windows*

Consumer Service Levels

Consumer service levels can significantly affect the efficiency of the supply chain, including through such sub-characteristics or proxy variables as

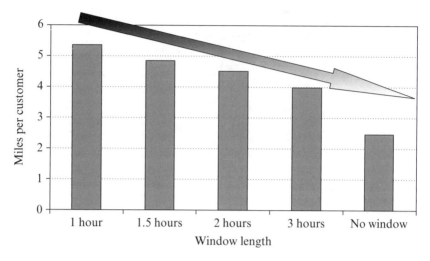

Source: Boyer et al. (2009).

Figure 3.5   Effects of delivery window size

delivery windows, delivery lead times, delivery frequency and the possibility of returning goods or packages to sender.

Boyer et al. (2009) have simulated various effects of delivery window size.[5] Figure 3.5 represents the relationship between window size and average mileage per delivery point. The purpose of their simulation was to gain insight into the impact of delivery window sizes on vehicle routing. To this end, they made use of Fleetwise Monitor by Descartes, a routing software application that, as the authors point out, is commonly relied on in the logistics and transport business.

Figure 3.5 indicates that the greater the window length, the smaller the number of miles per customer. It follows that cost will rise as more and tighter delivery windows are incorporated into the routing schedule.

A similar study or simulation by Kämäräinen (2001) found a cost difference of 42 per cent between a system of indefinite deliveries to reception and/or delivery boxes on the one hand and a method incorporating delivery time windows on the other. This difference in cost was calculated on the basis of data from a pilot project in the greater Helsinki area in Finland. The average cost of delivery within a time window was €2.1, as compared to an average cost of €1.2 for indefinite delivery to a box.[6]

Source: Punakivi and Saranen (2001).

Figure 3.6   Cost comparison between delivery with and without signed confirmation

Security and Delivery Type

The likelihood of non-delivery due to 'customer not at home' depends to a large extent on whether or not the consignee is required to sign for receipt. If not, perhaps the goods may be left in a closed box at the front door. Obviously the type of product to be delivered will co-determine whether this is a feasible option (e.g. frozen foods).

The sub-characteristics or proxy variables of security and delivery type are home delivery with and without signature for receipt, delivery to collection points, and the use of delivery lockers or boxes.

A simulation by Punakivi and Saranen (2001) found that the cost difference between delivery with and without signature for receipt can amount to a factor of 2.5 (see Figure 3.6).

Consignments requiring signature for receipt tend to have a high non-delivery rate. In other words, they generate a greater likelihood of couriers needing to return several times to the same address before being able to successfully deliver the parcel. Each failure to deliver represents a substantial cost increase for the last-mile logistics provider. This increased cost through non-delivery is also represented in Figure 3.6. Fernie and McKinnon (2004) assert that the average proportion of failed deliveries amounts to around 30 per cent, depending on the type of product involved.

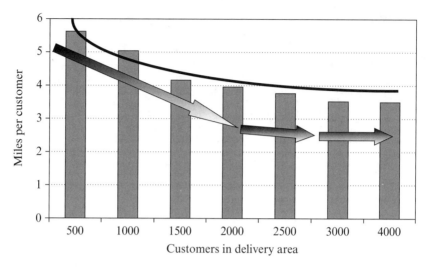

Source: Based on Boyer et al. (2009).

Figure 3.7   Effects of consumer density

Geographical Area and Market Penetration and Density

In certain regions, market penetration may be crucially important for attaining a sufficient critical mass. Here, the main sub-characteristics or proxy variables are the density of the region or market and the average distance between the various delivery points, as well as the extent to which goods may be pooled during routing.

As in the case of delivery to traditional outlets such as supermarkets and shops, market size is an important economic parameter in the context of last-mile deliveries. If just one parcel needs to be collected or delivered in a particular region, cost will increase substantially in consequence of the (empty) mileage involved. Yet the population density of the delivery area usually does not affect the delivery price.

Boyer et al. (2009) have simulated the relationship between population and market density on the one hand and mileage per delivery point on the other (see Figure 3.7).

In this simulation, the delivery area was assumed to measure one square mile. It shows that there is an unequivocal declining relationship between mileage per delivery address on the one hand and the number of consumers in the delivery area on the other. The associated cost increases as the number of customers in the delivery area declines. It should be noted, though, that the relationship is one of decreasing marginal miles per delivery address. The optimum[7] for this simulation is between 3000 and 5000 persons per square mile.

Vehicle Fleet and Technology

The vehicle fleet operated by the logistics provider can significantly affect cost in various ways, including through fuel consumption, the (optimum) loading capacity, loading and unloading methods, safety and so on. The sub-characteristics or proxy variables are type of van and/or truck.

A less obvious, but equally important, proxy variable is the type of information and communication technology (ICT) used. It is essential to optimum routing that the logistics provider should be able to respond quickly and accurately to fluctuations during collection and delivery. By relying on situation-specific ICT systems, one can save time, paperwork and fuel.

The Environmental Factor

Consumers and service providers are becoming increasingly aware of the environmental impacts of economic activities, transport operations and logistics services. As a result, many consumers expect suppliers to apply or introduce environmentally friendly methods. However, consumers' willingness to pay for environmentally sound delivery methods is low or virtually non-existent. Similarly, as mentioned earlier, consumers are not prepared to accept longer service times in exchange for greener delivery.

Within the context of last-mile services, suppliers need to balance against each other the need for quick and limited delivery windows on the one hand and the striving for environmentally viable delivery on the other. The smaller the delivery window, the greater the negative environmental impact of the delivery method is likely to be.

In the future, logistics providers will need to offer different delivery options (quick versus slow, with time window versus unrestricted etc.) and they will need to raise consumers' awareness of the cost implications of their choice for a green delivery method.

LAST-MILE TYPOLOGY FROM AN INNOVATION PERSPECTIVE

Next, we wish to draw up a typology based on the previously discussed last-mile characteristics. Clearly, existing typologies (such as that proposed by Boyer et al., 2005) are not satisfactory from an innovation

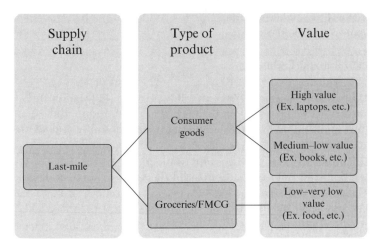

Note: FMCG = fast moving consumer goods.

Source: Own diagram.

Figure 3.8   Typology of last-mile subflows

perspective, as they do not distinguish appropriately between subflows. In this context, a last-mile typology can be adequate only if it allows a detailed analysis of the relevance of the aforementioned characteristics. Only then does it become possible to determine where innovation can help optimize cost and efficiency, and minimize environmental impact. To this end, we propose a typology that distinguishes between subflows on the basis of product value, as presented in Figure 3.8.

The last mile may be subdivided into three value-based flows: high-value/durable products (such as laptops), durable goods of medium value (such as DVDs and books), and finally goods with a low to very low unit value (such as groceries or daily consumer goods).

Table 3.1 categorizes the subflows according to the relevance of the various sub-characteristics or proxy variables.

Sub-characteristic or proxy variables that apply to a particular subflow are marked 'x' in the appropriate box of Table 3.1. Moreover, if the sub-characteristic greatly affects cost, efficiency and/or environmental performance (in either a positive or a negative sense), then the corresponding cell has been hatched.

We now analyse the proposed classification in greater detail. For the characteristic 'consumer service', the time window, the short lead time and the delivery frequency can significantly affect last-mile efficiency

Table 3.1   Assignment of characteristics/proxy variables to subflows

	Low value	Medium value	High value
Consumer service			
Time window	x		
Lead time	x	x	x
Frequency	x		
Return		x	x
Security & delivery type			
Home delivery with signature		x	x
Home delivery without signature	x		
Collection points		x	x
Boxes	x		
Geographical area & market density / penetration			
Density	x	x	x
Pooling of goods	x	x	x
Fleet & technology			
Type of delivery vehicle	x	x	x
Information & communication technology / informatics	x	x	x
The environment			
Packaging	x	x	x
Trade-off between time factors and environmental impact	x	x	x

Source: Own analysis.

and cost for the subflow of low-value products. This is due to the fact that, when ordering low-value products such as groceries online, the consumer is generally not prepared to wait as long as he would be if he were ordering a laptop or a book. Moreover, long lead times can give rise to problems of freshness if the products concerned are perishable. In the case of groceries, the customer may expect delivery before a certain time, for example lunch (time window), and several times per week (frequency).

In the case of high- and medium-value goods, such time-related factors are far less relevant, as the consumer's willingness to wait for delivery of these kinds of goods will generally be greater. Within the subflows of high- and medium-value goods, it is primarily the delivery return rate that significantly affects the efficiency of the last mile. This is primarily due to the fact that, in Europe, e-commerce legislation is extremely customer-friendly, which translates into a high proportion of goods delivered through direct sales channels being returned to the supplier.

As regards security and delivery type, clearly a courier is unable to leave high- and medium-value goods unattended and without the customer's signature for receipt. Hence, for these types of product, issues such as 'customer not at home' come into play. This is far less the case for low-value goods, as these can be left without signature for receipt, for example in a box at the front door. In order to reduce the proportion of home deliveries with signature requirement, one can opt for a system of collection points, for example newspaper agents, petrol stations and the like, where the goods are delivered for the customer to pick up upon signature. This will strongly reduce the rate of delivery failure due to 'customer not at home'. Collection points offer the greatest potential for efficiency gains and cost savings within the subflows of high-value and medium-value goods (Punakivi et al., 2001; Van Oosterhout, 2004; Weltevreden, 2008).

As previously mentioned, time-sensitive deliveries are particularly problematic or cost-inducing within the subflows of low-value products. This has implications for the aspects 'geographical location' and 'market penetration or density'. After all, time-sensitive deliveries, with narrow windows or short lead times, leave less scope for pooling of goods, which in turn results in rising cost, including through more empty trips. It follows that urban environments on average imply lower delivery costs thanks to their greater market density. Cities also tend to offer greater possibilities than rural areas for home delivery of low-value goods such as food.

The proxy variable ICT – an aspect of vehicle fleet and technology – is relevant to all flows, but its effect is potentially greater for low-value commodity flows, due to the fact that routing decisions for such goods need to take greater account of time-related factors.

Likewise, in so far as the variable 'environment' is concerned, the previously referred to trade-off between environmental effects and time-sensitive delivery is mainly problematic in the case of low-value goods. After all, the willingness to pay for green delivery methods will tend to be lower for such commodities: the lower the value of the goods, the more quickly the cost of the delivery method is likely to become disproportionate in the eyes of the consumer; conversely, in the case of high-value goods, the consumer will be more readily prepared to pay extra for green delivery, as here the delivery cost represents just a fraction of the total price (Smithers, 2007).

THE RELATIONSHIP BETWEEN LAST-MILE CHARACTERISTICS/PROXY VARIABLES AND THE URBAN ENVIRONMENT

As far as the characteristic 'consumer service level' is concerned, the greatest opportunities in an urban environment would appear to lie in the proxy variables delivery window and frequency, due to the dense (delivery) network that the city offers. Hence the most substantial efficiency gains are to be achieved in the subflow of low-value goods.[8]

Looking at the characteristic 'security and delivery type', there would appear to be possibilities for enhancing efficiency by making use of collection points in order to reduce the delivery failure rate. Hence we are talking mainly about high- and medium-value durable goods.

As a characteristic, 'geographical area and degree of market penetration' offers opportunities for significant efficiency improvements in urban environments, especially if one focuses on the effects of the proxy variable 'pooling of goods' and 'market density'. This implies that the greatest efficiency gains are to be realized in the subflow of low-value goods.

In so far as the characteristic 'ICT' is concerned, the most substantial opportunities for optimization again lie in the flow of low-value goods, as it displays the most pronounced fluctuations during delivery rounds.

In an urban environment, the delivery routes are generally less environmentally damaging than in rural areas. Hence green delivery methods may be assumed to be more appropriate for low-value product groups. With regard to the characteristic 'environment', one can therefore surmise that the cost of more environmentally-friendly delivery methods in urban environments is more acceptable for low-value products than it is in rural regions.

CONCLUSION

The research question considered in this chapter was as follows: which characteristics do private companies and public authorities need to take into account when implementing innovative concepts in last-mile logistical subflows with a view to optimizing efficiency gains and cost reductions?

In this survey of last-mile logistics, we first focused on its definition and problematic nature. The last mile is generally recognized as one of the least efficient legs in the supply chain, contributing substantially to a higher overall cost. In order to gain a better understanding of the issue at hand, we first considered a last-mile typology proposed in the academic literature. However, it soon emerged that, from an innovation perspective, this commonly applied typology does not represent the specific character-istics of the last mile in an adequate and unequivocal manner. Therefore we put forward a typology based on the value of the goods shipped, which allowed us to identify clear and meaningful last-mile subflows, namely low-value consumer goods, medium-value goods and high-value durable goods. Next, a number of characteristics and proxy variables were assessed for their relevance to each of these subflows.

The following areas were found to offer opportunities for optimizing last-mile efficiency and reducing cost: consumer service level; security and delivery type; the geographical region and market penetration or density; the vehicle fleet and technology; and the environment. For each of these areas, two to four proxy variables were specified.

The relevance of each of the proxy variables to each of the three sub-flows varied. Clearly, though, the determining factor for their applicability was the value of the goods concerned.

Further research needs to concentrate on measuring and quantify-ing the impact of the different last-mile characteristics on the basis of the proposed proxy variables. In this respect, it is also important that insights should be acquired into the underlying relationships between the various characteristics, with a view to further optimizing the alloca-tion of scarce resources in innovation management in the last mile of the supply chain.

NOTES

1. Operating (quasi-)empty vehicles.
2. This list of characteristics was drawn up on the basis of the scientific literature, interviews with experts and research into the cost structure of logistics providers.
3. The figures are based on data from integrators.
4. Figure 3.4, bottom, represents time-sensitive deliveries (delivery windows, short lead time etc.). In most cases, this implies a significant rise in the number of (tonne-)miles. This increase in mileage (and the associated ping-pong effect) is due to the greater number of non-optimal trips in between delivery points as compared to a routing sched-ule for non-time-sensitive deliveries.
5. This figure and the following ones are based on statistical models. In each of these models, the authors make a number of limiting assumptions. In the work by Boyer et al. (2009), one of the underlying assumptions was that the time windows were spread out over a nine-hour working day. This way, one obtains a relatively equal distribution of demand. In reality, suppliers may face different demand patterns, as the popularity of time windows may vary. For the full list of assumptions, we refer the reader to the articles in question.
6. Figures for 2000–2001, Kämäräinen (2001).
7. Figures generated by means of a simulation model.
8. That is not to say, though, that no significant efficiency gains can be achieved within the other subflows. This observation also holds in relation to the summary conclusion below.

REFERENCES

Boyer, K.K., M.T. Frohlich and G.T.M. Hult (2005), *Extending the Supply Chain – How Cutting-edge Companies Bridge the Critical Last Mile into Customers' Homes*, New York: Amacom.

Boyer, K.K., A.M. Prud'homme and W. Chung (2009), 'The last-mile challenge: evaluating the effects of customer density and delivery window patterns', *Journal of Business Logistics*, **30** (1), 185–201.

De Smedt, B. and R. Gevaers (2009), 'The economic feasibility of sustainable logistic real estate', in *Conference Proceedings ERES Conference 2009*, Stockholm, Sweden.

Fernie, J. and A. McKinnon (2004), 'The development of e-tail logistics', in *Logistics and Retail Management*, 2nd edn, London: Kogan Page, pp. 164–87.

Gevaers, R., E. Van de Voorde and T. Vanelslander (2008), 'Technical and process innovations in logistics: opportunities, barriers and best practices', *European Transport Conference*, Leeuwenhorst, the Netherlands.

Gevaers, R., E. Van de Voorde and T. Vanelslander (2009a), 'Innovations in last-mile logistics: the relations with green logistics, reverse logistics and waste logistics', in *Conference Proceedings of International Symposium on Logistics 2009*, Istanbul, Turkey, S.l.

Gevaers, R., E. Van de Voorde and T. Vanelslander (2009b), 'Technical and process innovations in green logistics: opportunities, barriers and best practices by using case studies', in C. Macharis (ed.), *Proceedings of the BIVEC–GIBET Transport Research Day*, Brussels: VUB Press, pp. 227–43.

Kämäräinen, V. (2001), 'The reception box impact on home delivery efficiency in the e-grocery business', *International Journal of Physical Distribution & Logistics*, **31** (6), 414–26.

Leavit, W. (2008), 'Unwrapping delivery', *Fleet Owner Magazine*, 13 November.

Madlberger, M. (2005), *The last-mile in an electronic commerce business model – service expectations of Austrian online shoppers*, available at http://is2.lse. ac.uk/asp/aspecis/20050078.pdf, European Conference on Information Systems, Regensburg, Germany.

Murphy, A.J. (2006), 'Grounding the virtual: the material effects of electronic grocery shopping', *Geoforum*, **38**, 941–53.

Onghena, E. (2008), *Integrators: werkwijze, strategieën en toekomst*, Universiteit Antwerpen.

Punakivi, M. and J. Saranen (2001), 'Identifying the success factors in e-grocery home delivery', *International Journal of Retail & Distribution Management*, **29** (4), 156–63.

Punakivi, M., M. Yrjölä and J. Holmström (2001), 'Solving the last mile issue: reception box or delivery box?', *International Journal of Physical Distribution and Logistics Management*, **31** (6), 427–39.

Smithers, R. (2007), 'Supermarket home deliveries service promotes its green credentials', *The Guardian*, 12 September.

Van Oosterhout, M. (2004), Prediction of e-economy impacts on transport – case Kiala: a new distribution concept for the home shopping market, Poet Research Project, DG Tren, European Commission, Brussels.

Weltevreden, J.W.J. (2008), 'B2C e-commerce logistics: the rise of collection-and-delivery points in the Netherlands', *International Journal of Retail & Distribution Management*, **36** (8), 638–60.

PART II

Possible Methodologies

4. Urban freight policy innovation for Rome's LTZ: a stakeholder perspective

**Amanda Stathopoulos, Eva Valeri,
Edoardo Marcucci, Valerio Gatta,
Agostino Nuzzolo and Antonio Comi**

INTRODUCTION

City logistics is defined as 'the process for totally optimising the logistics and transport activities by private companies in urban areas while considering the traffic environment, the traffic congestion and energy consumption within the framework of a market economy' (Taniguchi et al., 1999, p. 17). In other words, city logistics can be considered a branch of transport modelling that deals with the typical problems relating to urban freight transport, such as congestion, time-window regulations, on-street loading and unloading of goods and environmental emissions caused by freight vehicles. Recent literature points towards the importance of explicitly considering different stakeholders' unique perspectives. Indeed, recognizing and understanding the concerns of different stakeholders and their problem identification with respect to urban freight is a key factor to successfully introduce urban freight policies. This chapter contributes to the understanding of practical issues relating to stakeholder evaluation of urban freight policies. The empirical section of the chapter presents evidence from stakeholder focus groups set in a specific and complex political and urban environment: the Limited Traffic Zone (LTZ) in Rome. In surveying the problems surrounding goods movements in Rome's LTZ, we focus on three main questions:

- Which are the principal problems associated with freight transport, according to the main stakeholders?
- What is the view of the current regulatory context and how does this modulate the problem perceptions?

● Which are the main policy proposals that stakeholders promote to tackle these problems?

To explore these points, surveys were carried out with three types of stakeholders: freight carriers; local policy-makers; and retailers localized in the LTZ. The survey results indicate that stakeholders perceive the problems in different ways. Despite general agreement regarding the shortcomings in the current regulation, important differences in the policy proposals by each group of stakeholders were discovered. Such results are critical for the formulation of freight policies. Indeed to ensure efficiency, city logistics measures need to recognize areas of potential conflict associated with the different interests held by the various stakeholders involved in the supply chain. Failing to account for preference heterogeneity and stakeholder-specific problem perceptions may jeopardize not only the successful introduction of innovative policies, but also their continuation in time.

The chapter is organized as follows. In the following section we outline the main research findings on urban freight distribution, including problems and policy solutions. Then the Roman LTZ and freight distribution context is overviewed. A further section describes the focus-group results from both aggregate and stakeholder-specific perspectives. Final sections close with discussion and conclusions.

URBAN GOODS DISTRIBUTION

Movement of Goods

City logistics is concerned with ensuring efficient transport of goods within the urban area, that is, from production sites to shops, and lastly to final consumers. To adequately understand this issue it is essential to study the delivery of goods according to their importance, in terms of flow and incidence. According to the Civitas project, in some European cities commercial transport makes up 30 per cent of the total traffic volume (Becker et al., 2008). In the case of Rome, the deliveries of goods make up 6 per cent of traffic volumes (Comi et al., 2008; Comi et al., 2011; Filippi and Campagna, 2008). Moreover, different goods types are organized into different supply chains depending on their characteristics and service requirements (Danielis et al., 2009). Generally these goods are transported from production sites to specific logistic centres, located near the city limit, where a first load rearrangement is performed. Then the goods are carried to shops within the city either by logistic service providers, typically using an adequate fleet of vehicles to provide the last-mile delivery service, or by autonomous transporters, often owning a single vehicle. In the final step, the goods are purchased by private citizens, who personally bring them home. The common practice in Rome has been that of a large number of micro operators (the so-called *padroncini*), often viewed as a factor that aggravates the critical issues of inefficient routing, low load factors, use of old vehicles and lack of innovation in urban freight. Another prevalent feature in the Italian, in general, and Roman, in particular, logistic system is the quantity of own-account[1] transport associated with problems such as inefficient load factors and the prevalence of goods that are unlikely to be incorporated in city logistics initiatives (Vaghi, 2008).

Problems Generated by Urban Freight

The rapid growth in freight vehicle activity in urban and metropolitan areas contributes to congestion, air pollution, noise and increases in logistic costs, and hence the price of products. In addition, the combination of different types of vehicles on the road increases the risk of accidents. The efficiency of the freight distribution system plays an important role in ensuring the competitiveness of urban areas, and is in itself an important element in the urban economy (Browne et al., 2007b). Some European surveys indicate that urban freight transport accounts for 14 per cent of urban vehicle-kilometres and 19 per cent of energy use (Schoemaker et al., 2006). Technical improvements to vehicles are reducing the environmental impacts of individual vehicles, but these results have often been compromised by growth in transport demand. In general, the share of total traffic emissions from freight vehicles is about 20 per cent to 30 per cent, depending on the local context. More specifically, in larger European urban areas, freight vehicles are responsible for 21 per cent of CO_2 emissions, half of particulate matter (PM) and a third of transport-related NO_x emissions (Dablanc and Rodrigue, 2009). What is more, urban freight is more polluting than long-distance freight transport owing to an older vehicle fleet and the frequency of short trips and stops (Dablanc and Rodrigue, 2009). Fuel consumption increases sharply if the vehicle has to stop frequently: with five stops in 10 km, fuel consumption increases by 140 per cent (Mårtensson, 2005). The following subsection gives an overview of the main policy proposals put forth to minimize these negative features of urban goods distribution.

Urban Freight Policies

The aim of city logistics schemes is to rationalize and increase the efficiency of urban freight transport systems as well as to reduce environmental impact and congestion. However, to effectively deploy the new technologies and policy measures needed to reach these aims, some questions must be answered. Urban freight logistics policies need to take into account the conflicting objectives and interests of the different stakeholders involved in urban goods delivery. To mitigate the identified problems, several measures are typically contemplated, such as route optimization, optimal location of logistics terminals and depots, load-factor controls and cooperative delivery systems (e.g. Russo and Comi, 2011). To facilitate the orientation among these single policies, we refer to the UK Department for Transport's guide on the implementation of freight quality partnerships (DFT, 2007). Here five main policy areas are identified:

1. Information policies
2. Distribution system policies
3. Accessibility policies
4. Loading/unloading (l/u) facilities
5. Vehicle policies.

Moreover, the policy instruments may be classified as rule-based or incentive-based. In the field of regulations, besides time windows and vehicle restrictions, rules on the emission and load factor of vehicles may be employed. Controlling for the load factor implies an objective of efficiency maximization, but entails important problems in its application (START, 2008). Differentiation according to emission factors indicates that the goal is of environmental efficiency along the lines of Milan's Ecopass scheme (Rotaris et al., 2009). Overall, urban freight management is progressively incorporated in the wider notion of sustainable urban development (Allen et al., 2000; Allen et al., 2003; Anderson et al., 2005). In the case of Rome the main concern in the policy architecture has been the environmental impact of freight movements in central areas and discouraging the use of own-account transport (Filippi et al., 2010). The presumption here is that third-account transport is more efficient. The problem of empty running in one leg of the delivery trip (return leg) and of the collection trip (outward leg) typically occurs in own-account operations and is indicative of poor efficiency. Following this brief account of problems and policies affecting urban freight, the next subsection reviews the literature characterizing the main stakeholder types present in the logistic chain.

Studying Actors and Interaction: Difficulties and Lessons Learnt

In the study of urban supply chains, we need to establish the main driving forces behind the behaviour of freight agents. Beyond mapping the main problems and policy solutions surrounding urban freight, the concern in this chapter is the perspectives and roles of different agents that have stakes in the logistic chain. A first distinction that needs to be drawn is between the responsibilities of private and public agents. For the current study, concentrating on the movement of commodities, it is important to distinguish between private operators (retailers, wholesalers or freight companies) and public ones such as local government (Visser et al., 1999). Since the decisions that generate the flows of goods in the urban area originate from the private sector, policy-makers have the task of facilitating/ restraining these flows or regulating the wider transport system (Harker and Friesz, 1986). Typical public measures include pricing, licensing or regulations, in line with the policy instruments listed above. However, the private subjects are responsible for fine-tuning the collaboration with their commercial partners, including decisions on shared use of l/u facilities and adoption of new technologies and delivery routines.

In general, freight behavioural analysis and data collection are particularly difficult, in part due to the large quantity of decision-makers that need to be surveyed (Hutchinson, 1985; Musso, 2006; Nuzzolo et al., 2010; Pan, 2006; Russo and Comi, 2010). Among the actors traditionally identified in the goods movement system are receivers, carriers and forwarders (Ogden, 1992). Here we concentrate on representing three main agent types that influence the functioning of the logistic chain. The first two, transport operators (carriers and forwarders) and retailers that receive the goods, are well identified in the literature. However, the current analysis is extended to include policy-makers, since they dictate the policy scenario in which the private agents operate. Other essential stakeholders, such as residents and consumers, are not surveyed due to their lack of direct influence over urban freight policies. In line with Muñuzuri et al. (2005), the interests of these agents may be viewed as represented by the local policy-makers. Once the main actors have been identified, one has to address the more complex problem of analysing the interaction between them in the act of delivering/receiving goods in the city. At this stage we need to account for the different needs and constraints associated with each type of agent in complying with city logistics policies. Indeed, possible asymmetries of power in dictating the rules of the freight distribution game determine the level of adherence to the policy and the degree of cooperation among actors, as well as the distribution of costs and benefits among actors. In the following we give a brief overview of the results from empirical studies concerning each agent type.

Freight transport operators
City logistics may be analysed in more detail from the point of view of each agent type. In considering *freight operators*, the most relevant aspect

is minimizing the cost of transportation (Danielis and Marcucci, 2007). Therefore the main problems revealed in the literature are related to the planning of collection and delivery, and the vehicle routing and operational costs such as fuel cost oscillations. The movement of goods involves several decision levels proper to the freight chain. The *consigner* hands the goods over to a *forwarder*, who may subcontract a *carrier* for the carriage of the merchandize. However, the choices of the *driver* of the vehicle also count as there is some autonomy in routing the delivery before handing the goods to a *consignee* (Friedrich et al., 2003). Numerous stated-preference and other questionnaire surveys have explored the behaviour of freight operators. Regarding the choice of distribution services, Fowkes et al. (1989) show, by performing a stated preference (SP) choice experiment on 50 English companies, that a low value of the goods carried correlates with choosing a lower-quality transport service. There is a rich literature on mode choice among freight operators (García-Menéndez et al., 2004; Marcucci and Scaccia, 2004; Norojono and Young, 2003; Shinghal and Fowkes, 2002). In particular, the importance of reliability for freight carrier operations is overviewed in several sources (Danielis et al., 2005; Fowkes, 2007; Fowkes et al., 2004). A more limited number of papers look into the choice between own-account and externally purchased transport (Marcos and Martos, 2004).

Receivers of goods
The literature on logistic decision-making among retailers is ample and developing quickly due to innovative technologies and organizational approaches. The receivers of goods need to respond, on their part, to the demands of final consumers. Along these lines, they require shorter delivery times along with the progressive elimination of warehouse spaces due to the elevated cost of rent in the urban area (Anderson et al., 2005; Maggi, 2001). However, a general classification to relate commercial establishments to urban freight movement is complex due to the large differences between essential features such as types of goods moved, store size and employment structure in different urban areas (Filser and Paché, 2005; Van Binsbergen and Visser, 2001). A main component in studies of retailer behaviour is the type of goods moved. For instance, in Rome, hotel, restaurant and catering (HoReCa) make up 71 per cent of all retailers in the LTZ area (Filippi and Campagna, 2008). In addition, the choice of externally purchased versus internally managed transport is still a scantily understood issue (Fridstrom and Madslien, 2002). Concerning policy preferences several studies have explored the influence of time-window regulations on retailer operations (Holguín-Veras, 2008; Quak, 2008; Quak and de Koster, 2009). Empirical studies often reach the conclusion

that retailers dictate many of the dimensions of contracting between retailers and carriers of goods (Melo, 2010). However, there is a low degree of agreement concerning which policy dimensions are most effective in influencing the behaviour of receivers.

Local policy-makers

From the point of view of the public administration, the most important aspect is that of moderating the social costs generated by freight movement in the urban area. Here the concern lies primarily with the impact on traffic congestion and planning problems connected to the provision of l/u facilities for freight in competition with other uses of the road capacity (Maggi, 2001). The identified problems are managed by designing policies for the effective regulation of freight traffic. This may imply imposing temporal and/or spatial limitations to circulation and/or parking of freight vehicles and by creating dedicated stopping areas for l/u manoeuvres.

Browne et al. (2007a) compare the freight policy approaches in London and Paris. Common policy issues of focus are l/u, hours of access, cleaner vehicle technology and modal shift promotion. What is more, the participation of stakeholders in policy planning phases, such as operators and trade organizations, is a central feature in both cities. For instance, Paris simplified its access regulations following the discovery that the low level of compliance was due to the extreme complexity of the scheme. Likewise the introduction of congestion charging in London was accompanied by extensive consultation with both the general public and freight stakeholders (Browne et al., 2003). Urban freight policy, in the UK context, is described as reactive towards problems that arise rather than the result of careful planning (Browne et al., 2007b). In general, European urban freight policy innovation is described as stuck in a *status quo* position where no specific stakeholder group is willing to take the lead (Dablanc, 2007).

Besides the difficulty of fully identifying the actors involved in the supply chain, several papers contribute towards giving us a more complex characterization of the relationships among agents. This issue is studied further in the next subsection.

On the Joint Study of Stakeholders

Another essential point is the acceptance on the part of the freight community of policy measures and innovations, and what sort of reactions can be expected. To gain a deeper understanding of these points, we need to bear in mind that freight chains are made up of agents with specific, and sometimes irreconcilable, needs and expectations along with specific sets of constraints (Puckett, 2009). Wisetjindawat et al. (2007) study interactions between freight actors at the urban scale and put forward a model for urban freight movement incorporating the behaviour of freight actors and their interactions in the supply chain. Moreover, Taniguchi and Tamagawa (2005) develop a method for evaluating city logistics measures considering the behaviour of several urban freight transport stakeholders. In all, five stakeholder types are considered: administrators, residents, shippers, freight carriers; and urban expressway operators. From this brief overview it can be argued that the relevance of including specific agent types for policy assessment should be decided in view of the specific context and problem studied.

Analysis and selection of practicable policy measures need to consider such interactions and find an optimal compromise between the interests of the actors involved. This is a critical factor in the success of each city logistics measure, as confirmed by several UK studies. Indeed, UK Freight Quality Partnerships (FQPs) can be considered a key factor in studying and implementing successful city logistics initiatives (DFT, 2007). An FQP group will typically aim to identify problems and policy solutions, examine sustainable best practices, and help implement them. This is an effective way to foster and promote collaborative solutions. As Van Binsbergen and Visser (2001) have underlined, the overarching objective of these methods is to create a 'supporting environment' for defining and implementing city logistics measures.

ROME'S LIMITED TRAFFIC ZONE

Freight Distribution Context

The successful introduction of city logistics requires a thorough knowledge of the context in which the stakeholders operate. In the Roman context the most comprehensive investigations for the aims of the current study are STA (1999) and Filippi and Campagna (2008). The STA study found that the historical centre of Rome is affected by the daily passage of 25 000 goods vehicles, among which about 10 000 (40 per cent) are through traffic (STA, 1999). In total, 35 000 instances of loading and unloading of goods are carried out daily. Moreover, two-thirds of the operations take place in the morning, between 7.00 and 13.00, the same hours during which passenger work travel is concentrated. Regarding l/u practices, there is a scarce use of the designated l/u bays. Indeed, 57 per cent carry out their operation while illegally double-parked and 36 per cent do so while parked by the roadside rather than in the bays. Concerning environmental impacts, 86 per cent of freight vehicles are diesel-fuelled. Also, it is noted that the share of road haulage carried out externally by contractors is 67 per cent, implying that a third of all freight operators use own-account transport. This is in line with the average national statistics, indicating that 59 per cent of road freight is carried out as own account (Confetra, 2001). Own-account transport is even more prevalent at the urban level, where it reaches 88 per cent. Rome has witnessed an inversion of this tendency, with a large decrease of own-account transport, dropping from 54 per cent in 1999 to 21 per cent in 2008. In the same period the vehicle size for this category has shrunk significantly, with 69 per cent using a car rather than heavy vehicles, compared to 61 per cent in 1999 (Comi et al., 2011). Possibly these changes are due to the structure of Rome's LTZ legislation, which tends to discourage the practice of managing freight consignments as own account. The STA study also focused on the receivers of goods. In particular, it is noted that most of the companies situated in the centre belong to the HoReCa sector (STA, 1999). Moreover, 80 per cent retain store spaces of less than 100 m^2. The interviews reveal that among larger operators the main concern is related to loading and unloading of goods, such as the lack of l/u bays (36 per cent) and difficulty of vehicle access to the historical centre (33 per cent). For smaller craft businesses, the main shortcoming of current legislative set-up is the lack of adequate trolleys and lifting equipment for the unloading of goods (39 per cent). An interesting finding in the more recent 2008 survey is that the l/u problems are perceived as having deteriorated, with 69 per cent of retailers regarding it as the main freight problem (Comi et al., 2011).

Regarding the interplay between supply and demand agents, the available studies offer little guidance. In general, it appears that the market for transport services is strongly influenced by the characteristics of the demand sector. In fact, the strong presence of small and medium-sized enterprises implies a reliance on traditional freight services. A survey by ISFORT (2003) emphasizes that the demand side appears inelastic in its choice of logistic services and is reluctant to stimulate its supply-side partners to innovate its services and organizational structure. According to ISFORT, three main factors, common to freight supply and demand operators, can explain the lack of modernization of the freight system:

- the prevalence of small operators;
- cultural backwardness;
- a low degree of internationalization of logistic activities.

In particular, restricted company size, combined with widespread cultural backwardness, leads to a poor capacity to innovate products and processes. What is more, reluctance to delegate out functions that do not belong to the core business appears to be widespread in the Italian context.

Rome's LTZ Legislation

The historical city centre of Rome has been subject to an LTZ since the late 1980s. The institution of a formal LTZ in Rome can be traced back to 1989, when a 5 km² area was restricted to non-resident vehicles. The current bans on traffic apply to both passenger and freight vehicles. Access and circulation in the larger peri-central area termed 'ZTL Anello Ferroviario' is prohibited for pre-Euro-1 and Euro-1 light and heavy vehicles. Instead, the central LTZ area, which is the focus of this study, has more detailed legislation in place. The current LTZ corresponds to a 4 km² area in the historical centre. The scheme can be described as a hybrid form of regulation and pricing, comprising elements of congestion control alongside environmental dispositions. For instance, entry is reserved for the least polluting vehicles (Euro-1 and later). At the same time, the system of time windows mimics a peak-hour system, albeit with a flat fee. The scheme operates during daytime hours for passengers (06:30–18:00 Monday to Friday and 14:00–18:00 on Saturday). The passenger LTZ largely overlaps with the 'LTZ for goods', an area aimed at goods vehicles that operates between 10:00–14:00 and 16:00–20:00. The charge for the annual permit is €550.[2] A notable development is the large increase in the entry fees introduced in 2007, from €33 annually (for nine vehicles) to €550 (for one vehicle numberplate). This increase by a factor of ten was originally designed to be accompanied by a series of improvements in l/u conditions. The latter proposals, however, remain unrealized. Initially the police enforced the scheme manually, but this caused many vehicles to enter the zone illegally. The system has subsequently become automated based on the use of electronic gantries and camera surveillance. Table 4.1 gives a synthetic summary of the access and parking regulations that apply to freight vehicles in the goods LTZ. It should be noted that some freight operators are exonerated from the system of time windows (see Table 4.1). Indeed, not only maintenance and cleaning vehicles but also vehicles carrying valuables, perishables, pharmaceuticals, newspapers and even operators with third-account licences can enter at any time.

On the whole, the regulation appears designed essentially to create incentives for third-account operators while discouraging lengthy parking of own-account vehicles, given the shortage of on-street parking space in the area. Currently the time-window regulations are not systematically enforced. Due to the many exceptions and the lack of time-of-day differentiation, the scheme can hardly be characterized as a congestion-reducing

Table 4.1   Current regulatory regime for urban goods distribution in the Rome LTZ

General regulation

Laden weight < 35 quintal (100 kg)	Laden weight > 35 q
Transit and parking allowed from 20:00 to 10:00 and 14:00 to 16:00; prohibited otherwise	Transit and stopovers permitted from 20:00 to 7:00; prohibited otherwise

Exceptions from time window (around the clock transit and parking)

Laden weight < 35 quintal (100 kg)	Laden weight > 35 q
1. Transport of perishable foods, pharmaceuticals, newspapers and precious goods 2. All courier and transport companies operating as third account (if enrolled in the National Registry of Auto Transporters) 3. Trucks involved in cleaning and maintenance services on account of the municipality or ATAC	1. Trucks with justified request detailing time, place and route (e.g. house moving)

Reductions of fee

50% reductions offered for electric cars and 25% reduction for CH_4, LPG and hybrid motor/fuel

---

Source: LTZ municipal resolution no. 44 from 2007; own table.

Note: ATAC = Rome's mobility agency.

policy. Neither can it be classified as an environmentally justified low-emission zone (LEZ) since the vehicle emissions standards are not currently part of the scheme. However, the exclusion of Euro-1 vehicles and below, along with the fee reductions for alternative fuels, implies that environmental objectives prevail over economic efficiency ones.

STAKEHOLDER SURVEY

Description of Survey

Stakeholders were interviewed using focus-group meetings to establish the problem identification surrounding freight delivery in Rome's LTZ.

Table 4.2   Stakeholder categories involved in focus-group survey

Category of stakeholder	Type of stakeholders involved	Number of stakeholders
Demand	Representatives of associations for traders and producers, Rome's industrialist and enterprises association	2
Supply	Associations of transporters, forwarders, freight transport companies, industrial freight association	6
Local policy-maker	Transport Department, local authorities, urban planners, local public transport company	6
Total		14

Source: Own elaboration.

Discussion-based surveys are a precious tool to gain understanding of how supply chains may react to new policy measures and what effect they will have on freight activity. Moreover, the group context provides a good indicator of differences in opinions among participants as opposed to single interviews. Clearly, attention needs to be given to the selection of the respondents who effectively have a stake in determining the behaviour of freight chains. The classic definition of a 'stakeholder' is that of any group that affects or is affected by the behaviour of the studied entity (Freeman, 1984). Typically the vagueness of the term generates some difficulty in identifying the main stakeholders in the problem under study (Mitchell et al., 1997). To ensure an adequate selection of stakeholders to participate in the focus groups, the selection was carried out in concert with experts at the Centre for Logistics and Transport studies at Rome Sapienza University. The key stakeholders were then divided into three main categories (see Table 4.2).

In the demand category, several trade organizations and retail representatives were contacted. However, there was limited interest in participating, as may be observed by the low number of participants in this category. Instead a strong interest on the part of local policy-makers and the freight supply sector was encountered. Overall the participation of 14 interviewees was secured. The interviews were conducted between June and July 2009.

Separate stakeholder meetings
The stakeholder consultation was carried out in two stages. In the first phase each stakeholder group was interviewed separately. The rationale

for this was to obtain a more uninhibited description of the groups' own ideas concerning the relevant problems and issues. In particular, it was essential to keep the problem description of operators separate from that of policy-makers, to allow expressions of discontent with current regulatory regimes. In the second phase, all stakeholders were gathered and interviewed jointly. The aim was to stimulate a wider discussion, partly based on the results obtained from the individual surveys (see below).

The single-category meetings were carried out in the following manner. The interviews were organized with between two and five participants. In most cases the invited stakeholders were officials in executive positions within their administrative or professional organization. Stakeholders were first introduced to the stages of the meeting and given a brief explanation of the aim of the research. The description was kept neutral to avoid influencing the responses. The separate meetings were structured as follows:

1. identification and definition of the main problems associated with urban freight distribution (UFD) in Rome's LTZ;
2. assessment of current UFD regulations and potential shortcomings in dealing with the perceived problems;
3. selection of the most preferred policy solutions, in view of the subjective problem perception and current regulation.

At the outset of the meetings each participant was invited to list what they perceived to be the main problems associated with goods distribution in Rome's LTZ. This problem description was used as a point of departure for a semi-structured discussion regarding the current and past problems with attention to revealing the behavioural targets and constraints of each type of stakeholder. For the last point it proved necessary to use a paper-based questionnaire given to the participants to fill out at home. Thus, following the meeting, each participant was given a questionnaire that asked them about possible policies to improve the current freight regulation in Rome's LTZ. In particular, the questionnaire solicited their views on the most adequate policies to solve, or contribute towards solving, the problems identified in the first phase of the interview. To structure the task, each single policy was allocated to one of five macro categories. These were: access policies; information measures; delivery policies; distribution system policies; and vehicle policies (DFT, 2007). Each respondent was given 100 points to allocate to specific policy measures within each macro category according to their perceived importance. On average, each interview lasted for approximately one hour.

Joint stakeholder meeting

All previously interviewed stakeholders were invited to attend a joint meeting. Overall, 11 stakeholders participated. The aim of this meeting was twofold. First, it was an occasion to gain confirmation of the information gathered in the first meeting and to confront each stakeholder group with their counterpart's (anonymous) preferences and policy proposals. Second, it was an opportunity to build the basis for a wider empirical analysis based on stated-preference (SP) experiments with retailers and carriers concerning the acceptability of freight policy innovation in the LTZ. The information gained is essential for the overall aim of the research project regarding empirical assessment of the acceptability on the part of the various parties to variations of the current regulatory regime governing goods distribution in Rome's LTZ.

In line with the first aim, the participants were presented with the aggregate outcome from the previous meeting and were requested to comment freely on the problem description and proposed policies. The discussion was centred around the 'top 12' policies.

Corresponding to the second objective, each participant was given a brief questionnaire on the main policy measures identified from the previous phase. The joint focus group provided an important input to the definition of attributes and levels later used to characterize different policy mixes presented in the follow-on SP experiment. The final joint meeting lasted three hours. All interviews were conducted by a study team with members from the University of Trieste, the University of Roma Tre and University of Rome 'Sapienza'.

General Problem Identification

The problem perception among stakeholders proved quite difficult to analyse due to the tendency of the experts to immediately propose various solutions rather than identify the main problems. Based on *ex post* examination of the results, we identify two main types of problems that appeared to be most widely shared among respondents. On the one hand we identify more general problems, which are not coupled with a specific solution:

- lack of data collection and updating on goods flows and vehicle movements;
- lack of correspondence between long-term plans and short-term projects;
- conflicting objectives among urban stakeholders regarding traffic flows and parking spaces.

The problem with freight data collection is widely observed in the literature (Ogden, 1992; Pan, 2006). What was underscored in these meetings was uncertainty as to who should be responsible for continuous data collection and updating. For the case of Rome it was noted how data gathering was based almost solely on the effort of ATAC, Rome's mobility agency, which has carried out large surveys on problems and characteristics of freight mobility in the central area surrounding the LTZ, and the above-cited Comi et al. (2011) and STA (1999). However, the surveys are far apart and uncertainty about current conditions remains, including the lack of timely updating of the data. The planning problem refers to the lack of reconciliation between the plans considering the movement of people and that of goods, along with short-term plans conflicting with long-term ones. The third issue relates to the preservation of open space, and competing uses of urban space among stakeholders. In these meetings a clear distinction was made between own-account freight supply and third-account operators. Several stakeholders were quick to point out that own-account is on average less efficient than externalized transport.

On the other hand, a series of more specific problems, matched by specific solutions, was proposed across agent types:

- loading/unloading bays;
- time windows;
- entrance fee.

The l/u bays were regarded as too few by all stakeholders, and the main problems surrounding them were illegal occupation, lack of surveillance, distance from shop and an inadequate structure for certain freight vehicles. Regarding the time windows, the most common objection concerned the presence of several exemptions, making the policy ineffective. Most operators agreed with the explicit aim of discouraging own-account transport using time-window restrictions in view of the difficulty of using any other policy to ensure that their operations are efficient. Few agreed with the current fee level, proposing a lowering or a different articulation according to vehicle type and weight/dimension. Lastly, a few innovative proposals were mentioned in the discussions, namely, introduction of urban distribution centres (UDCs) and reserved lanes for goods distribution. These last issues are closer to a policy proposal than simple problem recognition since they do not yet exist in Rome.

Problems as seen by policy-makers, retailers and freight operators
The discussion has, thus far, focused on the overall problem perception, but it is also important to look at agent-specific perspectives. It can be

Table 4.3   Most important problem areas by type of agent

Policy-makers	Freight demand	Freight supply
1. Inefficiency of distribution system * (lack of control of load factors and number of entries)	1. Fluidity of traffic * (congestion)	1. Loading/unloading bays ** (lack of surveillance)
2. Loading/unloading bays ** (illegal parking)	2. Loading/unloading bays ** (illegal parking)	2. Time windows *** (problem with unfair distribution of authorizations)
3. Time windows*** (too many exemptions)	3. Urban distribution centres and pick-up points †† (placement and fees)	3. Annual fee † (perceived as too high)

Notes: Asterisks indicate problem type: * general traffic system, ** l/u practices, *** time windows, † access fee, †† UDC.

Source: Own elaboration.

expected that different types of operators will have quite dissimilar needs and experiences of the current regulatory scheme. Table 4.3 evaluates the three most preferred policies according to each stakeholder type.

It can be noted that the policy-makers tended to take a more social stance, valuing general efficiency and worrying about illegal occupations of l/u bays and the complexity of the time-window regulation. The demand side tended to include a note on the lack of distribution centres. Lastly, the supply sector looks at the problems influencing their operations more directly. That is, they criticize the lack of control by the municipality over the illegal/improper use of the l/u bays. Considering the time-window regulation, there is concern regarding unfair allocation of exemptions to numerous private operators based on the type of goods distributed and to municipal postal distribution carrying express mail in competition with commercial operators. The entrance fees are, not surprisingly in view of the large increase in recent years, regarded as too high.

Aggregate Policy Proposals by Stakeholders

As described above, each agent received a questionnaire to fill in at home. The form described five macro policy areas, each associated with a list of

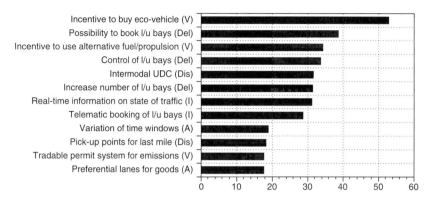

Notes: Normalized for number of respondents in each stakeholder group and referred to specific macro category (a maximum of 100 would mean all agents had given all the points to a single policy within a category). Parentheses refer to policy area: A = Access policies, I = Information, Del = Delivery policies, Dis = Distribution system policies, V = Vehicle policies.

Source: Own elaboration from focus-group surveys.

Figure 4.1   Top 12 policy proposals from aggregate stakeholder evaluation

specific policy measures that the respondents were asked to assess according to importance (DFT, 2007). In correspondence with each macro category between 6 and 9 specific policy measures were listed along with a space dedicated to own proposals. Each stakeholder was asked to allocate 100 points among the specific policies belonging to each macro category. The aggregate result from this exercise is given in Figure 4.1.

It can be noted how each of the five macro categories is represented among the policies that gathered the most support. Not surprisingly, among the top-rated policies we find those incurring least costs to users, such as vehicle incentives, in line with the well-known equity/efficiency trade-off. Fundamentally, these policies require minimal behavioural adjustment and imply an equal distribution of costs among agents. Policies of control of l/u bays and monetary incentives have gathered from a third to almost half of the available 100 points in their macro category. Looking further down the list, we find policies requiring a larger amount of behavioural adaptation on the part of operators in order to be effective. This includes variations in time-window regulation and the set-up of a UDC. An interesting feature of the aggregate list is the inclusion of innovative policies such as preferential lanes for goods and public transport, and a tradable permit system among the top 12 policies. These policies, however, gathered less than a fifth of the available points in their macro category. On the whole this aggregate analysis provides only limited insight, as it does not explicate single stakeholder preferences. In fact, any potential differences and latent conflicts are simply hidden in the aggregate average policy ranking. In the following subsection the results for each stakeholder are examined.

Policy proposals as stated by retailers, policy-makers and freight carriers
A disaggregate approach allows us to reveal the distinctive preferences of each stakeholder group. For instance, it can show which among the stakeholders are behind the collective support for any specific policy. Figure 4.2 illustrates the distribution of responses for each agent type.

Looking in more detail at the results from the policy-maker's selection, the main feature is the similarity to the aggregate responses. Indeed, the four top prioritized policies are the same as in the average results. This suggests that this group is most in line with the overall evaluation and may see their preferences satisfied to a greater extent.

Instead, supply agents and retail representatives are further from the collective results on account of their distinctive preferences, partially based on their diverse characteristics. Considering the freight supply stakeholders, a group including institutional representatives along with operators, it is clear that several typical transport features find their way into this agent type's priorities. The fact that three out of five top policies belong to the vehicle macro category is a clear indication of this. As an example, a narrow policy such as a change in the entrance requirements to allow trucks over 5 tons to enter the LTZ is the second most preferred policy for freight stakeholders. In the third position we find the policy of limiting access for vehicles with low load factors, a policy not currently in place. These preferences can be explained by the fact that the interviewed stakeholders are large, highly efficient third-account operators that could easily satisfy the requirement. Instead, such a policy would deter entry by own-account operators. This testifies to the importance of gathering stakeholder specific data to grasp the particular needs and requirements of each agent type. Overall, freight stakeholder preferences appear to be guided by their operational needs.

Regarding retailers, the policy ranking is less tied to own needs and instead focuses on typical carrier problems. Indeed, the preferred policies belong to all macro categories. Among the top policies we note vehicle incentives, preferential freight lanes and an increase in the number of l/u bays. These are all oriented towards facilitating the work of freight operators. Only indirectly may such policies influence the daily activity of retailers.

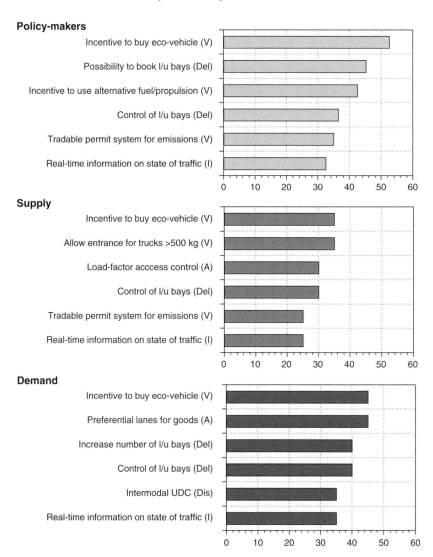

Notes: See Figure 4.1.

Source: Own elaboration from focus-group surveys.

Figure 4.2 Top six policies within policy macro area per stakeholder type

DISCUSSION OF RESULTS

An essential feature behind the success of freight policies is the consideration of the roles and needs of the different stakeholders in the logistic chain and their acceptance of the policy scenarios envisioned. This chapter studies which policies are the most appropriate to ensure a sustainable management of freight in the urban area considering regulatory decisions, technological innovation and available methods to optimize the movement of goods. In particular, due recognition is given to the fact that active consultation between stakeholders is crucial to define coherent and realistic city logistics policy mixes. The empirical section of the chapter presents evidence from stakeholder focus groups from Rome's LTZ. We examine the problem structure as identified by three main stakeholder types – freight carriers, local policy-makers and retailers. The discussions are structured around the hypothetical introduction of new policy measures to improve the current management of freight distribution in Rome's LTZ. Following the characterization of each stakeholder's preferences, the next objective is to look at the level of shared support for a policy. This feature, as outlined throughout this chapter, would facilitate the introduction and continuation of a policy. Notably the results indicate that some policies have strong and mutual support. These include: the eco-vehicle incentive; the service to obtain information concerning l/u bays; and the increase in the number of l/u bays. However, accounting for differences in the stakeholder-specific rankings generates some realignment of priorities when accounted for. Looking at stakeholder-specific judgements, several policies receive unbalanced support. This includes the intermodal UDC and preferential lanes for goods and public transport. Regarding the delicate question of time windows, retailers were overall reluctant to propose this policy, causing its position to drop in the aggregate evaluation. This result is in line with the common observation defining city-access and delivery-time restrictions as a core issue in generating disagreement among buyers and sellers of freight. Likewise, compared to the aggregate results, the position of fuel incentives drops considerably, reflecting the low interest on the part of supply stakeholders.

One policy in particular gains only unilateral support on the part of policy-makers – the tradable permits policy. Indeed, the policies where support is concentrated with a single agent, or, as with time windows, with only policy-makers and freight operators, run the risk of not securing the necessary support to be implemented, let alone voted through to political agenda-setting. For the case of tradable permits to gain access, the lack of interest by carriers and retail stakeholders is probably due to insufficient understanding of the policy. Another feature that determines acceptability, as discussed for the aggregate results, is the amount of behavioural adaptation required to comply with the policy. Notably policies that require a joint effort among operators, such as time windows and pick-up points, fare badly in our survey. It is important to understand how the stakeholder-specific evaluations connect to the feasibility of policies. For instance, during the in-depth interviews it was revealed how retailer representatives were overall positive towards innovative freight policies as long as retailers sustained none of the costs of keeping them alive. The allocation of points on the part of the demand for typical transportation issues may also reflect the lack of core retailer issues among the policies. On the other hand, the freight carriers are interested in typical transport-oriented problems such as vehicle standards and l/u bays. This implies a more realistic stance on the part of freight suppliers towards the policies that influence their daily operations. These operators have a negative view of both UDC and pick-up points, policies that introduce a rupture in the chain of distribution. Reasons for this reluctance, revealed in the focus discussions, are a fear of losing control and legal responsibility of the goods transported, as the interviewed institutional operators and couriers tended to have a highly specialized and efficient distribution chain. Other reasons for the limited enthusiasm are lack of clarity over who should cover the operational costs and the inappropriateness of many goods typically moved in the urban area (e.g. fresh foods). Policy-makers had a highly distributed support comprising incentives, pricing and technological innovation, reflecting their broad-spectrum vision of the problems. However, from the discussion we can also trace a long line of failed policy innovation and infrastructure melioration for the historical centre of Rome. This leads us to apply caution in the positive evaluation of the more innovative initiatives to come out of the aggregate stakeholder survey exercise.

CONCLUSIONS

To ensure the performance of freight policy strategies, there is a need to investigate in depth the preferences of various stakeholder types and to relate the findings to the characteristics of the actors, urban context and goods transported. In order to introduce city logistic policies successfully, it is important to recognize and adequately understand the concerns and problem identification of different stakeholders with respect to urban freight transportation. This chapter examines the problem structure as identified by three main stakeholder types in the discussion surrounding the hypothetical introduction of new policy measures to improve the current scheme of managing freight distribution in Rome's LTZ.

A number of in-depth interviews were carried out to investigate the problem perceptions and positions of key players in the Roman city logistics sector. The interviews revealed differences in the problem identification among stakeholders. A main point emerging in the consultations was the high degree of interdependence among stakeholders in the introduction of more economically and environmentally sensible policies. This inability or reluctance to act independently of other stakeholders is described well by Dablanc:

> However, changes are slow, and on the whole, it appears as though none of the stakeholders are willing to make fast progress: on the one side, city governments expect business to set up new logistic services fit to the emerging needs of the customers and retailers as well as beneficial to the environment; on the other side, logisticians are waiting for municipalities to initiate (and subsidize) new services before starting businesses which could prove poorly profitable and highly risky. (Dablanc, 2007, p. 280)

The results illustrated here give a first indication to policy-makers in identifying the policy issues for which there is consensus and also in distinguishing policies that are negatively perceived by certain freight stakeholders. Explaining and understanding carriers' and retailers' responses will lead to policy development that better reflect the complex and diverse needs of the freight sector. Indeed, this leads us to consider the importance of a wide participation among agents. The need for an integrated approach in dealing with the problems afflicting urban freight is one of the core issues in the notion of city logistics. The basic idea is that, to be able to define a comprehensive framework for planning and developing efficient freight distribution systems in urban areas, a broad spectrum of authors needs to be involved, ranging from government policy-makers, transport operators, freight forwarders, retailers and residents. In this chapter we have undertaken a study, rooted in the specific experiences of a complex goods distribution context, to discover points of consensus and discord from the perspective of three main types of stakeholder. Such efforts point the way towards increasing the rate of success of urban freight measures. Future research needs to both amplify the range of stakeholders considered and associate the finding with different operational contexts.

ACKNOWLEDGEMENTS

We gratefully acknowledge funds from Volvo Research and Educational Foundation, project SP-2007-50 on 'Innovative solutions to freight distribution in the complex large urban area of Rome', along with contributions from PRIN 2008 project 2008YEPPM3_005 on 'Methods and models for efficient estimation of urban freight distribution strategies'. We would also like to thank the participants in the CREI seminar 2009 (Rome) and the NECTAR Cluster 3 meeting in Porto 2009, along with the interviewees participating in the various stakeholder surveys.

NOTES

1. Own-account operators are defined as operators: (1) for whom goods transport is not the main economic activity; (2) where the goods belong to the firm; and (3) where the transportation is carried out by own vehicles.
2. Temporary permits on a daily basis can be purchased for a charge of €35.

REFERENCES

Allen, J., S. Anderson, M. Browne and P. Jones (2000), 'A framework for considering policies to encourage sustainable urban freight traffic and goods/service flows', Transport Studies Group, University of Westminster, London.
Allen, J., G. Tanner, M. Browne, S. Anderson, G. Christodoulou and P. Jones (2003), 'Modelling policy measures and company initiatives for sustainable urban distribution', Transport Studies Group, University of Westminster, London, http://www.wmin.ac.uk/transport.
Anderson, S., J. Allen and M. Browne (2005), 'Urban logistics – how can it meet policy makers' sustainability objectives?', *Journal of Transport Geography*, **13** (1), 71–81.
Becker, H.-J. B., D.R. Runge, U. Schwedler and M. Abraham (2008), 'Commercial transport in European cities. How do European cities meet the challenges of commercial transport? Experiences and case studies from the CIVITAS Programme of the European Commission', *IVP-Schriften*, No. 21, Technische Universität Berlin, Berlin.
Browne, M., J. Allen and M. Attlassy (2007a), 'Comparing freight transport strategies and measures in London and Paris', *International Journal of Logistics Research and Applications*, **10** (3), 205–219.
Browne, M., T. Nemoto, J. Visser and T. Whiteing (2003), 'Urban freight movements and public–private partnerships', 3rd International Conference on City Logistics.
Browne, M., M. Piotrowska, A. Woodburn and J. Allen (2007b), 'Literature review WM9: Part I – urban freight transport', University of Westminister, London.
Comi, A., P. Delle Site, F. Filippi, E. Marcucci and A. Nuzzolo (2008), 'Differentiated regulation of urban freight traffic: conceptual framework and examples from Italy', 13th International Conference of Hong Kong Society for Transportation Studies, Hong Kong, China, 9–10 June.
Comi, A., P. Delle Site, F. Filippi and A. Nuzzolo (2011), 'Ex-post assessment of city logistics measures: the case of Rome', in U. Crisalli and L. Mussone (eds.), *Proceedings of SIDT International Conference*, Milan: Franco Angeli.

Confetra (2001), 'Profilo dell'autotrasporto di cose in italia', Milano.

Dablanc, L. (2007), 'Goods transport in large European cities: difficult to organize, difficult to modernize', *Transportation Research Part A: Policy and Practice*, **41** (3), 280–85.

Dablanc, L. and J.-P. Rodrigue (2009), 'City logistics', in J.-P. Rodrigue, C. Comtois and B. Slack (eds), *The Geography of Transport Systems*, New York: Routledge, pp. 174–204.

Danielis, R. and E. Marcucci (2007), 'Attribute cut-offs in freight service selection', *Transportation Research Part E: Logistics and Transportation Review*, **43** (5), 506–15.

Danielis, R., E. Marcucci and L. Rotaris (2005), 'Logistics managers' stated preferences for freight service attributes', *Transportation Research Part E: Logistics and Transportation Review*, **41** (3), 201–15.

Danielis, R., L. Rotarsi and E. Marcucci (2009), 'Urban freight distribution policies and supply chains: a discussion based on Italian evidente', mimeo.

DFT (2007), 'A guide on how to set up and run Freight Quality Partnerships', Department for Transport, http://www.freightbestpractice.org.uk/case-studies.

Filippi, F. and A. Campagna (2008), 'Indagine sulla distribuzione delle merci a Roma, nell'ambito dello Studio di settore della mobilità delle merci a Roma', CTL: Centre for Studies on Transport and Logistics and ATAC.

Filippa, F., A. Nuzzolo, A. Comi and P. Delle Site (2010), 'Ex ante assessment of urban freight transport policies', *Procedia – Social and Behavioral Sciences,* **2** (3), 6332–42.

Filser, M. and G. Paché (2005), 'Can we speak of a "wheel of retail logistics"? The contribution of the wheel of retailing model', LEG – CERMAB, CNRS UMR 5118, Université de Bourgogne.

Fowkes, A.S. (2007), 'The design and interpretation of freight stated preference experiments seeking to elicit behavioural valuations of journey attributes', *Transportation Research Part B: Methodological*, **41** (9), 966–80.

Fowkes, A.S., P.E. Firmin, G. Tweddle and A.E. Whiteing (2004), 'How highly does the freight transport industry value journey time reliability – and for what reasons?', *International Journal of Logistics*, **7** (1), 33–43.

Fowkes, A.S., C.A. Nash and G. Tweddle (1989), 'Valuing the attributes of freight transport quality: results of the stated preference survey', Working Paper 276, Institute of Transport Studies, University of Leeds, UK.

Freeman, R.E. (1984), *Strategic Management: A Stakeholder Approach*, Englewood Cliffs, NJ: Prentice Hall.

Fridstrom, L. and A. Madslien (2002), 'A stated preference analysis of wholesalers' freight choice', in R. Danielis (ed.), *Freight Transport Demand and Stated Preference Experiments*, Milano: Franco Angeli, pp. 223–50.

Friedrich, M., T. Haupt and K. Noekel (2003), 'Freight modelling: data issues, survey methods, demand and network models', *Proceedings of 10th International Conference on Travel Behaviour Research*, Lucerne.

García-Menéndez, L., I. Martiinez-Zarzoso and D.P. De Miguel (2004), 'Determinants of mode choice between road and shipping for freight transport: evidence for four Spanish exporting sectors', *Journal of Transport Economics and Policy*, **38** (3), 447–66.

Harker, P.T. and T.L. Friesz (1986), 'Prediction of intercity freight flows, I: Theory', *Transportation Research Part B: Methodological*, **20** (2), 139–53.

Holguín-Veras, J. (2008), 'Necessary conditions for off-hour deliveries and the effectiveness of urban freight road pricing and alternative financial policies in competitive markets', *Transportation Research Part A: Policy and Practice*, **42** (2), 392–413.

Hutchinson, B. (1985), 'Freight surveys', in E.S. Ampt, A.J. Richardson and W. Brög (eds), *New Survey Methods in Transport, Proceedings of International Conference*, Hungerford Hill, Australia, 12–16 September 1983, Utrecht: VNU Science Press.

ISFORT (2003), 'Osservatorio nazionale sul trasporto e la logistica: le dinamiche della domanda e dell'offerta', ISFORT and Milan Polytechnic University, Milan.

Maggi, E. (2001). *City logistics: un approccio innovativo per la gestione del trasporto urbano delle merci*, Milan: DIAP Politecnico di Milano.

Marcos, B.A. and L.P. Martos (2004), 'Analyzing the determinants of freight shippers' behavior: own-account versus purchased transport in Andalusia', Documentos de trabajo, Serie 1, No. 76, Centro de Estudios Andaluces.

Marcucci, E. and L. Scaccia (2004), 'Mode choice models with attribute cutoffs analysis: the case of freight transport in the Marche region', *European Transport/ Trasporti Europei*, nos 25–26, 21–32.

Mårtensson, L. (2005), 'Volvo's environmental strategy for next generation trucks', Proceedings of BESTUFS Conference, Volvo Truck Corporation, *Environmental Affairs*, June.

Melo, S. (2010), 'Evaluation of urban goods distribution initiatives towards mobility and sustainability: indicators, stakeholders and assessment tools', Ph.D. thesis, Faculty of Engineering da Universidade do Porto, Porto, Portugal.

Mitchell, R.K., B.R. Agle and D.J. Wood (1997), 'Toward a theory of stakeholder identification and salience: defining the principle of who and what really counts', *The Academy of Management Review*, **22** (4), 853–86.

Muñuzuri, J., J. Larrañeta, L. Onieva and P. Cortés (2005), 'Solutions applicable by local administrations for urban logistics improvement', *Cities*, **22** (1), 15–28.

Musso, A. (2006), 'Report on urban freight data collection in Italy', produced for workpackage 3.1 BESTUFS project.

Norojono, O. and W. Young (2003), 'A stated preference freight mode choice model', *Transportation Planning and Technology*, **26** (2), 195–212.

Nuzzolo, A., U. Crisalli, A. Comi and S. Galuppi (2010), 'Demand models for the estimation of urban goods movements: an application to the city of Rome', in J.M. Viegas and R. Macario (eds), Selected Proceedings of 12th World Conference on Transportation Research-WCTR 2010.

Ogden, K.W. (1992), *Urban Goods Movement: A Guide to Policy and Planning*, Aldershot, UK: Ashgate.

Pan, Q. (2006), 'Freight data assembling and modeling: methodologies and practice', *Transportation Planning and Technology*, **29**, 43–74.

Puckett, S.M. (2009), 'Improving our understanding of freight travel decision making: motivations, constraints, incentives and interactions', Resource Paper, IATBR Conference, Jaipur, India, December.

Quak, H.J. (2008), 'Sustainability of urban freight transport: retail distribution and local regulations in cities', Erasmus University Rotterdam.

Quak, H.J. and M.B.M. de Koster (2009), 'Delivering goods in urban areas: how to deal with urban policy restrictions and the environment', *Transportation Science*, **43** (2), 211–27.

Russo, F. and A. Comi (2010), 'A modelling system to simulate goods movements at an urban scale', *Transportation*, **37** (6), 987–1009.

Russo, F. and A. Comi (2011), 'Measures for sustainable freight transportation at urban scale: expected goals and tested results in Europe', *Journal of Urban Planning and Development*, **137** (2), article in press.

Rotaris, L., R. Danielis, E. Marcucci and J. Massiani (2009), 'The urban road pricing scheme to curb pollution in Milan: a preliminary assessment', Working Paper no. 122, University of Trieste.

Schoemaker, J., J. Allen, M. Huschebek and J. Monigl (2006), 'Quantification of Urban freight transport effects', BESTUFS Consortium.

Shinghal, N. and T. Fowkes (2002), 'Freight mode choice and adaptive stated preferences', *Transportation Research Part E*, **38** (5), 367–78.

STA (1999), 'Studio per la mobilità delle merci nel Centro storico di Roma', STA (Rome's Mobility Agency), in Italian.

START (2008), 'Final report. Future solutions for goods transport', http://www.start-project.org/downloads.html.

Taniguchi, E. and D. Tamagawa (2005), 'Evaluating city logistics measures considering the behavior of several stakeholders', *Journal of the Eastern Asia Society for Transportation Studies*, **6**, 3062–76.

Taniguchi, E., R.G. Thompson and T. Yamada (1999), 'Modelling city logistics', in E. Taniguchi, R.G. Thompson and T. Yamada (eds), *City Logistics I*, Kyoto: Institute of Systems Science Research, pp. 3–37.

Vaghi, C. (2008), 'La city logistics dagli approfondimenti metodologici agli aspetti operativi', in M. Spinedi (ed.), *Primo quaderno della logistica urbana. I progetti di City Logistics: dagli aspetti teorici alle applicazioni pratiche. Esperienze italiane ed europee a confronto*, Studio Lavia, Regione Emilia Romagna, Italy.

Van Binsbergen, A. and J. Visser (2001), 'Innovation steps towards efficient goods distribution systems for urban areas', TRAIL Thesis Series no. 2001/5, Delft University Press, Delft.

Visser, J., A. van Binsbergen and T. Nemoto (1999), 'Urban freight transport policy and planning', in E. Taniguchi and R.G. Thompson (eds), *City Logistics I*, Kyoto: Institute for City Logistics.

Wisetjindawat, W., K. Sano, S. Matsumoto and P. Raothanachonkun (2007), 'Micro-simulation model for modeling freight agents interactions in urban freight movement', TRB 2007 Annual Meeting, Washington, DC.

5. Multi-actor multi-criteria analysis: a case study on night-time delivery for urban distribution

**Cathy Macharis, Ellen Van Hoeck,
Sara Verlinde, Wanda Debauche and
Frank Witlox**

INTRODUCTION

This chapter presents the multi-actor multi-criteria analysis (MAMCA) that, as a stakeholder-oriented tool to evaluate transport projects, was developed at the Department of MOSI – Transport and Logistics of the Vrije Universiteit Brussel (Macharis, 2004). In this chapter it is used as a tool for measuring public support for night-time delivery in urban surroundings as it enables incorporation of the views of different stakeholders, in this case the receiver, the transport sector, society as a whole and the employee, and their criteria. These stakeholders were interviewed on their attitude towards five different scenarios in which the time periods for deliveries and/or the accompanying measures differ. In the case of city distribution, different stakeholders are involved, which can make difficulties. For example, the given alternatives are hard to implement because of different constraints of optimization (Menge and Hebes, 2009). Some of the stakeholders are resistant to alternatives given by other stakeholders. Therefore an appropriate methodology to handle the constraints is required, which is possible with the MAMCA.

This chapter presents both the MAMCA approach and the results of the case study. In a later section, we focus on the MAMCA methodology, which allows the points of view of several stakeholders and their goals to be incorporated into the analysis. Then we present a case study of the MAMCA used in night-time distribution. The final section summarizes the conclusions.

MAMCA METHODOLOGY

Evaluating (new) transport projects (either new infrastructure or new initiatives) implies having a method that is able to take into account different
conflicting objectives and can reconcile tangible and intangible criteria.
Today, five commonly used methods exist: the private investment analysis
(PIA); the cost-effectiveness analysis (CEA); the economic-effects analysis
(EEA); the social cost–benefit analysis (SCBA); and the multi-criteria
analysis (MCA) (Macharis et al., 2007). The latter two are the most frequently used. Recently, however, both in management literature and practice, the concept of stakeholder and stakeholder management has become
very important. A technique that combines the MCA technique with the
notions of stakeholder and stakeholder management in an explicit way is
the so-called multi-actor multi-criteria analysis (MAMCA) (developed by
Macharis, 2004). This approach takes the advantages of an MCA (namely
the fact that effects may be expressed in different units and that trade-offs
become more explicit) and those of stakeholder management (the fact that
stakeholders are crucial actors in contributing to the success or failure of
the implementation of a policy).

In a classical multi-criteria decision analysis (MCDA) approach the
following steps are taken: problem definition; developing the alternatives;
developing a set of criteria and an evaluation matrix; the general evaluation of the alternatives; and finally the implementation (Nijkamp et al.,
1990; De Brucker et al., 1998). The first step in the MAMCA approach is
the definition of the problem and the identification of the alternatives (step
1). The methodology differs from the classical approach of MCDA in the
explicit introduction of stakeholders at a very early stage (step 2). These
stakeholders will be key to identifying the criteria, which are here equal to
the objectives of the stakeholders. The weights that have to be given represent the importance the stakeholders attach to these objectives (step 3). The
stakeholders will also get the opportunity to discuss the alternatives. New
alternatives can be entered as requested by the stakeholders (step 1). In the
fourth step, for each criterion, one or more indicators are constructed (e.g.
direct quantitative indicators such as money spent, number of lives saved,
reductions in CO_2 emissions achieved and so on, or scores on an ordinal
indicator such as high/medium/low for criteria with values that are difficult
to express in quantitative terms etc.) (step 4). The measurement method
for each indicator is also made explicit (e.g. willingness to pay, quantitative scores based on macroscopic computer simulation etc.). This allows us
to measure the performance of each alternative in terms of its contribution
to the objectives of specific stakeholder groups. Steps 1 to 4 can be considered as mainly analytical, and they precede the 'overall analysis', which

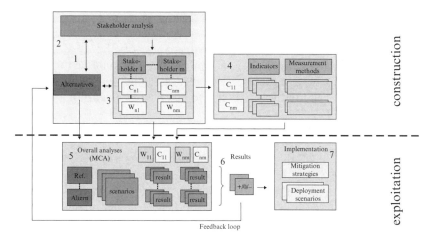

Source: Macharis et al. (2004).

Figure 5.1   Methodology for a multi-actor multi-criteria analysis

takes into account the objectives of all stakeholder groups simultaneously and is more 'synthetic' in nature. The fifth step is the construction of an evaluation matrix, aggregating each alternative contribution to the objectives of all stakeholders. Next, the MCDA yields a ranking of the various alternatives and reveals the strengths and weaknesses of the proposed alternatives (step 6). The stability of this ranking can be assessed through a sensitivity analysis. The last stage of the methodology (step 7) includes the actual implementation. The overall methodology of the MAMCA is shown in Figure 5.1. The various steps are discussed in more detail below.

Step 1: Define Alternatives

The first stage of the methodology consists in identifying and classifying the possible alternatives submitted for evaluation. These alternatives can take various forms according to the problem situation. They can differ for infrastructure investments, technological solutions, possible future scenarios together with a base scenario, different policy measures, long-term strategic options and so on.

Step 2: Stakeholder Analysis

This stage identifies the stakeholders. Stakeholders are people who have an interest, financial or otherwise, in the consequences of any decisions taken.

An in-depth understanding of each stakeholder group's objectives is critical in order to appropriately assess the different alternatives. Stakeholder analysis should be viewed as an aid to properly identify the range of stakeholders who need to be consulted and whose views should be taken into account in the evaluation process. Once identified, they might also provide new ideas on the alternatives that have to be taken into account.

Step 3: Define Criteria and Weights

The choice and definition of evaluation criteria are primarily based on the identified stakeholder objectives and the purposes of the alternatives considered. A hierarchical decision tree can be set up. In the MAMCA methodology, the criteria for the evaluation are the goals and objectives of the stakeholders, and not the effects or impacts of the actions *per se*, as is usually the case in a multi-criteria analysis. In a natural way, these impacts will be reflected in the goals of the stakeholders (if all relevant stakeholders are included). The weights are then determined by the importance the stakeholder attaches to each of his or her objectives. For determination of the weights, existing methods can be used, such as the allocation of 100 points, direct allocation and so on (for an overview see Nijkamp et al., 1990 and Eckenrode, 1965). The approach followed here, taken from a stakeholder perspective, also solves one of the main problems in multi-criteria analysis, namely the (in)dependence of the criteria. In MCDA theory, methods can only be used if the general assumption of independence between criteria is fulfilled. In the literature it is widely recognized that in many decision problems (and certainly in transport-related problems) there is interdependence between the criteria (Öztürk, 2006; Carlsson and Fuller, 1997). By defining the weights as the importance the stakeholder attaches to his/her goal, there may be interdependence between the criteria, as long as the stakeholder wants to give it the (summed) weight he or she is attaching to it. A new problem occurs, however. When creating an extra layer of different stakeholders in the analysis, it is often felt necessary to give a weight to the stakeholders as well. In order to show that the points of view of all stakeholders are equally important, the weights are usually set equal for every stakeholder (group). Performing a sensitivity analysis on these weights can lead to new insights. When the government is one of the stakeholders, which is usually the case in the evaluation of transport projects, one could say that this stakeholder represents the society's point of view and therefore is the right one to follow. Analysis of the points of view of the other stakeholders, such as users, local population, manufacturers and so on, may then show if a certain measure may be adopted or rejected by these groups.

Step 4: Criteria, Indicators and Measurement Methods

At this stage, the previously identified stakeholder criteria are 'operationalized' by constructing indicators (also called metrics or variables) that can be used to measure whether, or to what extent, an alternative contributes to each individual criterion. Indicators provide a 'scale' against which a project's contribution to the criteria can be judged. Indicators are usually, but not always, quantitative in nature. More than one indicator may be required to measure a project's contribution to a criterion, and indicators themselves may measure contributions to multiple criteria.

Step 5: Overall Analysis and Ranking

Any MCDA method can be used to assess the different strategic alternatives. In fact, the second-generation multi-criteria analysis methods, the group decision support methods (GDSM), are well suited for use in the MAMCA methodology as they are able to cope with the stakeholder concept. The PROMETHEE method has, for example, been extended in Macharis et al. (1998), the analytical hierarchy process (AHP) method in Saaty (1989) and ELECTRE in Leyva-López and Fernández-González (2003). These GDSM methods allow each stakeholder group to have their own criteria, weights and preference structure, and only at the end of the analysis are the different points of view confronted.

In this step, the evaluation of the different alternatives should be inserted into the evaluation table. Depending on the method, these evaluations must be given in a cardinal, ordinal or ratio scale (De Brucker et al., 1998). In the AHP method, a similar pair-wise comparison procedure is followed for the determination of the weights. An intermediate step can be introduced in the form of a profile chart in case there is a large number of criteria, making it more difficult to work with the pair-wise comparisons. In the profile chart, the alternatives are directly evaluated in terms of very good (+++) to very bad (−−−) and later on translated towards the Saaty scale (see Dooms et al., 2004). In the Group Decision Support System (GDSS)–PROMETHEE procedure the evaluations can be completed directly in the evaluation table on a cardinal scale.

Step 6: Results

The multi-criteria analysis developed in the previous step eventually leads to a classification of the proposed alternatives. A sensitivity analysis is performed at this stage in order to see if the result changes when the weights are modified. More important than the ranking, the multi-criteria analysis reveals the critical stakeholders and their criteria. The MAMCA compares different strategic alternatives, and supports the decision-maker in making his final decision by pointing out for each stakeholder which elements have a clearly positive or a clearly negative impact on the sustainability of the considered alternatives.

Step 7: Implementation

When the decision is made, steps must be taken to implement the chosen alternative by creating deployment schemes. The information on the points of view of each stakeholder, received from the previous steps, helps enormously in defining the implementation paths.

APPLICATIONS OF MAMCA

The MAMCA methodology has been applied in a very broad range of applications. In the area of transport it was used to cope with an intermodal terminal location decision problem (Macharis, 2000), for the evaluation of transport policy measures (e.g. the evaluation of mobility rights (Crals et al., 2004)), transport technologies (e.g. the evaluation of advanced driver assistance systems), the choice of the best alternative for a possible modal shift of waste transport in the Brussels region (BRUGARWAT: Brussels Garbage by Water) (Macharis and Boel, 2004) and the location of a new high-speed train terminal in Brussels (Meeus et al., 2004). For the development of a port master plan the methodology also proved very helpful (Dooms et al., 2004). The MAMCA methodology is also applied in the evaluation of DHL's hub strategy at Brussels airport (Dooms et al., 2006; Dooms and Macharis, 2005) and the evaluation of policy measures in the framework of Flanders in Action (Macharis et al., 2009). In the case of city distribution, the objective was to examine whether there was public support for an overall implementation of night-time deliveries.

CASE STUDY: MEASURING PUBLIC SUPPORT FOR NIGHT-TIME DELIVERIES IN BELGIAN CITIES

In this section one application of the methodology will be discussed in more detail to illustrate the different steps of the MAMCA method.

Step 1: Define Alternatives

In this case, there are two alternatives: delivering businesses in cities during the daytime or at night. Based on a profound study of the problems of urban distribution and of the typical characteristics of night deliveries, the alternatives are defined and then translated into five possible scenarios.

Scenario 1: Day deliveries
Scenario 1 assumes that deliveries in cities are made during the day in compliance with currently imposed time windows. The actual practice shows that this would be mainly between 9 am and noon (Stad Gent, 2004; Schoemaker et al., 2006). This scenario can be seen as the reference scenario.

Scenario 2: Night deliveries between 7 pm and 7 am
In scenario 2 all deliveries are shifted to the late evenings, nights and early mornings, when demand for transport is low. At these times commuter traffic virtually stops. Most commuters leave their homes between 6:30 am and 8:45 am, with a peak between 7 am and 8:15 am (Verhetsel et al., 2007). Statistics on everyday congestion in Belgium point in the same direction: the earliest traffic jams appear at 6:30 am and end around 9:15 am (www.touring.be, 12 March 2009). They are at their longest at 8:35 am. The evening rush hour is more spread out. People arrive home between 4:30 pm and 8 pm, with an early peak between 4:30 pm and 6 pm. From 7 pm, the number of commuters still on the way drops dramatically. According to Touring Mobilis, the evening traffic jams reach their peak between 6 pm and 6:30 pm. This shows that in Belgium the hours between 7 pm and 7 am can be considered as off-peak.

Scenario 3: Off-peak deliveries between 7 pm and 11 pm
As previously mentioned, off-peak deliveries have several undesirable side effects. They are generally directly linked to night-time delivery, for example the higher nuisance caused by loading and unloading trucks and the higher wages for drivers and workers. To find out whether a well-thought-out partial use of the off-peak hours to deliver goods might mitigate these side effects, two alternative scenarios were introduced.

In scenario 3, deliveries are allowed only between 7 pm and 11 pm, based on the following:

- At 9:30 pm only 9 per cent of Belgians are already in bed (Glorieux et al., 2008). Another 3.5 per cent are getting ready to do the same.

- At 11 pm more than half of the population is asleep (56 per cent). One hour later, 83 per cent are sleeping and at 2 am, nearly everybody has gone to bed (96.1 per cent).
- Labour legislation is less strict on companies introducing night work when it is performed before midnight (http://www.belgium.be, 12 March 2009).

Scenario 4: Off-peak deliveries between 3 am and 7 am

In scenario 4 deliveries can only be carried out between 3 am and 7 am. We can assume that some stakeholders might prefer these hours because they are the off-peak hours closest to the 'normal' delivery hours in the morning.

Scenario 5: Night deliveries between 7 pm and 7 am, combined with noise standards and a subsidy scheme

Literature on night-time deliveries and pilots shows that the noise nuisance caused by trucks driving, loading and unloading is an important obstacle to introducing off-peak deliveries in cities (Dassen et al., 2008). Therefore, in this scenario, as in scenario 2, all deliveries are shifted to the late evenings, nights and early mornings. But this time, this shift is combined with a specific set of measures aimed at mitigating the nuisance. The scenario refers to the Dutch Piek programme. At the end of 1998 the renewed 'Decree Retail Trade Environmental Protection' came into force (www.piek.org, 12 March 2009). It stipulated that the noise emission generated when loading and unloading goods between 7 pm and 7 am must comply with strict peak noise standards. Given the products used at that time, industry and commerce could not comply with these strict standards. They were forced to come up with innovative measures. The Dutch government supported the implementation of these new products with a long-term subsidy scheme, also called the Piek programme.

Step 2: Stakeholder Analysis

In most urban settings, there is spatial integration of the different qualities that city life incorporates. This is often encouraged by local governments because these hybrid neighbourhoods generate a vibrant, attractive and safer city (De Munck and Vannieuwenhuyse, 2008). Therefore, in addition to the 'economic' stakeholders, one should also take into account the needs of the different 'social' stakeholders. Concerning urban distribution, there are three groups of stakeholders: (i) trade and industry; (ii) society; and (iii) public policy-makers (Witlox, 2006). Trade and industry include suppliers, carriers, receivers, wholesalers and distribution companies. Society consists of inhabitants, employees, commuters, consumers and tourists. Public policy-makers are local, regional and national governments. When evaluating night-time distribution, this general categorization is still valid, although the sub-categories should be slightly rearranged according to the mutually different or coinciding objectives within or between the different groups. This leads to four separate stakeholders: the receiver; the transport sector; society as a whole; and the employee. All these stakeholders, each with their own, often conflicting, interests, take measures to mitigate the adverse effects of urban distribution to them personally (or as a group), which in turn often cause additional nuisance to the other stakeholders. Therefore governments aim for a sustainable urban distribution, which means that they want to establish a framework within which the various aims and objectives of the stakeholders are reconciled as much as possible.

The receiver

The attitude of the receiver is a very decisive success factor (Holguín-Veras et al., 2005). Receivers determine delivery time and usually prefer to take deliveries in the morning right before or right after opening up. Although they are very divergent, the different types of receivers are considered to be one group due to their common objectives concerning deliveries, which are:

- competitiveness
- customer satisfaction
- smooth delivery (just-in-time deliveries, without delays, right in front of the shop, at a convenient time)
- attractive urban shopping environment
- goods safety (both delivered goods and stock)
- motivated employees.

The transport sector

The second group of stakeholders is the transport sector. This group comprises carriers, but also logistic suppliers, the distribution sector and other related stakeholders, for example suppliers and harbours. These are the objectives that the transport sector uses to evaluate every possible change in their delivery operations:

- delivery cost
- customer satisfaction
- technical feasibility
- organizational feasibility
- motivated employees.

Society
The third stakeholder is society as a whole. Since the users of the urban space (inhabitants, commuters, tourists, shoppers) and the government have the same objectives regarding urban distribution, they are considered as one group for this analysis. Their objectives are the following:

- efficient urban distribution
- cost-efficient accompanying measures
- attractive urban environment
- smooth traffic
- traffic safety
- limited noise nuisance
- limited emissions of pollutants.

The employee
The fourth group of stakeholders are the employees. It concerns all the employees, truck drivers, employees working in the stores, at the port and so on. Their objectives for their work environment are:

- health
- safety
- wages
- flexibility
- social life
- stress.

Steps 3 & 4: Translate the Objectives into Criteria and Indicators, and Allocate a Weight to Each Criterion

After identifying the alternatives and the different stakeholders with their key objectives, the next five steps of the MAMCA methodology aim to obtain and to process information on the impact of the different alternatives on the stakeholders' objectives. When analysing the advantages and disadvantages of night-time deliveries, most of the defined criteria cannot be expressed in numbers or are not the subject of existing statistics, for example an attractive shopping environment or motivation of the employee. Therefore this information was gathered through 18 interviews with representatives of the different stakeholder groups.

The interviews were held along established lines and included three phases. First, the above-defined objectives were presented while asking for possible gaps. Second, the interviewee could indicate the importance of each of the objectives by assigning points. A total of 100 points had to

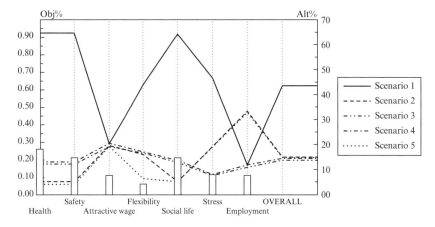

Source: MOSI-T, VUB.

Figure 5.2 Results for the stakeholder 'employee'

be spread over the different objectives. Finally, a score between −2 and +2 had to be given to each scenario for the different objectives. Afterwards, the different scores for objectives were transformed in order to get pair-wise comparisons, which are used to establish the weights for the criteria. Furthermore, an evaluation matrix was constructed that aggregates each alternative contribution to the objectives of each stakeholder group.

Step 5: Overall Analysis and Ranking

In order to carry out the overall analysis and ranking, we use Expert Choice™, specialized software that makes use of the AHP method. The results of this analysis are shown in the next section.

Step 6: Results

Employee
Figure 5.2 shows the results for the stakeholder 'employee'. The figure can be interpreted as follows: the objectives are represented by vertical bars and the alternatives (scenarios) are displayed as horizontal line graphs. The intersection of the alternative line graphs with the vertical objective lines shows the priority of the alternative for the given objective, as read from the right axis labelled Alt%. The objective's priority is represented by the height of its bar as read from the left axis labelled Obj%.

For the stakeholder 'employee', the overall best scenario is scenario

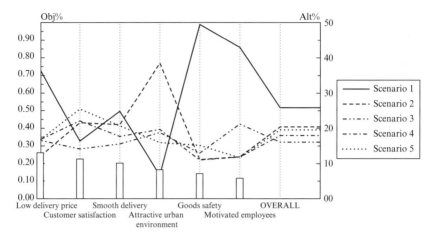

Source: MOSI-T, VUB.

Figure 5.3   Results for the stakeholder 'receiver'

1. The second best is scenario 2, followed by scenarios 5, 3 and 4. This means that the stakeholder 'employee' prefers day deliveries and considers them the best alternative. In general the employee has three objections to night distribution. First, the safety of the driver, for example the risk of robberies. The chance of accidents with pedestrians or bike-riders becomes higher, given that truck drivers are less attentive because they do not expect this type of road users at night. The second objection is that the social life of the truck driver is jeopardized. Night distribution will not lead to shifts but to longer working days, which has an effect on the health (third objection) of the truck driver. These three objections occur in the figure as the three highest bars, meaning that these objectives have the highest relative importance. In the case of the objective 'employment', night deliveries are preferred (scenario 2 and scenario 5).

Receiver
The results for the stakeholder 'receiver' are shown in Figure 5.3. Again, scenario 1 comes out as the overall best alternative. Subsequently, we have the four other scenarios with very close scores. Scenario 1 is the best scenario in view of the objectives 'low delivery price', 'smooth delivery' and 'goods safety'. One of the respondents mentioned that the just-in-time principle is only possible in the case of day deliveries; it makes sure that inventories are limited to a minimum, which can result in a low delivery price. The disadvantage of night distribution is that few employees are

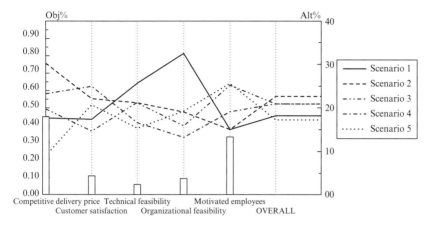

Source: MOSI-T, VUB.

Figure 5.4 Results analysis for the stakeholder 'transport sector'

motivated to work during the night. The safety of the goods is also better guaranteed in the case of day deliveries. Also for hypermarkets such as Colruyt, night deliveries are more advantageous because the shelves can be filled up during closing time, which improves customer satisfaction.

Transport sector
The model seen from the perspective of the stakeholder 'transport sector' is shown in Figure 5.4. The results are remarkably different from those of the previously discussed stakeholders. Scenario 2 (night deliveries between 7 pm and 7 am) is overall perceived as the best option. Subsequently scenario 3 (off-peak deliveries between 7 pm and 11 pm) and scenario 4 (off-peak deliveries between 3 am and 7 am) are good alternatives. With regard to the less important objectives 'technical feasibility' and 'organizational feasibility', scenario 1 (day deliveries) scores best. The advantage of night distribution is the low delivery price that can be adopted. According to an interviewed representative, night distribution brings a higher cost (truck driver) but due to the lower (no) congestion costs, the advantage of night deliveries is still higher than the cost it brings. Another advantage of night deliveries is motivated employees. Truck drivers are prepared to start their work day earlier, unlike the trade unions. The disadvantage of night deliveries is organizational feasibility. The transport company has to be at the truck driver's disposal during the night. From the results, the objective 'organizational feasibility' turned out to be less relatively important.

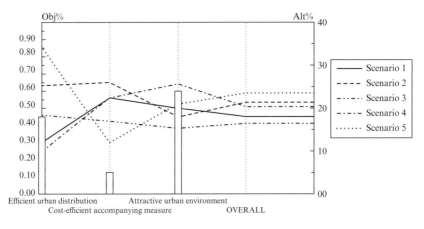

Source: MOSI-T, VUB.

Figure 5.5   Results for the stakeholder 'society'

Society
With regard to urban deliveries, the stakeholder 'society' aims for three
objectives, namely 'efficient urban distribution', 'cost-efficient accompanying measures' and an 'attractive urban environment'.

For these three objectives scenario 5 receives the best score, followed
by scenario 2 and scenario 4. Strikingly, scenario 1 (day deliveries) is not
considered as the best alternative. The objective 'attractive urban environment' has the highest relative importance. For this objective, scenario
4 (deliveries between 3 am and 7 am) is preferred. Remarkably, society,
which includes the citizens, gives a high relative weight to the objective
'efficient urban distribution', in contrast to the expectations of the other
stakeholders. As for this objective, scenario 5 has the highest preference
(Figure 5.5).

Sub-criteria within society
According to the interviewed representatives of the stakeholder group
'society', the objective 'attractive urban environment' is defined by six sub-
criteria, being 'transport safety', 'limited emissions of pollutants', 'noise
nuisance', 'smooth traffic flow', 'visual nuisance' and the question whether
it is desirable to shift to a 24-hour economy, called the 'social component'.
The results of the analysis for these sub-criteria are shown in Figure 5.6.
Overall, the best scenario is scenario 4 (off-peak deliveries between 3 am
and 7 am). With regard to the objectives 'noise nuisance' and 'social component', day deliveries are preferred because of the noise caused by the

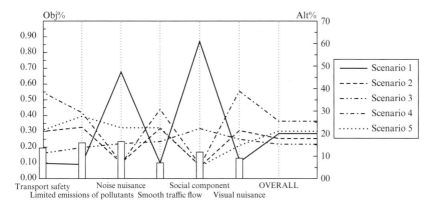

Source: MOSI-T, VUB.

Figure 5.6   Results for the 'stakeholder society', sub-criteria

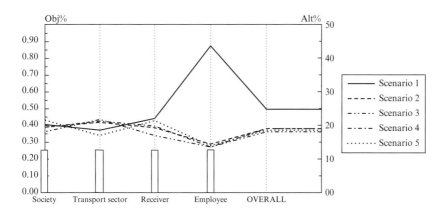

Source: MOSI-T, VUB.

Figure 5.7   Sensitivity analysis for all stakeholder groups

loading and unloading operations and the issue whether a further shift to a 24-hour economy is desirable. As far as the other objectives are concerned, society prefers scenario 4, off-peak deliveries between 3 am and 7 am.

Overall optimal scenario

Figure 5.7 shows that the optimal scenario, considering the preferences of all stakeholder groups as of equal importance, is scenario 1 (day deliveries), followed by scenario 4 and scenario 2 respectively. As mentioned before, scenario 1 is the optimal scenario for the stakeholders 'employee' and 'receiver'. Scenario 3 is the scenario with the highest score for the stakeholder 'transport sector' and scenario 5 for 'society'. The figure also reveals that the four alternative scenarios are close to each other. The stakeholders are open to change in delivery times but do not have an expressed preference for one of the alternatives.

The analysis of these results shows clearly the conflicting interests of the different stakeholder groups. Employees prefer day deliveries, since here 'health', 'social life' and 'safety' prevail. Receivers choose day deliveries as well, because the primary objectives here are 'smooth delivery' and a 'low delivery cost'. In contrast, for the stakeholder 'transport sector', totally different results were observed. Day deliveries are only ranked fourth and instead scenario 2 is considered the best alternative. This can be explained by the fact that a 'competitive delivery price' is very important for this stakeholder group. This is in contrast with the receiver, who does not prefer scenario 3. It is important in implementing night distribution that the opinions of these two stakeholders are tuned in to each other. Also striking is the fact that the 'transport sector' considers scenario 5 to be the most appealing one to its employees, as the stakeholder group 'employee' indicates that it prefers scenario 1. Like the 'transport sector', 'society' does not choose day deliveries as the best option. They consider scenario 2, scenario 4 and scenario 5 to be optimal, which can be explained by the fact that for 'society' the objectives 'efficient urban distribution' and an 'attractive urban environment' are the most important objectives. It is very obvious that day deliveries have a low score for these objectives.

Step 7: Implementation

In the last step new alternatives or modified ones are proposed for further analysis as more insight into the advantages and disadvantages of a certain alternative for each stakeholder is generated. This then creates a feedback loop towards the beginning of the procedure.

CONCLUSION

The MAMCA method makes the objectives of the various relevant stakeholders explicit, thereby leading to a better understanding of the objectives of these stakeholders by all parties concerned. Allowing the stakeholders (whether representatives of business firms or government agencies) to reflect on their own objectives and involving them in the pair-wise comparisons also provides added value in the individual stakeholders' internal decision-making processes. It expresses the concerns of the individual stakeholder. The MAMCA approach forces them to reflect on what they really want and on the rationale for these wants. Moreover, the fact that the stakeholders know that they are included in a comprehensive evaluation alters their way of thinking, and motivates them to make proper assessments. The MAMCA performed on night-time deliveries gave the following results: two of the four stakeholder groups, 'employee' and 'receiver', prefer deliveries to be carried out as they are today, namely by day. The opinion of the stakeholder group 'transport sector' is completely the opposite, as they prefer to deliver between 7 pm and 7 am. The fourth stakeholder group, 'society', prefers night deliveries as well, but only when accompanied by a subsidy scheme and noise standards. These findings suggest that public support for an overall implementation of night-time deliveries is rather low. Overall the term 'night-time deliveries' is not yet well known by the most of the stakeholders. But at the same time, the research shows that there is some room for implementation in Belgian cities, but only if the time period, the type of business and the accompanying measures are carefully selected.

REFERENCES

Allen, J., S. Anderson, M. Browne and P. Jones (2000), 'A framework for considering policies to encourage sustainable urban freight traffic and goods/service flows: summary report', London: University of Westminster.

Carlsson, C. and R. Fuller (1997), 'Problem solving with multiple interdependent criteria, Consensus under Fuziness', in J. Kacprzyk, H. Nurmi and M. Fedrizzi (eds), *The Kluwer International Series in Intelligent Technologies: Consensus under Fuzziness*, Vol. 10, pp. 231–46.

Crals, E., M. Keppens, C. Macharis, R. Ramboer, L. Vereeck and I. Vleugels (2004), 'Nog te veel vragen en te weinig mogelijkheden. Resultaten onderzoek naar verhandelbare mobiliteitsrechten', *De Verkeersspecialist*, **110**, 15–18.

Dassen, R., P. Colon, L. Kuipers and E. Koekebakker (2008), *Dagrand-distributie supermarkten*, Nijmegen: BCI.

De Brucker, K., A. Verbeke and W. Winkelmans (1998), *Sociaal-economische evaluatie van overheidsinvesteringen in transportinfrastructuur*, Leuven: Garant.

De Munck, L. and B. Vannieuwenhuyse (2008), 'Duurzame stedelijke distributie', Report, Vlaams Instituut voor de Logistiek.

Dooms, M. and C. Macharis (2005), 'Introducing the concept of stakeholders in the evaluation of transport infrastructure projects: The DHL case at Brussels National Airport', paper presented at the 45th Congress of the European Regional Science Association, 23–27 August, Vrije Universiteit Amsterdam.

Dooms, M., C. Macharis, A. Verbeke in cooperation with Ecorys, BGDA and COOPARCH-RU (2004), 'Masterplan van de Haven van Brussel: Interimrapport 5', Report, Port of Brussels.

Dooms, M., A. Verbeke, C. Macharis and R. S'Jegers (2006), *De zaak DHL. Het regionaal hub project van DHL in Brussel-Nationaal: een socio-economische en maatschappelijke evaluatie*, Antwerpen/Apeldoorn: Garant.

Eckenrode, R. (1965), 'Weighting multiple criteria', *Management Science*, **12** (3), 180–92.

Glorieux, I., J. Minnen and T.P. van Tienoven (2008), 'Het collectieve ritme van België: Evoluties in het levensritme van de Belgen op basis van tijdsbestedingsonderzoek uit 1966, 1999 en 2005', Report Brussels, Vrije Universiteit Brussel.

Holguín-Veras, J., J. Polimeni, B. Cruz, N. Xu, G. List and J. Nordstrom (2005), 'Off-peak freight deliveries: challenges and stakeholders' perceptions', *Transportation Research Record*, **1906**, 42–8.

Leyva-López, J. and E. Fernández-González (2003), 'A new method for group decision support based on ELECTRE III methodology', *European Journal of Operational Research*, **148**, 14–27.

Macharis, C. (2000), 'Strategische modellering voor intermodale terminals: socio-economische evaluatic van de locatie van binnenvaart/weg terminals in vlaanderen', Ph.D. thesis, Vrije Universiteit Brussel.

Macharis, C. (2004), 'A methodology to evaluate potential locations for intermodal barge terminals: a policy decision support tool', in M. Beuthe, V. Himanen, A. Reggiani and L. Zamparini (eds), *Transport Developments and Innovations in an Evolving World*, Berlin: Springer Verlag, pp. 211–34.

Macharis, C. and B. Boel (2004), 'BRUGARWAT: Brussels Garbage by Water', conference paper in *Bijdragen vervoerslogistieke werkdagen*, ed. Hoeven, Nederland; in C. Ruijgrok and R. Rodenburg, Delft: Connekt.

Macharis, C., J. Brans and B. Mareschal (1998), 'The GDSS Promethee procedure', *Journal of Decision Systems*, **7**, 283–307.

Macharis, C., A. De Witte, and J. Ampe (2007), 'The multi-actor, multi-criteria analysis methodology (MAMCA) for the evaluation of transport projects: theory and practice', *Journal of Advanced Transportation*, **43** (2), 182–202.

Macharis, C., A. De Witte and L. Turcksin (2010), 'The multi-actor multi-criteria analysis (MAMCA): application in the Flemish long term decision making process on mobility and logistics', *Transport Policy*, **17**, 303–11.

Meeus, T., C. Macharis and M. Dooms (2004), 'Inplanting van tweede HST-terminal te Brussel: scenario Brussel-Nationaal moet verder worden onderzocht', De Lloyd. Universiteit and Transport.

Menge, J. and P. Hebes (2009), 'Dealing with constraints of urban logistics – assessment of an optimisation project', German Aerospace Center (DLR) in the Helmholtz Association, Institute of Transport Research (IVF).

Nijkamp, P., P. Rietveld and H. Voogd (1990), *Multicriteria Evaluation in Physical Planning*, Amsterdam: Elsevier Science Publishers.

Öztürk, Z.K. (2006), 'A review of multi criteria decision making with dependency between criteria', paper presented at MCDM 2006, Chania, Greece, 19–23 June.

Saaty, T. (1986), 'Axiomatic foundation of the analytic hierarchy process', *Management Science*, **32** (7), 841–55.

Schoemaker, J., J. Allen, M. Huschebeck and J. Monigl (2006), Quantification of Urban Freight Transport Effects I. BESTUFS II.

Stad Gent (2004), 'Stadsdistributie: van bezorgd naar bezorgen: Alternatieven voor de bevoorrading van handelaars in de Gentse binnenstad', Report, City of Gent.

Verhetsel, A., I. Thomas, E. Van Hecke and M. Beelen (2007), Pendel in België: Deel I: de woon-werkverplaatsingen. Brussel, FOD Economie, K.M.O., Middenstand en Energie.

Witlox, F. (2006), 'Stadsdistributie, dé oplossing voor de tanende (groot)stedelijke mobiliteit?', in M. Despontin and C. Macharis (eds), *Mobiliteit en (groot) stedenbeleid*, Brussel: VUB.

Internet Sources

http://www.touring.be/nl/dagelijks-leven/onderweg-leren-rijden/alternatieve-mobiliteit/artikels/analyse-files/index.asp, accessed 12 March 2009.
http://www.belgium.be/nl/publicaties/publ_wegwijs_nachtarbeid.
   jsp?referer=tcm:117-16007-64, accessed 12 March 2009.
http://www.piek.org/engels/home_eng.htm, accessed 12 March 2009.
http://www.un-documents.net/wced-ocf.htm, accessed 12 March 2009.

6. Definition of a set of indicators to evaluate the performance of urban goods distribution initiatives

Sandra Melo and Álvaro Costa

INTRODUCTION

In the past, the topic of urban goods distribution (UGD), as well as the closely related subject of freight traffic, has been overlooked by researchers and planners. It has been treated mainly as a marginal issue of passenger traffic and usually studied in an inappropriate geographical scale, not taking into account the specificities of freight. However, during the last decade the negative impacts of UGD on the quality of life, mobility and attractiveness of cities have contributed to an increasing attempt to reverse this tendency. More research on this topic has been conducted and the primary key findings on the topic have been made. The tendency has been to look at solutions inspired by other perspectives already studied and analysed in more detail (e.g. passenger transport) and apply them to a new specific context (e.g. freight). In some situations, this procedure leads to alternative initiatives that could be seen as 'good practice' in supplying cities, based on the theoretical or empirical results its implementation would produce. These examples of 'good practices' in UGD initiatives, however, present heterogeneous methodologies of evaluation and diverse types of output indicators, making it unfeasible to extrapolate general lessons from them.

This chapter, which arises from broader research on UGD, tries to contribute to defining an objective methodology for the study of the topic. It proposes that the perspectives of public and private stakeholders should be considered, given the specificities of the topic of freight and that of the local intrinsic characteristics of implementation. To support the inclusion of stakeholders' interests, a set of indicators is defined here according to the structure presented in the following paragraph.

The chapter begins with a short preface on the stakeholders' views of the topic of UGD. With this conceptual overview in mind, the ensuing section emphasizes the main criteria considered for the purpose of evaluation: mobility and sustainability. Subsequently we identify qualitative and quantitative criteria underlying good practices in the selection of indicators. The consideration of both these criteria is then combined and refined in light of the stakeholders' main interests. The result of this methodology leads to a final compilation of indicators, whose validation is described in the last section. The final set of indicators suggested in this chapter allows us to quantify 'good practices' in UGD and support the evaluation of policies through the use of modelling tools.

INTERESTS AND CRITERIA OF STAKEHOLDERS

The overall UGD system consists of stakeholders interacting according to their own interests – influencing and being influenced by the urban environment in which regional economy, legal conditions, transport infrastructure and the surrounding environment play a relevant role. The main challenge of studying the UGD system with this chapter's approach is that the bearing effects of one group of stakeholders might be the causing effects of another group. Therefore finding a balance between different stakeholders' interests requires understanding their role and preferences within the system.

The following description tries explicitly and sufficiently to reflect stakeholders' preferences and needs, and their relative role and expectations.

The main group of stakeholders to be considered in city logistics includes suppliers, residents (community), receivers/shopkeepers, other road users and (local) administrators, all of them with different and complex transportation and consumption needs (Schoemaker et al., 2006).

The group labelled as suppliers consists of shippers and freight carriers. Shippers (manufacturers, wholesalers, retailers) operate from warehouses and are the customers of transport companies that send or receive goods from companies or persons. Although shippers usually determine pick-up time, they do not have absolute control of delivery time. Freight carriers (transporters, warehouse companies) usually decide on the time and route that is more efficient to meet the delivery constraints imposed by receivers. Freight carriers establish the connection between shippers and receivers, and must satisfy both. They are usually contracted in outsourcing agreements and are expected to provide higher levels of service within the framework of just-in-time (JIT) transportation systems with lower costs. The main interests of suppliers are to minimize the costs of collecting and delivering goods to customers and to maximize their profits, within a given regulatory framework and a given transport infrastructure. They try to provide higher levels of service (profitability, safety, user satisfaction and shipper satisfaction) at the lowest cost.

Residents and users (community) are the people who live, work and shop in cities. Their concern is to minimize traffic congestion, noise, air pollution and accidents close to their homes, workplaces and recreational areas. Residents and users perceive goods vehicles in a negative way: these are the vehicles that obstruct passenger circulation, make noise, park illegally, pollute and so on. So they do not appreciate goods vehicles using local roads, even if these goods are meant for resident's and users' consumption.

Goods are delivered to receivers, who set delivery times, most frequently in mutual agreement with the carriers. A survey carried out in Portugal (Melo, 2010) shows that when preparing the schedules and routes for supply trips to urban areas, 96 per cent of the transporters take into account the congestion levels at the destination, whereas 56 per cent state that the determinant decision factor is the schedule imposed by receivers. Receivers want goods to be delivered on time and according to what was previously established. Usually they do not care much about how goods arrive as long as their requirements are fulfilled. They prefer a smooth, frequent, easily accessible, relatively cheap, punctual, reliable, safe and secure door-to-door service and, at the same time, minimum disturbance caused by the transport of goods. In the main, they establish delivery requirements based on their needs and profits. Therefore it is difficult to involve receivers in initiatives that do not prove in advance to be profitable for them. Examples of receivers are individual consumers and shopkeepers.

Administrators and in particular local authorities and policy-makers attempt to create and implement policies that will regulate the system operations at local (community) level and subsidize some services of public interest. They are mostly interested in raising overall socioeconomic welfare and controlling the externalities of transport operations (Janic, 2006). On the one hand, they attempt to promote the economic development of the city, which requires taking into account the industry stakeholders' interests. On the other hand, they want to alleviate traffic congestion, improve the environment and reduce traffic accidents, which can require the implementation of restrictions on the operations of suppliers. Their role is difficult, especially when it comes to making some politically hard decisions about transport, as well as when it is necessary to implement effective – but vote-losing – initiatives (Begg and Gray, 2004).

Each stakeholder, in its own role, tries to optimize its functioning according to its own interests, independent of its neighbours interests. This generates problems and conflicts in the achievement of consensual initiatives to be implemented in a limited space and infrastructure within an urban area. These difficulties can be narrowed down to a simple distinction between the objectives of the public – the city – and the private – the transport chain – stakeholders (STRATEC, 2005).

Public objectives reflect administrators', receivers', residents' and users' (visitors, tourists, employees) concerns relative to the promotion of the public good. Public objectives are often related to the well-being of all stakeholders in a specific area, such as quality of life (accidents, noise, emissions, nuisance etc.) and economic vitality.

Private objectives reflect suppliers' and the transport industry's worries about improving the efficiency and profits of their service. Private objectives are often related to turnover levels, such as sales levels, customer levels, cost levels (operation and driving), service levels and competition.

The balancing act of considering both public and private objectives for the establishment of more sustainable strategies in UGD has proved difficult. It involves bringing together stakeholders with different expectations and objectives, who usually advocate different approaches and measures. Therefore the challenge of developing and promoting initiatives within these circumstances 'is not only finding an appropriate strategy but also one that all stakeholders will want to own and invest in' (Hensher and Brewer, 2001, p. 1). Stakeholders, regardless of whether their interests are public or private, must want to be involved and participate in UGD decisions in order more easily to find consensual strategies and indicators that play a determinant role in their perception of the initiative. The best way to get their support is to (a) understand and care for their needs and concerns, and (b) get them involved throughout the different stages of the process: problem analysis, objectives definition, selection of solution, implementation and evaluation (STRATEC, 2005).

In an attempt to understand different stakeholders' needs and concerns, a questionnaire was carried out, designed to obtain information about the particular understanding of stakeholders' perceptions of UGD. In the light of this aim, two target groups were selected to reply to the questionnaire: (a) urban planners at local administrations in the north of Portugal, who reflect social (i.e. public) perspectives; and (b) associate members of the National Association of Portuguese Freight Carriers (ANTP – Associação Nacional de Transportadores Portugueses) to better understand the perspectives of transporters and suppliers (i.e. private parties). The analysis of the responses to the questionnaire shows that the determinant factors on decision-making regarding UGD for public interests are the sustainability of the city, followed by environmental pollution, costs of transport and, lastly, urban mobility issues. Private interest parties (i.e. transporters) prioritize it differently, indicating costs of transport as the most determinant factor for decision-making, followed by environmental pollution, urban mobility and, lastly, sustainability issues.

With this overview in mind, the study establishes the criteria of mobility and sustainability as the two key pillars of evaluation for public and private objectives in UGD. Environmental pollution will be included in the environmental sustainability dimension and costs of transport will be included in the economic sustainability category. This categorization does not overlook the social sustainability dimension, also considered in this study.

SCOPE OF MEASUREMENT: MOBILITY AND SUSTAINABILITY CRITERIA

With such different priorities of heterogeneous stakeholders' perspectives, it may be difficult to keep a flexible attitude towards diverse and almost conflicting interpretations of mobility and sustainability criteria. To overcome some blurred interpretation, this section establishes what degree of mobility is expected to be achieved and what issues from the three dimensions of sustainability (environmental, economic and social) should be considered in the development of a general set of indicators.

Both concepts (mobility and sustainability) strongly rely on a negotiated balance between private interests (operations efficiency) and public interests (economic costs, environmental pressure and social equity). Mobility is understood as ease of movement, and the chosen indicators will reflect this interpretation. The ideal mobility is the one that allows economic and social activities to be carried out with a minimum external cost to society. The expected sustainability is the one that corresponds to the transport and distribution of goods with lower environmental impacts within the city, minimum costs for city and industry, and minimum externalities for society.

With these interpretations in mind, the measurement of mobility and sustainability is evaluated in a specific period, with no intention to predict its level in the future. Indicators differentiate passenger and freight mode, and try to reproduce different tendencies for each stakeholder considered. In addition, as it is not the objective of the chapter to predict and measure the level of mobility and sustainability at some distant point in the future, special emphasis is given to the goals whose current level will mean the most for the welfare of future generations. This assumption implies the following methodological effects: first, the environmental indicators consider two sets of issues: those of the global greenhouse effect and energy consumption, and local issues of local atmospheric pollution. The pollutants are attributed to their place of emission on the basis of the trip that generated them; this allows us to estimate rates of emission per km (and per area) within the city. Second, the economic indicators should in an ideal approach analyse the global costs of the UGD system. Due to technical restrictions and to the fact that such analysis was not an objective of this study, the economic indicators will focus on operational and internal costs of the community as a whole and also of the different stakeholders: suppliers, public authorities and citizens. It should also be noted that environmental pollution, such as atmospheric pollution, has been considered, but has not been taken into account from on economic point of views. The intention is to avoid the same element being taken into account twice – in the environmental sphere and in the economic sphere, within the same target analysis: Third, the social indicators attempt to observe which constraints and benefits would be attained for which stakeholders, in a time period when social equity issues are receiving increasing attention. Social indicators will incorporate both mobility and sustainability issues and will be used both as an input to characterize the problem and as an output to evaluate the effects of an initiative.

DEFINITION AND FUNCTIONS OF INDICATORS

The previous sections presented the main groups of stakeholders and the two key pillars of evaluation on the topic of UGD. This section describes the theoretical background to the selection of indicators to perform that evaluation. Indicators reflect society's values and goals, and are key tools to measure the performance of a system and the evolution of a process, or to evaluate the results of a particular action within a complex system.

There are many different definitions of indicators, which stem from different perspectives. An adapted definition of that presented by the Organization for Economic Cooperation and Development (OECD, 1994, p. 13) reads as follows: 'a statistic or parameter that, tracked over time, provides information on trends in the condition of a phenomenon and has significance extending beyond that associated with the properties of the statistics itself.' Unlike simple statistics, indicators provide a summary indication of a condition or problem and allow the observation of progress or change. This progress can be measured over time or against benchmarks, targets or visions for the future.

In other literature sources, indicators are defined as tools that can illustrate and communicate complex phenomena simply, while still including trends and progress over time (Henderson, 1996; Eckersley, 1997; Gilbert and Tanguay, 2000; EEA, 2005). Jacksonville Community Council[1] (1992), quoted by Foley (2004, p. 17), presented a similar definition quite simply:

'indicators are a way of seeing the "big picture" by looking at a smaller piece of it. They tell us which direction we are going: up or down, forward or backward, getting better or worse or staying the same.' Indicators are quantities that give schematic information by means of several representations of a complex and wide-reaching phenomenon, thereby making clear a situation or a characteristic that is not directly perceivable. They help to reduce a large quantity of data down to their simplest form, presenting the essential meaning of the questions being asked of the data (Ott, 1978). Additionally, indicators provide a useful tool for policy-making and for assessing policy implementation (Mega and Pedersen, 1998). They represent an empirical model of reality, assuming implicitly that a complex phenomenon could be represented by a limited number of variables (Musu et al., 1998).

While the definitions vary, there is consensus about the purpose: an indicator should be more than just a simple statistic or measurement. Indicators' purposes are then reflected in several functions, such as helping to identify trends, predict problems, assess options, set performance targets and evaluate a particular system. The primary purposes of indicators should be: (a) to reduce the number of measurements needed to give an exact representation of a process or a situation and (b) to facilitate the information communication process to the end-users and stakeholders.

To achieve such essential purposes, the selection of indicators should consider quality and quantitative criteria.

Qualitative Criteria for Indicators

Although indicators can be very different, depending on the use for which they have been elaborated, common criteria are used by a range of groups and organizations for the purpose of their selection. In general, indicator quality criteria mentioned in policy documents of some relevant international organizations (EU,[2] Eurostat,[3] EEA,[4] UN[5] and WHO[6]) and in scientific literature (Mitchell et al., 1995; Mega and Pedersen, 1998; Ditor et al., 2001; Cybernetix and STRATEC, 2003; Nicolas et al., 2003; Marsden and Snell, 2006; Litman, 2007) commonly state that indicators must be clear and understandable, policy-relevant, significant, accessible and reliable. Also, they should aid in comparing, evaluating, predicting and decision-making at various levels.

In terms of quality criteria, indicators must also cover the most essential issues at stake, be strongly consistent with the statistical database, presented simply so that they may be used by all those concerned, and adequately represent the selected geographical or political area. Results from the above-mentioned literature sources lead to the definition of the following principles (ideally to be applied) when selecting performance indicators on UGD:

(a) *Scientific validity*   Scientific validity is an important factor to consider, particularly when using causal frameworks, because a scientific basis for links between the stress indicators and the condition indicators selected must be established. Some degree of uncertainty is inevitable when establishing these relations and thus it is important to understand exactly how well it will describe the impacts, and how great is the consensus on the validity of the indicator.

(b) *Representativeness*   A representative indicator represents the issue of concern (mobility and sustainability). Representativeness is an important characteristic because of the frequently stated requirement that the number of indicators should be manageable and therefore relatively small (Ditor et al., 2001).

(c) *Relevant and easy to understand*   Indicators must measure what they are supposed to measure. The selected indicators should represent what needs to be known and should be easily understood by decision-makers and the general public. How well does the indicator display a move towards or away from sustainability and mobility? How useful is the indicator for the end-users? How comprehensible is the indicator to the public/decision-makers?

(d) *Evidence of links of cause and effect*   A good indicator is not only representative of an issue, but it also highlights the links and inter-relationships of the stress–condition–response cycle.

(e) *Responsiveness to change*   A responsive indicator can be expected to respond to the external stimuli's changes, such as policy interventions. An example of responsive indicator often used is the air pollutants emitted resulting from the implementation of an initiative in comparison with a 'do-nothing' situation.

(f) *Comparability to target, thresholds or standards*   The use of thresholds or targets in indicator development is an effective tool for measuring progress towards a variety of goals and is therefore important from a policy perspective. Data collection should be standardized so that the results are suitable for comparison between various times and groups.

(g) *Transferability*   An indicator that can be used at different times and in different geographical scales can help users to relate their own behaviours and decision-making to the local context and regional and national issues. How well can the indicators be used in different time periods and in different geographical areas?

(h)   *Accuracy, time-series data availability or collection*   Indicators must be measurable, and the uncertainty of the measure must be as small as possible. It is useless to have a conceptually very good indicator if the methods used to measure its values give very uncertain results, from which no conclusion can be drawn.

(i)   *Cost-effectiveness*   The set of indicators should be cost-effective to collect. The decision-making value of the indicators must outweight the cost of collecting them.

(j)   *Net effects*   Indicators should differentiate between net (total) impacts and shifts of impacts to different locations and times.

The definition and selection of indicators should attempt to accomplish the mentioned principles. However, it is difficult to find indicators that satisfy all these principles simultaneously. Consequently, judgements must be made about their relative importance. Throughout this study, the level of significance for stakeholders will be the first priority in the list of selection criteria. Data availability limitations exclude certain otherwise desirable indicators.

The defined quality criteria presented above will be used, together with quantitative criteria (see next subsection), as guidelines for the development of the final indicator set.

Quantitative Criteria for Indicators

The definition of quantitative criteria for transport indicators requires the identification of the consequences or impacts that need to be measured and how those effects are related to a set of causes. In the transport area and related to the mobility and sustainability criteria, this approach typically leads to the measurement of safety, congestion, fuel consumption and environment. Due to a lack of adapted data, this study will not integrate questions linked to safety. Consequently, the scope of the analysis is narrowed to that shown in Figure 6.1.

For road transport as the main mode used for city distribution, Figure 6.1 presents a causal-based framework for a representation of the influence of urban goods movement on society and environment. Each of the referred impacts has variables that affect them, factors that affect these same variables and so on. The arrow associated with each variable represents its direction of influence. In this way, to select indicators that point to a positive direction towards better mobility and sustainability, it is necessary to change the variables that influence the impacts, which are measured by indicators. Fuel consumption, congestion and environment levels are impacts influenced most directly by land use, truck fuel

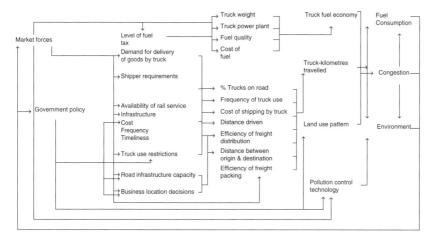

Source: Richardson (2005).

Figure 6.1   Freight factors affecting distribution system

economy and truck vehicle-kilometers travelled. Beyond these factors, many others (some even interrelated) can be found, but the illustration presented by Richardson (2005) is a first step to understanding the causal linkages among factors, reflected by the respective impacts that can be measured by the indicators. In this example, possible indicators to evaluate a truck use restriction policy would be travel times (unit of time), fuel consumed on the area (litres), vehicle delays (unit of time) and CO_2 emissions, respectively. Travel times and vehicle delays can be a measure of mobility, CO_2 emissions can be a measure of social and environmental impacts and fuel consumption can be a measure of economic and environmental impacts (driver costs and natural resources depletion).

The quantitative comparison of these indicators between a scenario *ex ante* and *ex post* makes it possible to assess whether the policy that was (or is about to be) implemented was (or will probably be) positive or not in terms of mobility and sustainability targets.

SELECTION OF INDICATORS

Table 6.1 presents a general list of mobility and sustainability (economic, social and environmental) indicators based on the relations shown in Figure 6.1, as well as on the established review from qualitative and

Table 6.1 *Indicator framework for the evaluation of transport sustainability and mobility performance*

Dimension	Theme	Indicators
Economic	Transport demand and intensity	1. Volume of transport relative to GDP (tonne-km; passenger-km)
		2. Road transport (passenger and freight; tonne-km and passenger-km)
		3. Railway transport (passenger and freight; tonne-km and passenger-km)
		4. Maritime transport for goods and passengers (tonne-km and passenger-km)
		5. Inland waterway transport (passenger and freight; tonne-km and passenger-km)
		6. Air transport (passenger and freight; tonne-km and passenger-km)
		7. Intermodal transport (tonne-km and passenger-km)
	Transport costs and prices	8. Total per capita transport expenditures (vehicle parking, roads and transit services)
		9. Motor vehicle fuel prices and taxes (for gasoline and gas/diesel)
		10. Direct user cost by mode (passenger transport)
		11. External costs of transport activities (congestion, emission costs, safety costs) by transport mode (freight and passenger)
		12. Internalization of costs (implementation of economic policy tools with a direct link with the marginal external costs of the use of different transport modes)
		13. Subsidies to transport
		14. Taxation of vehicles and vehicle use
		15. % of GDP contributed by transport
		16. Investment in transport infrastructure (per capita by mode/ as share of GDP)
	Infrastructure	17. Road quality – paved roads, fair/good condition
		18. Total length of roads in km
		19. Density of infrastructure (km/km^2)
Social	Risk and safety	20. Persons killed in traffic accidents (number of fatalities – 1000 vehicle-km; per million inhabitants)
		21. Traffic accidents involving personal injury (number of injuries – 1000 vehicle-km; per million inhabitants)

Table 6.1   (continued)

Dimension	Theme	Indicators
	Health Impacts	22. Population exposed to and annoyed by traffic noise, by noise category and by mode associated with health and other effects
		23. Cases of chronic respiratory diseases, cancer, headaches. Respiratory restricted activity days and premature deaths due to motor vehicle pollution
	Affordability	24. Private car ownership
		25. Affordability (portion of households income devoted to transport)
	Employment	26. Contribution of transport sector (by mode) to employment growth
Environ-mental	Transport emissions	27. NOx emissions (per capita)
		28. VOC emissions (per capita)
		29. PM10 and PM2.5 emissions (per capita)
		30. SOx emissions (per capita)
		31. O_3 concentration (per capita)
		32. CO_2 emissions (per capita)
		33. N_{20} emissions (per capita)
		34. CH_4 emissions (per capita)
	Energy efficiency	35. Energy consumption by transport mode (tonne-oil equivalent per vehicle-km)
		36. Fuel consumption (vehicle-km by mode)
	Impacts on environmental resources	37. Habitat and ecosystem disruption
		38. Land take by transport infrastructure mode
	Environmental risks and damages	39. Polluting accidents (land, air, water)
		40. Hazardous materials transported by mode
	Renewables	41. Use of renewable energy sources (numbers of alternative-fuelled vehicles) – use of biofuels
		42. Total expenditure on pollution prevention and clean-up
		43. Measures taken to improve public transport
Mobility	Mobility	44. Average vehicle journey time
		45. Average vehicle journey length per mode
		46. Quality of transport for disadvantaged people (disabled, low incomes, children)
		47. Personal mobility (daily or annual person-miles and trips by income group)
		48. Volume of passengers

Table 6.1 (continued)

Dimension	Theme	Indicators
	Service provided	49. Daily number of trips
		50. Structure of trip purposes
		51. Daily average time budget
	Organization of urban mobility	52. Modal split
		53. Average distance travelled
		54. Average speed (global and per person)

quantitative criteria on the topic. This review identified common indicator sets from the EC Sustainable Development Strategy, the EC ETIS, the EEA TERM, Eurostat, the OECD, the US EPA, the World Bank, UNECE, VTPI and the JRC Well-to-Wheels study, and was complemented with scientific inputs from Dobranskyte-Niskota et al. (2007), Nicolas et al. (2003) and Schoemaker et al. (2006). Differences among the organizations and authors are thought to provide a sufficient degree of diversity and offer the overall comprehensive picture necessary to define an indicator set.

Table 6.1 provides an indicator framework for the evaluation of transport sustainability and mobility performance in general. It includes all the modes of transport and even themes, which are not analysed throughout the study. Such a detailed list provides an overall picture of the indicator framework and, simultaneously, allows the extraction of the specific indicators that are to be used to evaluate the UGD initiatives.[7]

Although in terms of mobility and transport emissions, Table 6.1 provides useful inputs for the analysis of mobility and sustainability applied to UGD, these indicators are clearly not enough to evaluate alternative initiatives, or include stakeholders' perspectives. Therefore an additional review focused on illustrating public and private interests and objectives on the evaluation of UGD sustainability and mobility performance was carried out. Table 6.2 illustrates the set of indicators that results from that review. It provides an indicator framework to evaluate the performances of UGD initiatives considering stakeholder interests. It includes specific goods distribution indicators and takes into account the dimensions of mobility and sustainability.

The 'interests' identified in the last column refer to the indicator's ability to measure the main (public or private) stakeholder's interest. For instance, within the dimension of mobility, one of the proposed indicators is the use of load capacity, which, on the one hand,

Table 6.2   Indicator framework for evaluating UGD initiatives considering stakeholders' interests

Dimension	Theme	Indicator	Interest
Economic	Transport demand	Volumes transported into urban areas	PU, PR
	Logistics	Goods receivers	PR
		Logistics costs	
		Share of urban transport costs compared to total supply chain	
		Salaries in urban freight transport	
	General delivery character- istics	Combined shipments	PU, PR
		Delivery days and times	
		Regularity of trips	
		Origin of delivery trips	
		Number of stops per tour per day	
		Trip length	
		Distance between shops	
		Trip times	
		Travel time to and within city centre	
	Employment percentage in transport and logistics	Number of jobs in transport	PU, PR
		Number of transport related companies	
Social	Freight vehicles	Number of vehicles according to GVW and age	PU
		Proportion of goods vehicles in total traffic	
		Ownership of vehicles	
		Vehicles operating in cities	
	Accidents and causalities in urban freight transport	Number of accidents	PU, PR
		Number of fatalities	
		Involvement of freight vehicles in accidents	
		Weekly distribution of accidents involving HGVs	
	Road user type	Cyclists	PU
		Pedestrians	
		Car drivers	

Table 6.2 (continued)

Dimension	Theme	Indicator	Interest
Environment	Energy use	Typical fuel consumption by vehicle type	PU , PR, C
		Energy consumption in urban freight transport	
		Consumption of non-renewable fuel resources	
	Exhaust emissions	Typical emission factors by vehicle type	PU, PR, C
		Share of urban freight in exhaust emissions	
	Noise	Noise levels driving truck	PU, PR
		Noise levels loading/unloading truck	
Mobility	Urban traffic flow	Number of vehicles entering cities	PU, PR
		Distribution of freight vehicles movements over day	
	Performance	Freight vehicle-kilometres	PU, PR
		Use of load capacity	
	Home delivery	Home delivery services offered by shops	PU
		Number of km covered by inhabitant	

Note: PU – Public interests; PR – Private interests; C – Citizens (community): in some situations their interests are private, public or both.

Source: Adapted from Schoemaker et al. (2006).

demonstrates the efficiency of the service and in that way it is a good indicator to illustrate private interests. On the other hand, a low use of load capacity has impacts on overall mobility, and thus affects society in terms of congestion and air pollution. In that way, this indicator is also adequate to illustrate public interests. The interests labelled as merely 'private' or simply 'public' are not exclusive, but concern mostly the chosen label.

The contents of Table 6.1 and Table 6.2, added to the literature review, and discussions devoted to this topic and empirical evidence provide the needed input to the final selection of indicators, illustrated in Table 6.3.

Table 6.3   Indicator framework for evaluating UGD initiatives mobility and sustainability performance considering stakeholders' interests

Indicator (unit)	Stake-holders	Description of the use of the indicator	Examples of project/ organization using the indicator
Economic			
Delivery times	PR	Delivery service is subdivided into the components of delivery time, delivery reliability, delivery condition and delivery flexibility.	Schoemaker et al. (2006)
Supplier operational costs		Delivery time can therefore be used as parameter of supplier delivery performance; it extends from the point at which the supplier parks to the point at which he leaves. Delivery times are related to supplier operational costs in a direct way: lower delivery times can contribute to lower operational costs.	
Deliveries/day trip length		Lower delivery times and lower operational cost are better.	
		Deliveries/day and trip length are descriptive indicators.	
Environmental			
Energy intensity (fuel consumption in litres by vehicle type)	PU, PR	As motor vehicles are the main users of transport fuel, the indicator is highly correlated with motor vehicle usage, which in turn measures indirectly the pressure on the environment through use of resources, energy consumption, air pollutant emission (particularly ozone, particulate matter, carbon monoxide and nitrogen oxide), noise pollution. This indicator has many linkages to others, for example, to the emission of sulphur oxides (SO_x) and nitrogen oxides (NO_x), reductions in the emissions of greenhouse gases, energy use, and land-use change.	(Henry and STRATEC, 2003) DfT TEBPP projects

Table 6.3 (continued)

Indicator (unit)	Stake-holders	Description of the use of the indicator	Examples of project/ organization using the indicator
		In consequence, there are implications for ambient concentration of pollutants in urban areas, human health, ozone depletion, and expenditure on air pollution abatement. No international targets have been established, although some countries have fuel consumption targets for the automobile vehicle fleet.	
Emissions g per area or km per vehicle type (NO_x; VOCs, CO)	PU, PR, C	Lower fuel consumption is better. There are non-CO_2 emissions limits established by EU directives (see case study). Nitrogen oxides are good marking elements of combustion engine processes, having at the same time various impacts on all levels. The exhaust of NO_x emissions results in the souring that affects historic buildings in cities. For heavy, diesel engines the current EU level of 0.7–0.9 g/tonne-km could be reduced by 70% to 0.2–0.25 g/tonne-km, which is a feasible level for sustainability. VOC emissions are strongly dependent on the composition of the fuels used (Remy and Gee, 1995). They can be emitted by incomplete combustion (70%), during refuelling (10%) or by evaporation from strong units (20%), particularly gas tanks. Many of them have direct toxic effects on humans and ecosystems: first, benzene and butadiene have carcinogenic effects, while most of them have greenhouse and photochemical impacts.	Mészáros (2000); Litman (2007); Schoemaker et al. (2006); Perry and Gee (1995)

Indicator	Description	References
	Carbon monoxide (CO) is a toxic gas that results from an incomplete combustion of diesel. High concentrations can be lethal, small concentrations can result in cardiovascular disorders and corrosion of the repiratory tract.	
CO_2 emissions (g per area or km)	The higher the number, the more damaging emissions are emitted. CO_2 is a basic indicator of energy use and greenhouse effects. The European Parliament has suggested introducing mandatory CO_2 emission standards[1] to replace current voluntary commitments (140g/km by 2008) by the auto manufacturers (see ACEA agreement) and labeling. In 2007, the European Commission proposed a new law to limit CO_2 emissions by 120gCO_2/km (COM 2007 – 856 final) for passenger cars and light-duty vehicles.	Mészáros (2000); Litman (2007)
Share of urban freight in exhaust emissions	The higher the number, the more damaging emissions are emitted.	
Mobility and sustainability (social) PU, PR, C		
Average speed (excluding stops to make deliveries – km/hour)	The lack of mobility has a number of consequences, such as delays and unreliable journey times; thus it is often measured by speed, vehicle journey time, travel time, delay time, among others. Reduced urban congestion and delays deliver economic benefits that cut operator delivery costs and generate regional multiplier impacts. Potentially, urban decongestion generates time savings for operators and other road users.	Dinwoodie (2006) Litman (2007); Lomax et al. (1997); Cybernetix and STRATEC (2003); Litman (2007); TSS (2007)
Average vehicle journey time on the area		
Travel time (sec./km)	Higher average speed is a better way to analyse improvement in mobility when compared with a base case situation of congestion and within the capacity and speed limits of the network. Lower average vehicle journey time on the area, travel time and delay time are better.	
Delay time (sec./km)	The selected indicators are also descriptive indicators.	

Table 6.3 (continued)

Indicator (unit)	Stakeholders	Description of the use of the indicator	Examples of project/ organization using the indicator
Distance travelled by HGV, LGV and car (vehicle-km)	PU, PR	Reductions in lorry-km in urban areas offer environmental benefits and fewer vehicular emissions of airborne pollutants. Motor vehicle travel (measured as vehicle-kilometres travelled (VKT), and passenger-kilometres travelled (PKT) is sometimes used as a sustainability indicator, assuming that motorized travel is unsustainable because it is resource-intensive and environmentally harmful.	Browne and Allen (1999); Mega and Pedersen (1998); AEA Technology Environment et al., The validity of Food Miles as an Indicator of Sustainable Development; Litman (2007) TSS (2007) Schoemaker et al. (2006)
Use of load capacity		Increases in vehicle load-factor deliver mobility benefits, which increases operator delivery efficiency and other road users. It probably also reduces environmental impacts.	
Proportion of goods vehicles in total traffic		Descriptive indicator	
Mean flow (vehicle/h)		Higher is better	
Density (vehicle/km)		Lower is better	

Notes: PU – Public interests; PR – Private interests; C – Citizens (community), in some situations their interests are private, public or both.

This set corresponds to the final selection to be validated by a questionnaire and carried out within a targeted expert's database.

To interpret the table's selection, one should bear in mind that:

- indicators are an evaluation instrument and should always be presented together with other scientific information to avoid misinterpretation;
- indicators should always be interpreted in the original context, considering the specific environmental, social and economic conditions;
- the use of indicators is just one step in the overall planning process, which includes consulting stakeholders, defining problems, establishing goals and objectives; identifying and evaluating options, developing policies and plans, implementing programmes, establishing performance targets and measuring impacts (Litman, 2007).

Some system boundaries are worth mentioning in light of the choice of indicators presented in Table 6.3. Although proper aggregation of indicators would simplify the process of dealing with target conflicts and the prioritization of the various initiatives in the field of goods distribution, a scientifically valid method for the aggregation of environmental, economic and social indicators into a 'sustainability index' does not yet exist. In addition, such aggregation would involve a loss of transparency and render impossible the relative evaluation of the various indicators in the process of negotiation. Moreover, considerations were restricted to road transport, and the focus on the effects of transport on the environment, economy and society does not consider possible interactions or indirect effects. Another limitation is the fact that the only measured indicators of environmental sustainability are energy conservation and emissions. Sustainability is much more than energy conservation (fuel consumption) and emission of air pollution (CO_2 emissions), which are highly correlated.

On the basis of the current discussion, many more indicators could also enrich the set of suggested indicators, and clearly there is room for discussion and debate relative to this choice. Virtually anyone can develop a different set of variables consisting of indicators of sustainability and mobility performance. However, as the final definition of a set of indicators is always dependent on personal choices, an error of judgement can always occur – not in the information represented by every single indicator, but in the overall view provided by the set. In an attempt to overcome the subjectivity inherent in personal choices, an enquiry was carried out to validate the set of indicators illustrated in Table 6.3.

VALIDATION OF THE SET OF INDICATORS

The validation of the set of indicators illustrated in Table 6.3 was carried out with the assistance of scientific/technical experts. The support was obtained through a survey sent to 124 sampled experts. This sample was selected from the list of members of the Grupo de Estudos em Transportes (Portuguese Transport Studies Group), which assembles the main Portuguese research units on transports and related fields. The survey consisted of ten questions, and was available online between 27 July 2008 and 27 August 2008.[8] Thirty-six respondents (29 per cent) evaluated and validated the set of indicators according to the following description.

The respondents were from transports, logistics and environment fields (50 per cent working on research, 31 per cent technicians/consultants, 13 per cent were suppliers and 6 per cent were public administrators). A significant majority of the respondents have been working on these topics for fewer than ten years (88 per cent), but 62 per cent for more than five years, which ensures reliable technical knowledge. All respondents were familiar with the concepts of mobility and sustainability and 44 per cent state their experience in projects and studies closely related to these concepts. A share of 19 per cent even considered themselves experts on these topics. With respect to the respondents' knowledge regarding the selection of indicators to evaluate initiatives in terms of mobility and sustainability, results were encouraging: 87 per cent of the respondents claim to have had experience related to the task. Altogether, these figures provide a high degree of confidence when it comes to respondents' knowledge to validate the proposed set of indicators.

Concerning the principles listed in the section 'Quality criteria', those that are identified more often in the set are: 'relevance' (22 per cent), 'simplicity/easy to understand' (19 per cent), representativeness (16 per cent) and 'evidence of links and effects' (15 percent). All the indicators fulfil at least six of the eight principles listed on the quality criteria section and 60 per cent of the indicators fulfil seven of the eight principles. Those that fulfil more principles are the 'CO$_2$ emissions', 'Fuel consumption' and 'Emissions NO$_x$, VOCs and PM' as measures of 'environmental sustainability'.

In an overall evaluation, respondents validated the selected indicators in terms of measuring mobility and sustainability in its three dimensions. A total of 34 per cent considered the indicators to be 'good' for measuring the respective domain and 27 per cent even considered them 'very good'. A total of 24 per cent considered them neither 'good' nor 'bad'.

A total of 98 per cent of the respondents considered Table 6.3's indicators to be a good tool of evaluation and that they reflected both public and private interests, as well as validated the categorization presented in the column 'stakeholders'. A total of 81 per cent agree that the selected set is effective and appropriate to measure mobility and sustainability in transport activities and 93 per cent consider the use of indicators to evaluate the mobility and sustainability performance to be relevant to support policy statements and actions on urban transport systems.

It was thought helpful to use as many of these selected indicators as possible. However, after analysing survey results, it was decided that 'mean flow' was not a particularly appropriate indicator as: (i) 22 per cent of the respondents stated that they would remove it from the set, and (ii) it was thought that it wouldn't produce enough relevant added value to overcome the negative evaluation results it got in the survey.

Once proposed indicators underwent this initial round of scrutiny, it was considered that the following set of selected indicators had been validated to evaluate the UGD initiatives towards increasing mobility and sustainability in light of public and private perspectives:

- Delivery times
- Supplier operational costs
- Deliveries per day
- Energy intensity (fuel consumption in litres by vehicle type)
- Emissions g per area or km by vehicle type (NO_x, VOCs, particulate matter)
- CO_2 emissions (g per area or km)
- Average speed (excluding stops to make deliveries – km/hour)
- Average vehicle journey time on the area
- Travel time (sec./km)
- Delay time (sec./km)
- Distance travelled by HGV, LGV and car (vehicle-km)
- Use of load capacity
- Proportion of goods vehicles in total traffic
- Density (vehicle/km).

Results of the analysis reveal that this final set of indicators allows us to quantitatively evaluate each initiative towards a better mobility and sustainability, considering the main stakeholders' interests as illustrated in Figure 6.2. Although the figure does not incorporate a scale of measurement, it illustrates whether or not the initiative contributes to a lower/higher level for each of the indicators of mobility and sustainability compared to the current situation. The closer the values of the individual indicators are in relation to the outside limit, the higher the level of mobility and sustainability in the area.

The example illustrated in Figure 6.2 shows that the regulation of access

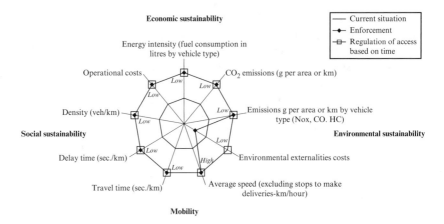

Source: Melo (2010).

*Figure 6.2   Evaluation framework for UGD initiatives towards mobility
and sustainability (illustrative example)*

based on time leads to a higher level of mobility and sustainability of the
area, through the improvement of all indicators. This improvement, which
goes from the centre to the outside limit, can correspond to lower or higher
levels of measurement. For example, a higher average speed than that of
the current situation represents an improvement in terms of mobility, as is
also the case of a lower travel time. Both are improvements (within specific
ranges of values) and, thus, are represented on the outside limit.

The selected set was successfully implemented in the evaluation of UGD
initiatives towards mobility and sustainability in a study carried out in
Porto, Portugal. The case study evaluated 16 scenarios in different geographical scales, distinguishing results by stakeholder group. Stakeholders
were analysed separately in order to add the effects on operational costs
and on environmental externalities to the analysis of public good (Melo,
2010). The group of stakeholders described earlier was narrowed to a distinction between public parties in the city and private parties in the transport chain, including suppliers, residents, shopkeepers, other road users
and local administrators. In the case study, the public good is reflected
by 'public transport' and 'citizens and users', whose interests are mainly
represented by local administrators. The private perspective is mostly
reflected by the group of 'suppliers'. In terms of model assumptions and
assignment, this categorization implied loading public transport networks
and respective dedicated lanes and stops (both for buses and taxis), private
transport flows and freight transport traffic (for both LGVs and HGVs

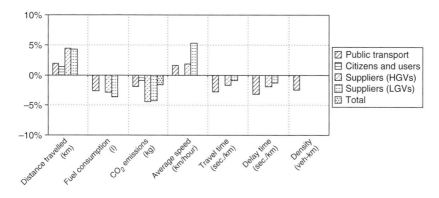

Source: Melo (2010).

Figure 6.3   *Evaluation of mobility and sustainability of UGD initiatives*
           (illustrative example of enforcement in Boavista area)

vehicles).[9] The fact that most of the results point in the same direction
in each initiative, not depending on the differences between the units of
study within Porto, indicates that most stakeholders would be affected in
a similar way by the initiative. The homogeneous results within each group
of stakeholders (as shown in Figure 6.3) is also a sign that the set of indicators clearly provides an objective tool of evaluation for the several groups
of stakeholders. The validity stems from such reasonable results and the
shared similarities with those of other studies described by Melo (2010) in
the compilation of good practices on UGD.

CONCLUSIONS

Very few comparable studies on UGD have been conducted and, therefore, this study is an attempt to make a valuable contribution to the
research carried out on the topic. Its singular approach represents an
original input to the research, overcoming some recognized gaps. The following findings reflect this study's main contributions.

First, there is not a common and objective methodology of evaluation
relative to UGD initiatives that reflects the main concerns of public and
private stakeholders, particularly in terms of mobility and sustainability.
Each initiative categorized as a 'good practice' according to the literature
review presents its own methodology of evaluation and respective indicators, making it impossible to generalize the approaches. Throughout this

chapter, an attempt was made to standardize the evaluation criteria by defining an objective tool of characterization and evaluation – the set of indicators. The questionnaire's results, as well as those of the case study carried out in Porto, validated the set of indicators as an objective tool to evaluate mobility and sustainability of UGD.

Second, the challenge in UGD is often to find a sustainable collective optimum of drawbacks and benefits for all actors. The set tool was built based on the few studies carried out on the topic, considering the determinant role stakeholders have in the performance of an initiative. With the development of a specific set of indicators, the success or failure of initiatives as regards mobility and sustainability can be evaluated on a stakeholder-based approach. The more each partner knows about other's expectations, the easier it will be to achieve win–win solutions (Melo, 2010). The study attempts to minimize the current lack of knowledge by suggesting the use of quantitative tools to predict stakeholders' effects and attitudes. Such an approach can be decisive to overcome an observed tendency in UGD in which freight industry has been largely ignored for planning purposes, given a presumed homogeneity of interests.

Lastly, the set is not only an instrument of comparative evaluation and evolution, but also potentially an accessory tool to be used by assessment tools such as simulation, surveys or empirical data collections. Its value relies on its ability to operationalize and quantify mobility and sustainability of UGD taking into consideration stakeholders' concerns and priorities. In this context, the suggested set of indicators may serve as a framework for the assessment of the performance of goods distribution initiatives, as well as for the analysis and comparisons of policy scenarios/strategies to mitigate negative impacts that originate from goods transport and distribution activities.

ACKNOWLEDGEMENTS

This chapter derives from Sandra Melo's Ph.D. thesis, which has been developed with financial support from Fundação para a Ciência e a Tecnologia (FCT). The grant SFRH/BD/18025 provided by FCT is gratefully acknowledged.

NOTES

1.　http://www.jcci.org/default.aspx.
2.　The EU Sustainable Development Strategy: a framework for indicators' and the

Communication from Mr Almunia to the member of the Commission, 'Sustainable Development Indicators to monitor the implementation of the EU Sustainable Development Strategy' (EC, 2005).

3. Assessment of quality in statistics' report (2003), Methodological documents: definition of quality in statistics.
4. EEA Core Set of Indicators – Guide' (EEA, 2005).
5. Indicators of Sustainable Development: Guidelines and Methodologies' (UN, 2001).
6. Monitoring reproductive health: Selecting a short list of national and global indicators' (WHO, 1997).
7. In the final categorization proposed in this study (Table 6.3), indicators such as 'external costs' may be considered within the social and mobility dimensions rather than within the economic dimension (Table 6.1). Such a difference of 'categorization' between tables is a result of the adopted approach in this research, which regards the impact of congestion (external costs) as a social effect rather than an economic effect.
8. http://FreeOnlineSurveys.com/rendersurvey.asp?sid=ex565b95lbmbk6z464272.
9. LGV (light goods vehicle) is the generic term for goods motor vehicles (like vans and pick-ups) with a maximum allowed mass of over 3.5 tonnes. HGV (heavy goods vehicle) is the generic term for goods motor vehicles (like lorries and trucks) weighing more than 3.5 tonnes.

REFERENCES

Begg, D. and D. Gray (2004), 'Policy instruments for achieving sustainable transport', *Issues in Environmental Science and Technology*, **20**, 65–80.

Browne, M. and J. Allen (1999), 'The impact of sustainability policies on urban freight transport and logistics systems', in *Transport Modes and Systems*, H. Meersman, E. Van de Voorde and W. Winkelmans (eds), Oxford: Pergamon, pp. 505–18.

Cybernetix and STRATEC (2003), 'CITY FREIGHT Inter and Intra City Freight Distribution Networks. Selection of the set of innovative systems or methods. Work package 3: Final report', Project funded by the European Commission on the 5th RTD Framework Programme.

Dinwoodie, J. (2006), 'Rail freight and sustainable urban distribution: potential and practice', *Journal of Transport Geography*, **14**, 309–20.

Dobranskyte-Niskota, A., A. Perujo and M. Pregl (2007), 'Indicators to assess sustainability of transport activities', JRC Scientific and Technical Reports, European Commission.

Eckersley, R. (1997), 'Perspectives on progress: is life getting better?', Resource Futures Program, Working Paper Series 97/27, Resource Futures Program, Commonwealth Scientific and Industrial Research Organisation, Canberra.

EEA (2005), 'EEA core set of indicators: Guide', EEA Technical Report, Copenhagen.

Foley, C. (2004), *Understanding the connection between People and the Land: Implication for the Social–Ecological Health at Iskatewizaagegan*, Canada: University of Manitoba.

Gilbert, R. and H. Tanguay (2000), 'Sustainable transportation performance indicators Project: brief review of some relevant worldwide activity and development of an initial long list of indicators', Center for Sustainable Transportation, Toronto.

Henderson, H. (1996), *Building a Win–Win–World*, San Francisco, CA: Berrett-Koehler.

Henry, A. and STRATEC (2003), 'PLUME – Planning and Urban Mobility in Europe', Draft Report, project funded by the European Commission on the 5th RTD Framework Programme, http://www.lutr.net/index.asp, accessed in November 2005.

Hensher, D.A. and A.M. Brewer (2001), 'Developing a freight strategy: the use of collaborative learning process to secure stakeholder input', *Transport Policy*, **8**, 1–10.

Janic, M. (2006), 'Sustainable transport in the European Union: a review of the past research and future ideas', *Transport Reviews*, **26** (1), 81–104.

Litman, T. (2007), *Well Measured: Developing Indicators for Comprehensive and Sustainable Transport Planning*, Victoria Transport Policy Institute, Canada. http://www.vtpi.org/wellmeas.pdf, accessed in May 2008.

Lomax, T., S. Turner, G. Shunk, H. Levinson, R. Pratt, P. Bay and G. Douglas (1997), 'Quantifying congestion: volume 1, final report', National Cooperative Highway Research Program (NCHRP) Report 398, National Academy Press, Washington, DC.

Marsden, G. and C. Snell (2006), 'Selecting indicators for strategic performance', *Proceedings from the 85th Transportation Research Board Meeting*, Washington, DC, January.

Mega, V. and J. Pedersen (1998), 'Urban sustainability indicators', Report for European Foundation for the Improvement of Living and Working Conditions.

Melo, S. (2010), 'Evaluation of urban goods distribution initiatives towards mobility and sustainability: indicators, stakeholders and assessment tools', PhD thesis, Faculdade de Engenharia da Universidade do Porto, Porto, Portugal.

Mészáros, P. (2000), 'Towards sustainable mobility – conflicts, impacts, principles, conditions, aspects of CEECs', *Periodica Polytechnica Ser. Transp. Eng.*, **28** (1–2), 65–75.

Mitchell, G., A. May and A. McDonald (1995), 'PICABUE: a methodological framework for the development of indicators of sustainable development', *International Journal of Sustainable Development and World Ecology*, **2**, 104–23.

Musu, I., E. Ramieri and V. Cogo (1998), 'Sustainability indicators: an instrument for Venice's Agenda 21', Working Paper 01.98 (in Italian), Fondazione ENI Enrico Mattei, Venice.

Nicolas, J., P. Pochet and H. Poimboeuf (2003), 'Towards sustainable mobility indicators: application to the Lyons conurbation', *Transport Policy*, **10**, 197–208.

OECD (1994), *Environmental indicators: OECD core set*, Paris; OECD.

Ott, W. (1978), *Environmental Indices: Theory and Practice*, Ann Arbor, MI: Ann Arbor Science Publishers.

Perry, R. and I. Gee (1995), 'Vehicle emissions in relation to fuel composition', *The Science of Total Environment*, **169**, 149–59.

Richardson, B. (2005), 'Sustainable transport: analysis frameworks', *Journal of Transport Geography*, **13**, 29–39.

Schoemaker, J., J. Allen, M. Huschebeck and J. Monigl (2006), 'BEST urban freight solutions', Report of Deliverable 5.1 – Quantification of Urban Freight

Transport Effects. Project funded by the European Commission on the 6th RTD Framework Programme.

STRATEC (2005), 'CITY FREIGHT inter and intra city freight distribution networks', Project funded by the European Commission on the 5th RTD Framework Programme.

TSS (2007), *AIMSUN 5.1 Microsimulator User's Manual*, TSS-Transport Simulation Systems.

PART III

Case Studies of European Cities

7. City logistics in Italy: success factors and environmental performance

Carlo Vaghi and Marco Percoco

INTRODUCTION

Some 80 per cent of the population in Europe is living in urban areas, and the economy and industrial production is also concentrated in urban areas. ECMT (1997) estimates that at least 20 per cent of the trips made by urban population are performed for shopping and retail goods procurement purposes; also that urban freight traffic performance (in tonne-km) weights for 30 per cent of the total freight traffic and that equivalent vehicles used for urban distribution account for 20 per cent of the total urban road congestion.

These data claim an active management of urban freight flows. Among the several approaches to address this issue, city logistics has now gained vast consensus among policy-makers. According to OECD (1996), city logistics is defined as 'measures for maximising the loading factor of vehicles and at minimising the number of vehicles per km, aiming at making goods distribution in the cities more environmentally sustainable'.

On this definition, city logistics implies the existence of a series of interconnected transport policies and measures aimed to reduce atmospheric pollution and congestion, and increase accessibility of cities. All those measures should in general aim to improve the quality of life in the cities.

In other words, urban centres should be attractive to inhabitants and city users (employees, business people, tourists etc.). Shops must be able to receive consumer goods with specific frequency (according to the type of goods, e.g. drugs must be distributed to pharmacies up to four times per day, supermarkets and groceries must receive fresh/perishable goods once per day etc.). On the other hand, residents must be able to find goods at a reasonable distance from their houses.

This situation is common to all cities; however, it is complicated by several factors, such as:

- the characteristics of urban centres and the presence of de-urbanization and re-urbanization processes in the inner zones;
- the characteristics of the population, for example the proportion of elderly people, who are less oriented to shopping in big shopping malls if they are far from home;
- city attractiveness for tourists, which implies a higher density of tourist-oriented shops, and a higher seasonality of the demand for goods distribution in the inner zones;
- the segmentation of products and the increase of seasonal cata-logues, for example clothes for which the traditional two seasons have been replaced by a continuous turnover of collections during the year;
- the increasing cost of commercial areas in the inner urban centres, which implies the maximum exploitation of the shop area and the minimization of the storage area;
- the success of just-in-time production, which is strongly linked to the two previous trends.

City logistics incorporates a number of activities and specific goals towards which different actors aim. The framework for city logistics is given by the local and regional economy, the transport infrastructure, and the surrounding environment, legal and regulatory conditions.

In this chapter we focus on Italy, a country that is experiencing dramatic problems due to deteriorated conditions of the urban environment and in which several cities are experimenting with city logistics integrated policies to govern urban freight flows.

In particular, we shall present a comparative analysis of the main city logistics systems in Italian cities and an in-depth cost–benefit analysis of the case of Padua. The case study of Padua will show the environmental and social effectiveness, measured in terms of social benefits versus costs, of the most successful and enduring city logistics experimentation in Italy. The next section will give a brief overview of urban policies for sustain-able development, together with information on the magnitude of external costs due to urban mobility in Italy. Afterwards, a comparative panel survey of the main features of the most relevant city logistics cases in Italy will be presented. In the final part of the chapter the main characteristics of Padua case study, together with the results of the cost–benefit analysis (CBA), will be described.

URBAN POLICIES FOR SUSTAINABLE DEVELOPMENT

In recent years, sustainable development has become a building block of economic policy at the local, national and international level. The urban environment is currently high on policy-makers' agendas both because of its importance in determining the quality of life in cities (Blomquist et al., 1988) and because of the central role played by urban governments in shaping environmental policies (Nijkamp and Pepping, 1998). In this context, the sustainability of transport activities is one of the main objectives pursued by the European Commission to improve environmental quality in the European Union.

Between 1995 and 2005, freight transport volumes and passengers grew by 34 per cent and 30 per cent respectively. However, during the same period, greenhouse-gas emissions grew by 24 per cent, whilst particulate matter has diminished by 30–40 per cent (EEA, 2006). Despite this evidence of a relative de-coupling of transport growth and environmental quality, the urban environment is still a source of concern for policy-makers. This concern is driven by the fact that in the past decade, both NO_2 and PM_{10} have shown a rising trend in concentration levels and, more disappointingly, annual average observations show that the concentrations of those substances are well above the European limits. In particular, in 2003, NO_2 and PM_{10} had an average concentration in European cities of 57 $\mu g/m^3$ and 42 $\mu g/m^3$ respectively, while the limit will be set in 2010 at 40 $\mu g/m^3$ (EEA, 2006). Arguably, one of the reasons for this unsatisfactory performance is probably related to the growing levels of congestion in urban areas, leading to driving at lower speeds and resulting in additional emissions.

In order to deal with the risks deriving from the high level of pollution in the cities, the European Commission has funded several projects aimed at studying and managing the transport–environment link (EC, 2001a, 2001b). One of the main goals of these projects is to identify best practices and appropriate policies to enhance sustainable transportation. However, different policies vary enormously in their effectiveness in achieving a reduction of pollution, and the time spans of the effects differ as well.

As recently reported by the Agenzia per l'Ambiente ed il Territorio (APAT, 2006), between 1993 and 2005, the quality of the environment in Italian cities dramatically deteriorated in terms of PM_{10} and NO_2 concentrations. Because of transport intensity, both pollutant matters constantly exceed the limit for almost three-quarters of Italian cities with more than 150000 inhabitants. From an economic point of view, the costs associated with transport externalities amounted, in 2004, to €107.1 billion (Bella et al., 2007). More than a half of this amount was due to greenhouse-gas emissions and atmospheric pollution.

In recent years, a number of interventions have been undertaken by local governments. However, all these policy actions have been of the 'command-and-control' type, whose economic efficiency is highly questionable (Fisher, 2000; Percoco, 2001).

The economic literature has convincingly demonstrated that efficient transport pricing results in the internalization of external costs. In accordance with these findings, urban governments have introduced various economic instruments for traffic control. Among them, the most widely used are fuel taxes (Harrington and McConnell, 2003; Parry et al., 2006), car taxes (Fullerton and West, 2002) and, in some cases, road pricing (Rouwendal and Verhoef, 2006).[1]

In Italy, fuel and car property taxes are set at central level,[2] so that they cannot be properly treated as urban transport policy instruments because of their lack of spatial variability (Rietveld, 2001).[3] Given this legal constraint, urban governments have long addressed transport issues by means of infrastructure and public transport planning. However, in the past two decades, transport policy in Italian cities has consisted mainly in imposing standards and land-use regulation measures, such as the definition of imited access or pedestrian areas, and in some sporadic cases, the construction of cycle lanes (especially in Northern cities). Since the 1990s, and because of the increasing concern over environmental quality, urban governments have continued to rely on parking policies and traffic-free Saturdays or Sundays.

FREIGHT TRANSPORT, CITY LOGISTICS AND SUSTAINABILITY

Specific goals can be listed in relation to 'city logistics actors' (see Table 7.1), assuming that some goals may lead to potential conflicts between actors. Hence city logistics policies have to be bound to the achievement of the social and environmental goals, taking into account specific goals brought by different stakeholder categories. Of course, the main role in this process is played by the public administration (municipality or similar), which holds the most important asset for any policy for urban distribution: the power to issue regulations.

As a broker of different specific goals of the 'city logistics actors', the public administration is:

Table 7.1   Actors and goals in city logistics

Actors	Goals
Retailers, traders, manufacturers	• Fast deliveries and known schedules • Acceptable costs • High frequency of deliveries
Consumers	• Accessibility of shops • Affordable prices in urban centres
Transport operators (on own account)	• Freedom of self-provision • Freedom of hawking • Freedom of supply services in urban centres
Transport operators (3PL)	• Freedom of provision of efficient and effective distribution services, with minimum restrictions • Participation in the decision process for issuing restrictions for most polluting vehicles • Recognize the organizational effort to keep loading factors high
Logistics, terminals, real-estate operators	• Involvement in city logistics programming • Supply of areas for urban distribution centres (inside and outside the city centre) • Supply of logistics services

Source: CERTeT-Bocconi.

• a public body representative of inhabitants and city users;
• a regulatory body for urban access, loading and unloading, issuing of Limited Traffic Zones (LTZ), timetables and so on;
• an owner of areas and buildings to be exploited as cross docking platforms, urban distribution centres and loading/unloading parking areas;
• an owner and manager of ICT tools for traffic management and monitoring.

In recent years, the debate on urban mobility issues in Italy has extended its scope to include the goal of rationalizing freight distribution in the cities.

The following subsections describe the main features of city logistics in Italy, starting from defining the scope of the survey, then evidencing success factors and detailing the main city logistics systems implemented in Italy.

City Logistics in Italy

The aim of rationalizing urban freight distribution can be achieved using the framework of Dasburg and Schoemaker (2009):

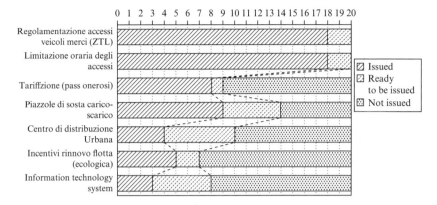

Source: Noia and Silva (2009).

Figure 7.1   City logistics measures in Italian cities, according to ATAC-Clickutility survey, 2009

- 'Single measures': policies classified under one of the following four categories:
  - Infrastructure, technology & equipment
  - Restrictions & incentives
  - Logistics & transport organization
  - Accompanying measures.
- 'Multiple measures': a coherent and shared combination of more 'single measures', implemented simultaneously by the public administration or equivalent local government, or by a public or private promoter.

The clustering of city logistics systems in the Italian literature has in several cases resulted in a survey of single measures implemented by cities. The survey is often completed by benchmarking with the main European city logistics experiences.[4]

A recent survey promoted by ATAC and Clickutility (Noia and Silva, 2009) demonstrated that almost all medium-sized towns and cities have issued policies and initiatives for managing urban distribution. Moreover, in a sample of 20 Italian cities (see Figure 7.1), almost all have issued limitations to freight traffic (time windows, LTZ). The adoption of more complex measures (charges, ICT tracking, UDC etc.) is nevertheless increasing.

A mere list of city logistics measures adopted by municipal administrations risks being hardly meaningful, since they tend to label as 'city

Source: CERTeT-Bocconi, 2010.

Figure 7.2 *Operating city logistics systems in Italy until 2009 (left) and new projects funded after 2007 (right)*

logistics system' even the implementation of a single measure. More often, the benchmark with city logistics experiences is often made also taking into account outdated systems; however, this is useful for verifying success and failure factors. In any case, those surveys often do not specify which 'city logistics projects' have resulted in the implementation of a real 'city logistics system', that is, in the adoption of a coherent combination of measures for rationalizing urban freight distribution.

In 2006, the Italian City Logistics Association (Spinedi, 2006 and Vaghi, 2008) recorded 28 'city logistics projects', of which only seven had already gone into operation, and one – Genoa – was dismissed due to the end of public financing. Eleven cases out of 28 were recorded in Emilia Romagna region, mainly due to the high number of studies triggered by European cooperation projects.[5]

CERTeT-Bocconi, in a survey of the actual status of city logistics in Italy (Bologna, 2010), assesses 40 city logistics studies and projects developed in the last ten years, and ten operating city logistics systems, defined as a bundle of regulatory, infrastructural and ICT measures, and a presence of a 'recognized' operator for last-mile distribution. The operating systems are concentrated in Northern Italy (see Figure 7.2). Other similar initiatives are about to start, while some services, once considered as 'best practices', are closing down.[6] A funding programme issued by the Ministry of Environment in 2007[7] has boosted further studies/initiatives: eight

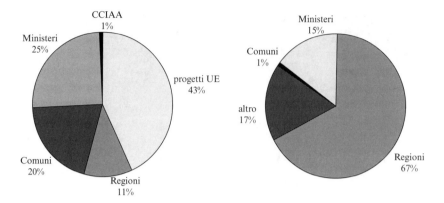

Source: CERTeT-Bocconi, 2010.

Figure 7.3   *Funds spent for city logistics by sponsor; projects (left) and*
operating systems (right)

existing systems have received additional funding, and ten cities got funds
for new projects, also in Central–Southern Italy. The total funding of city
logistics initiatives is estimated at €47 million up to 2008, with a big role of
European projects and ministerial funds (see Figure 7.3).

Main Business Models and Success Factors

The number of active Italian cases allows the definition of some recurring
logistic schemes and models of interaction between the local administration and the other actors that participate in the definition of the city logistics system.

First, it must be recognised that almost all successful cases rely on the
the presence of a logistic platform, or UDC,[8] where freight to be delivered
in the inner city shops is sorted by destination and carried on LEV or ZEV[9]
vans.

The business models described below are the main ways through which
the main stakeholders involved in the city logistics process agree upon:

●   freight traffic regulation (time windows, issuing of LTZ, exemptions
    for vehicles participating in the city logistics system, other fostering
    policies);
●   reciprocal supply of specific assets (regulatory power, logistic
    platform, infrastructure, expertise in logistics and cross-docking
    etc.).

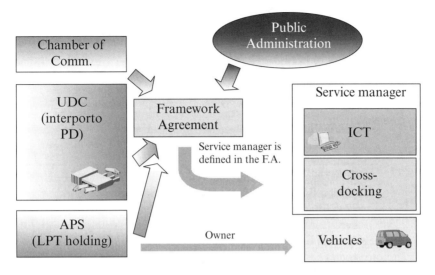

Source: CERTeT-Bocconi, 2010.

Figure 7.4   The Padua business model

Three main business models can be recognized (Bologna, 2010 and Vaghi, 2006): the 'Padua model' (Figure 7.4): the main public and private stakeholders (e.g. the municipality, the provincial administration, the local chamber of commerce on one side; associations of couriers and transport operators, on the other side) agree – through the signature of a Framework Agreement[10] – on regulations (implicitly accepted by all stakeholders while signing the FA), and reciprocal supply of specific assets. The specific fostering policy consists in the exemption of those vehicles from any time window or limitation of loading/unloading in a Limited Traffic Zone, issued in the city centre. The UDC is provided and managed by a in-house logistic operator.[11] The second model is the Venezia–Mestre model (Figure 7.5): the UDC-based logistic concept is the same as in the Padua model, but the UDC and last-mile transport service manager is selected by public tender. The service manager is endowed by its own UDC, and vehicles are owned (or granted) by the municipality. The third model is the Vicenza model (Figure 7.6): the UDC-based logistic concept is entirely managed by a NewCo, created as a public–private partnership between the municipality and private stakeholders.[12]

Some preliminary conclusions can be drawn about the preferred city logistics models adopted by Italian cities:

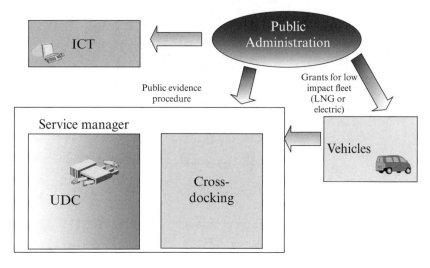

Source: CERTeT-Bocconi, 2010.

Figure 7.5   The Venezia–Mestre business model

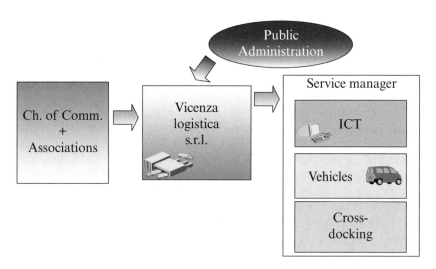

Source: CERTeT-Bocconi, 2010.

Figure 7.6   The Vicenza business model

- The total performance of city logistics systems active in Italy amounts to 22–25 000 deliveries per month, depending on the month surveyed. A total of 32 vehicles is deployed, 12 of which are electric powered (Bologna, 2010 and Vaghi, 2008). Those figures are rapidly increasing, in line with the growth of the active systems.
- Almost all systems include the use of a peri-urban UDC as cross-docking platform. Nevertheless, 93 per cent of feasibility studies of city logistics services concern the economic sustainability of a new UDC (Spinedi, 2006 and Vaghi, 2008).
- The UDC is always an already-existing infrastructure (existing warehouses or cross-docking surfaces in logistic platforms, under-used depots etc.), except in one case (Lucca), where effective fund-raising made the building of a new dedicated city logistics centre economically feasible.
- The Padua model is the most commonly adopted model. The 'Cityporto' brand has been exported from Padua to other medium-sized cities. A unique city logistics manager, responsible for the cross-docking at the UDC and for the last-mile delivery, is identified, either by service-level agreements between municipalities and their in-house companies, or by public evidence procedures in which private logistic operators were allowed to participate.
- Low- or zero-emission vehicles and ICT platforms are almost entirely funded by public grants.
- A lengthy and accurate concertation process between the public administration and all the stakeholder representatives (associations of shopkeepers, third-party transport operators etc.) is always a pre-requisite for the acceptability of the new system.
- City logistics is more diffused in medium-sized cities: the complexity and the wider dimension of the commercial areas in big cities make the implementation of a city logistics service more difficult.

The success of a city logistics system is almost always linked with the presence of fostering policies, regulatory incentives issued by the municipalities giving more favourable traffic rules to the city logistics manager in order to make participation of operators in the city logistics system more attractive, and in turn aiming at ensuring the economic and financial feasibility of the experience. The most effective fostering policy is the creation of an LTZ in which loading/unloading operations, or even the access, is allowed to specific vehicle categories only. A legal debate[13] is open on the possibility of limiting fostering policies to

Table 7.2 '*Cityporto Padova*'

Manager	Interporto di Padova S.p.A. (managing company of the local freight village), appointed after a Framework Agreement signed between the municipality and the province of Padua, the Chamber of Commerce, and APS Holding (multi-service in-house company owned by the municipality)
Main features	Urban distribution centre (Interporto)
	Last-mile delivery performed by natural-gas-powered and electric vehicles
	Limited Traffic Zone (LTZ)
	Time windows for loading/unloading in the city centre
Vehicles	8 natural-gas-powered (2 of which equipped for temperature-controlled goods);
	1 electric vehicle
Period	From March 2004
Deliveries performed	About 60 000 per year (2008)
Fostering policy	CITYPORTO vehicles (owned by the public holding APS) can enter reserved lanes with no limitations (such as buses) and have no time windows for loading/unloading
Main customers	33 couriers/forwarders/3PLs + 2 operators on own account outsource the distribution to VELOCE

vehicles identified by licences or logos, without extending those policies to all vehicles having the same technical characteristics (e.g. fuel, emission regime).

City logistics is often a peculiar aspect of traffic regulation programmes issued by the cities. The connection with info-mobility policies is more and more relevant, since access to LTZs is controlled by the same equipment used for controlling car traffic. Moreover, some city logistics systems (Parma, Bologna) foresee the assignment to drivers of hand-held computers where information on traffic, congestion and preferred routes for deliveries are shown.

The Main Italian City Logistics Systems

Tables 7.2–7.6 describe the main features of the most relevant city logistics systems in Italy. Figures on operating vehicles and deliveries performed are shown, with an indication of the business model and the fostering policy adopted. Some aspects raise the peculiarity of a couple of cases:

Table 7.3 '*Veloce Logistic Vicenza*'

Manager	Vicenza Logistic City Center s.r.l., NewCo owned by the Municipality of Vicenza (55%), by local freight transport operators and entrepreneurial associations (45%)
Main features	UDC
	Low-emission vehicles
	Total traffic restriction in historical centre, even for LEV (no limitations for transport of perishable goods)
Vehicles	5 (electric)
Period	From January 2005
Deliveries performed	5000 per month
Fostering policy	VELOCE vehicles only (identified by logo) can enter limited traffic area and use reserved lanes (such as buses)
Main customers	14 logistics operators outsource the distribution to VELOCE

Table 7.4 '*Ecoporto Ferrara*'

Manager	Coopser (local logistic operator, specialized in the distribution of perishable goods)
Main features	UDC (private)
	Low-emission vehicles (natural gas powered)
	Restrizioni al traffico (ZTL e aree pedonali)
	Road pricing (in fase di implementazione)
Vehicles	51 (natural-gas-powered)
Period	From 2002
Deliveries performed	140 000 per month[1]
Fostering policy	Discount (80%) on road pricing tariffs are issued for LEV and electric vehicles
Main customers	Main manufacturers of milk and other perishable goods

Source: [1] Coopser.

- Vicenza is the only city that has issued a total restriction on access, loading/unloading in the (narrow) LTZ, exempting Velocelogistic vans only. The measure was the object of legal debate,[14] although the claim against the measure, issued to the Italian Competition Authority (AGCM) by some express couriers, was not successful.

Table 7.5   'LIFE-CEDM Lucca'

Manager	Municipality of Lucca
Main features	UDC (peri-urban platform, under construction)
	Electric vehicles
	ICT platform for route planning and tracing of deliveries
	ZTL and progressive restriction to the access for more pollutant vehicles
Vehicles	One electric vehicle payload 1.6 tonnes
	One electric vehicle payload 3.5 tonnes
Period	From 2007
Deliveries performed	Average 110 per day (April 2008)[1]
Fostering policy	To be implemented: ZTL with access reserved to electric vehicles and vehicles with loading factor > 60%
Main customers	More than 30 couriers and logistic operators

Source: [1] LIFE-CEDM.

Table 7.6   'Ecocity Parma'

Manager	Centro AgroAlimentare Parma (PPP), supported by the Municipality of Parma
Main features	UDC: peri-urban platform at Centro Agroalimentare (food and vegetable general docks)
	Natural-gas-powered vehicles
	ICT platform for route planning and tracing of deliveries
	Implementation of a ZTL
Vehicles	Natural-gas-powered
Period	From March 2008
Deliveries performed	n.a.
Fostering policy	Transport operators have the opportunity to ask for authorization to load/unload and access the ZTL, if their vehicles are compatible with performance standards of Ecocity vehicles:
	• Emission class not lower than Euro 3
	• Max. payload 3.5 tonnes
	• Ecocity tracing devices applied on the vehicle
	• Loading factor higher than 70%
	Strong marketing action, with opportunity to accord 'Ecocity label' to shops.
Main customers	n.a.

- Parma is the only city that has issued a restriction to vans with a loading factor lower than a definite threshold. The measure entered into force very recently, and there is no evidence that it has been applied with effective results.

THE ENVIRONMENTAL PERFORMANCE OF CITY LOGISTICS: THE 'CITYPORTO PADOVA' CASE

The economic and environmental performance of measures for rationalizing urban logistics is a key issue. The main problem is the scarcity of active and successful cases, and the narrow operating period during which they can be monitored. Nevertheless, cost–benefit analysis made in feasibility studies for new city logistics systems have the usual degree of uncertainty of *ex ante* evaluations.

CERTeT-Bocconi performed in 2006 – on behalf of Interporto Padova, the service manager – the environmental performance evaluation of 'Cityporto Padova' city logistics system (Vaghi and Pastanella, 2006). The approach included the use of elements of cost–benefit analysis, and the exercise is the first CBA *ex post* made on a city logistics system in Italy.

'Cityporto Padova'

The city logistics service 'Cityporto-consegne in città' is a urban distribution service operating in the urban area of Padua, focusing on the local LTZ, having a size of 830 000m^2 (Stefan, 2009[15]). The manager is Interporto di Padova S.p.A., which also manages the local freight village as a in-house company controlled by the municipality. The deliveries are performed by eight LNG-powered and one electric vans; two of them are equipped for the deliveries of temperature-controlled goods. The UDC is a 1000 m^2 wide cross-docking platform located within the freight village. The service has been operating since 2004; it is undoubtedly the most relevant and successful city logistics system in Italy, recognized as one of the European best practices (Dasburg and Schoemaker, 2009). Cityporto has overcome the start-up phase successfully, and now performs almost 60 000 deliveries per year (see Figure 7.7) for 45 customers (the major part of couriers and forwarders operating in the city, but also SMEs that usually delivery their produce on own account).

The service was granted in the start-up phase (2004–07) by the City and the Province of Padua, and the local Chamber of Commerce, as stated in the Framework Agreement[16] (Comune di Padova, 2004). The amount of grants agreed was decreasing year by year, and the service

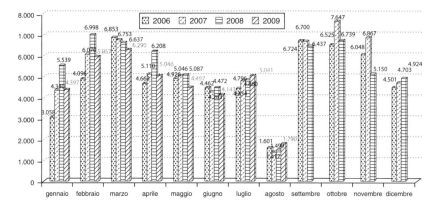

Source: Cityporto, 2009.

Figure 7.7 '*Cityporto Padova*' – *trend of deliveries per month, 2006–09*

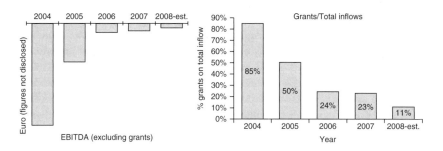

Source: CERTeT Bocconi on Cityporto data.

Figure 7.8 '*Cityporto Padova*' – *EBITDA (index) and grants/inflows ratio, 2004–08*

was complete in 2008 (see Figure 7.8) (Dasburg and Schoemaker, 2009; Vaghi, 2008).

Cityporto resumes the success factors listed earlier, and the model is nowadays replicated in other medium-sized Italian cities. However, Cityporto shows some peculiar success factors, such as the location of the UDC within the freight village, operating for decades, renowned among operators, near their logistic platforms and sufficiently far from inner-city shops.[17] Cityporto customers have been convinced about the neutrality of the service provided: no courier has priority in cross-docking operations or in delivery routes. The 'loss of the direct interface between suppliers and customers', stated by Allen et al. (2009, p. 71) as a potential failure factor for a UDC-based city logistics model, is solved by Cityporto. Drivers deliver to the receiver the bill of lading issued by its usual supplier, unless the latter trusts its freight to Cityporto for the last mile.

The Framework Agreement is the result of a lengthy and effective concertation process among public authorities and private stakeholders. During this time, specific aspects were investigated thoroughly, including the setting of tariffs. Finally, the public ownership of vans allowed the application of very effective fostering policies: Cityporto vans are exempted from time windows for entering the LTZ and can access the reserved lanes in the city.

The Evaluation of Environmental Performance: Methodological Aspects

The analysis, made through a CBA approach, aimed at assessing the external costs saved by the implementation of the Cityporto service in a defined period between September 2004 and December 2005. When the CBA was performed, that was the time horizon for which a complete tracing of deliveries and routes was available at the manager's premises. A database of more than 52000 records (one record per delivery) was built, covering 313 days and 1892 delivery trips, made by the four vans operating at Cityporto at that time.

The aim was to calculate the differential of externalities based on (i) trip length and (ii) vehicle emission factors, in *ex ante* and *ex post* scenarios. External costs for the main air pollutants (PM_{10}, CO, NO_x, SO_x, VOC), global warming (CO_2), noise pollution and accidents were applied in order to assess the social NPV (net present value) of the implementation of Cityporto in the defined time horizon. Value of time for goods was not calculated, and time cost benefits were not included, following a cautionary approach.[18] The monetary impact of reduced congestion was not included in the CBA either, although the municipality estimates a potential reduction of 5 per cent on the total number of vehicles accessing the entire municipal territory. However, in 2004–05 the impact on congestion was lower, if not negligible, due to the limited number of operating vehicles.

The two scenarios were built as follows:

● *Ex post* scenario: two databases provided by Cityporto were integrated (Figure 7.9 (a)). GIS software[19] was employed for tracing intermediate and end points of the deliveries and for calculating each trip distance. The final outcome was the visual tracing of each of the 1892 delivery routes (Figure 7.9 (b)) and the assessment of the average distance per trip (km) performed by Cityporto vans, by month.

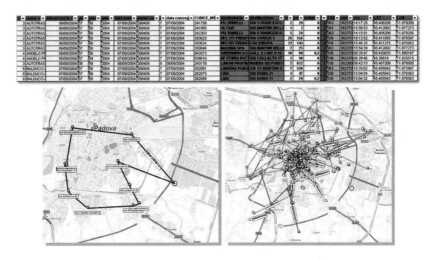

Source: Cityporto and TPS s.r.l.

*Figure 7.9   Example of Cityporto database of deliveries; (b) example of
              visual tracing of a delivery trip*

- *Ex ante* scenario: a questionnaire survey was performed. The panel
  of interviewed operators represented 88 per cent of Cityporto deliveries in the selected time horizon. The aim of the survey was the
  assessment of:
  - how many deliveries per trip operators were performed in the city
    centre before Cityporto;
  - how many vehicles (of which Euro category) were involved;
  - how long were the delivery trips.

The comparison between *ex ante* and *ex post* scenarios allowed the assessment of the global reduction of mileage performed by freight vehicles in
Padua after the implementation of Cityporto, and of the external costs
saved both by the reduction of trip length and by the adoption of LNG-
powered vehicles.

The CBA approach presented other methodological peculiarities:

- No investment costs were accounted: since no investment for infrastructure was needed, public grants – given by the public for the
  start-up and for the purchasing of LEV – were assumed as the cost
  side of the CBA.
- No differential between operational costs *ex ante* and *ex post* were

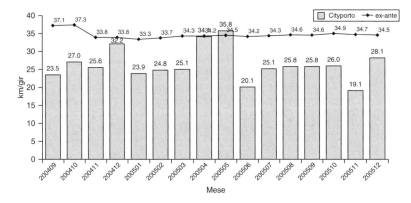

Source: Vaghi and Pastanella (2006).

Figure 7.10 *Average length of trips for deliveries (km/trip) – ex ante versus ex post*

assumed. The assessment of operational costs *ex ante* in the questionnaire survey gave few results, not significant for assessing the differential with the *ex post* scenario. On the other side, the tariff paid by the operators for cross-docking could be assumed as a proxy of the 'road user's producer surplus' in our CBA.[20] Following a cautionary approach, this category of possible 'internal benefit' was not considered.

The Evaluation of Environmental Performance: Results

The benchmark between scenarios showed a net decrease of the distance covered by freight vehicles in Padua: 11 000 km less per month, about 127 000 in the entire 15-month period. The average trip length decreased by 37 per cent, from 34 to 25 km (Figure 7.10). Impacts are also positive for fleet management: 12 trips per day are saved, and the corresponding vans used *ex ante* by the operators can be deployed on delivery areas other than the city centre.

As a first conclusion, the presence of Cityporto transit points allows a net reduction of the route length for deliveries in the inner city. Even without considering that Cityporto vehicles have less polluting engines, the service results in a significant reduction of emissions and congestion.

As regards the Euro emission category of vehicles used by the operators in the *ex ante* scenario, the survey reported common use of the pollutant Euro 0 vans:

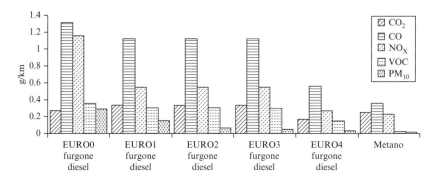

Source: COPERT2 data.

Figure 7.11   Emissions per engine emission class (g/km, mg/km for CO_2) – diesel van < 3.5 tonnes payload

Table 7.7   Quantities of polluting emissions saved in Cityporto 15-months observed period

Pollutant	Emissions saved (CO_2: tonnes; other pollutants: kg)
CO2	38,4
CO	202
NOx	163
SOx	16,3
VOC	58,1
PM10	41,4

Source: Vaghi, Pastanella, 2006.

- 19 operators used Euro 0 vans for delivery trips in Padua inner city;
- 2 operators used Euro 1 vans, one Euro 2 and one Euro 3.

The calculation of the differential of polluting emission was then based on COPERT2 emission coefficients, comparing reference (g/km) values of Euro 0–4 diesel vans[21] and LNG vehicles (Figure 7.11).

Taking into account the specific emissions of the vehicles employed, and the average trip length in the *ex ante* and the *ex post* scenario, the implementation of Cityporto led to a net saving of the following quantities of polluting emissions in the 15-month period considered (see Table 7.7).

The application of specific external costs (€/g) to these figures[22] led to the final outcome in terms of external costs saved, as shown in Figures 7.12

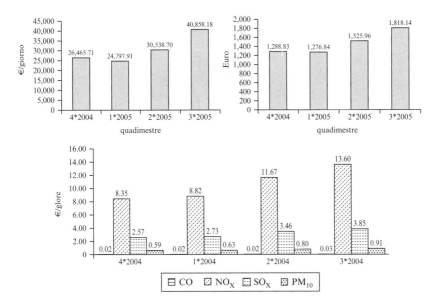

Source: Vaghi and Pastanella (2006).

Figure 7.12 *External costs saved for (a) PM_{10} emission decrease; (b) CO_2 emission decrease; (c) other pollutants emission decrease*

and 7.13. It should be noted that the average benefit per day amounts to €550 in the third quadrimester 2005, the period when the traffic managed by Cityporto is higher, that is, almost comparable to the traffic recorded in 2008 and 2009. The bigger contribution in terms of external benefits is given by the reduction of PM_{10} emissions, which accounts for €508/day, that is, about €122000 in the entire period.

Adding the external benefits in terms of noise pollution, congestion and accidents avoided,[23] the final results of the CBA imply a total benefit for the society of about €169000 in 15 months. The contribution of each benefit category is shown in the Figure 7.13.

As remarked above, Cityporto traffic in the third quadrimester 2005 can be used as a proxy for more recent years. Hence the value of benefits of third quadrimester 2005 has been spread over a five-year time horizon in order to assess and actualize the total amount of benefits gained even in the maturity period of the service.

On this assumption, the NPV of total benefits amounts to €728500. The NPV of total public grants (assumed as the cost side of the CBA), is €438000, leading to a positive benefit–cost ratio equal to 1.66.

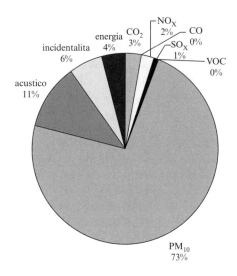

Source: Vaghi and Pastanella (2006).

Figure 7.13   External costs saved by category (%)

CONCLUSIONS

Starting from the definition of the scope and purpose of city logistics, the present chapter has presented an overview of the most advanced measures for rationalizing urban distribution in Italian cities. The survey shows that Italy, although a 'second mover' country in the city logistics European experience (started in the 1990s) has implemented very actively the concept of a city logistics system, defined as the implementation of multiple and cooperative measures of urban logistics. The large number of cities (almost all medium-sized) developing city logistics projects and the promising number of systems activated justify the assumption.

The analysis of the Cityporto Padova case study gives a promising outcome as concerns the environmental effectiveness of city logistics. The positive benefit–cost ratio show in Padua has indeed encouraged other Italian cities in the development of city logistics systems with the same features as Cityporto, leading to the activation of at least two other 'city-portos' in Central–Northern Italy.

However, the case study demonstrates how UDC-based city logistics systems are economically viable and environmentally effective only if some success factors are present, for example, the availability of a peri-urban platform, a thorough concertation process, and a fostering regulatory policy for access and loading/unloading, issued by the municipality.

The case study yields a controversial outcome as concerns congestion, suggesting that UDC-based city logistics system could lead to significant results in terms of congestion decrease if they manage to capture a big part of the urban freight traffic on third-party account. The Italian and European experience (e.g. Velocelogistic in Vicenza) suggests that it can be achieved only with the enforcement of major restrictions to access to LTZs.

NOTES

1. In recent years, however, tradable permits have begun to be considered in the case of transport as well, as well as greenhouse-gas emissions (Raux, 2004; Verhoef et al., 1997).
2. Regional governments can modify the tax on car ownership only within a very narrow range.
3. The economic literature has not yet reached consensus on the overall impact of environmental federalism. For a good survey of the literature on this point see Millimet (2003).
4. See Da Rios and Gattuso (2004), Maggi (2001), Ministero delle Infrastrutture e dei Trasporti (2006), Conti and Urgeletti (2004).
5. CITYPORTS and MEROPE projects, among others.
6. E.g. CITYPLUS in Milan, organized by ATM, the local public transport operator. Cityplus was presented as 'best practice' in a BESTUFS II Workshop in 2006 (Decio, 2006).
7. Ministero dell' Ambiente, 'Programma di co-finanziamento diretto alla riduzione dell' impatto ambientale derivante dal traffico nelle città con l'obiettivo di giungere ad un sostanziale miglioramento della qualità dell'aria', 2007.
8. Urban distribution centre. A complete definition of UDC (or UCC – urban consolidation centre) is given in Huschebeck and Allen (2005), pp. 3–5. Here also the Italian cases of Padua, Vicenza and Ferrara are quoted.
9. Low-emission vehicles or zero-emission vehicles.
10. The reference model of the FA is the one signed in Padua before the start of the 'Cityporto' service (see Comune di Padova, 2004).
11. Interporto di Padova S.p.A. – the local freight village manager – in Padua case (see www.cityporto.it).
12. Chamber of Commerce and Associations of Craftsmen and Shopkeepers, in the Veloce logistics case of Vicenza (see www.velocelogistic.it).
13. See AGCM (2009).
14. See footnote 13.
15. See also http://www.cityporto.it/.
16. Signed by the City and the Province of Padua, the local Chamber of Commerce and APS Holding S.p.A., the local public transport holding. See also above.
17. Many city logistics pratices demonstrate how a peri-urban UDC is more efficient, attractive to transport operators, and environmentally more effective than a platform located near the delivery area (see Allen et al., 2009, p. 72).
18. Assessment is still in progress, in a forthcoming monitoring phase.
19. PTV-Intertour®, run by TPS s.r.l.
20. A definition of road user's producer surplus is given in European Commission – DG REGIO (2008), p. 134.

21. Less than 3.5 tonnes of payload.
22. Unit external costs suggested by Federtrasporto (2002) for polluting and CO_2 emissions, for Northern Italy urban and metropolitan areas, were applied. Unit cost figures were appreciated to 2005 values.
23. The calculation was made taking into account unit external cost suggested for Italy by FS – Amici della Terra (2002).

REFERENCES

AGCM (2009), Parere AS499, 'Regolamentazione dell'accesso e del transito nelle zone a traffico limitato nel mercato dei servizi postali', 27/02/2009.
Allen, J., G. Thorne and M. Browne (2009), *BESTUFS Good Practice Guide on Urban Freight Transport*, European Commission, Project funded by the 6th Framework Programme RTD.
APAT (2006), *III Rapporto sull'ambiente urbano*, Agenzia per la protezione dell'Ambiente e del Teritono Rome.
Bella, M., C. Sensi, I. Caropreso, G. Casoni, M. Brambilla, L. Catani and M. Ponti (2007), 'Le stime e le previsioni dei costi sociali', in M. Bella (ed.), *Economia, misurazione e prospettive dei costi esterni del trasporto in Italia*, Bologna: IL Mulino.
Bologna, S. (ed.) (2010), *Documento del Gruppo 'Città' CNEL sulla mobilità urbana delle merci per lo sviluppo di un trasporto multimodale sostenibile*, CNEL V Commissione, Rome, February.
Blomquist, G.C., M.C. Berger and J.P. Hoehn (1988), 'New estimates of quality of life in urban areas', *American Economic Review*, **78** (1), 89–107.
Comune di Padova (2004), *Accordo di programma per l'attuazione della riorganizzazione della distribuzione urbana delle merci e per l'attivazione di una piattaforma logistica*, Padua, 5 April.
Conti, M.L. and G. Urgeletti (2004), *Esame e confronto di differenti soluzioni al problema del trasporto merci in ambito urbano*, Università degli Studi di Parma.
Da Rios, G. and D. Gattuso (2004), *La mobilità delle merci nell'area metropolitana milanese*, Milan: F. Angeli.
Dasburg, N. and J. Schoemaker (2009), *BESTUFS II – Best Urban Freight Solutions II; Deliverable 5.2 Quantification of Urban Freight Transport Effects II*, European Commission, project funded by the 6th Framework Programme RTD.
Decio, B. (2006), *Il caso Milano*, BESTUFS II 5th Workshop, Vienna, 20 September.
EC (2001a), *Clean Urban Transport*, Luxembourg: European Commission.
EC (2001b), *Sustainable Urban Mobility*, Luxembourg: European Commission.
ECMT (1997), 'Freight transport and the city', Report of Round Table 109, Paris: OECD, December.
EEA (2006), *Transport and the Environment: Facing a Dilemma*, Copenhagen: European Environment Agency.
European Commission – DG REGIO (2008), *Guide to Cost–Benefit Analysis of Investment Projects*, Final Report 16/06/2008.
Federtrasporto (2002), 'Fisco e pedaggi per ridurre i costi del trasporto: la metodologia', *Bollettino economico Federtrasporto*, no. 12, October.

Fisher, C. (2000), 'Climate change policy choices and technical innovation', Resources for the Future Climate Issue Brief No.20, Washington, DC.

FS – Associazione Amici della Terra (2002), *I Costi Sociali e Ambientali della Mobilità in Italia – Quarto Rapporto*, Ferrovie dello Stato.

Fullerton, D. and S.W. West (2002), 'Can taxes on cars and on gasoline mimic an unavailable tax on emissions?', *Journal of Environmental Economic and Management*, **43**, 135–57.

Harington, W and V. McConnell (2003), 'Motor vehicles and the environment', Resources for the Future Report, Washington, DC.

Huschebeck, M. and J. Allen (2005), *BESTUFS II – Best Urban Freight Solutions II; Deliverable 1.1 – Policy and Research Recommendations I*; European Commission, project funded by the 6th Framework Programme RTD.

Maggi, E. (2001), *City logistics: un approccio innovativo per la gestione del trasporto urbano delle merci*, DIAP Politecnico di Milano.

Millimet, D.L. (2003), 'Assessing the empirical impact of environmental federalism', *Journal of Regional Science*, **43** (4), 711–33.

Ministero delle Infrastrutture e dei Trasporti (2006), *Piano Nazionale per la Logistica*, Consulta Generale per l'Autotrasporto, Roma.

Nijkamp, P. and G. Pepping (1998), 'A meta-analytical evaluation of sustainable city initiatives', *Urban Studies*, **35** (9), 1481–500.

Noia, G. and C. Silva (2009), 'Misure e sistemi per la regolazione degli accessi e distribuzione delle merci nei centri urbani in Italia', Mobilitytech, Milan, 5 October.

OECD (1996), *Integrated Advanced Logistics for Freight Transport*, Paris: OECD.

Parry, I.W.H., M. Walls and W. Harrington (2006), 'Automobile externalities and policies', Resources for the Future Discussion Paper No. 06-26, Washington, DC.

Percoco, M. (2001), 'Physis e techne, nature e arte', *Equilibri*, **5** (1), 85–94.

Raux, C. (2004), 'The use of transferable permits in transport policy', *Transportation Research*, **9**, 185–97.

Rietveld, P. (2001), 'Pricing mobility: Experiences in the Netherlands', *European Journal of Transport and Infrastructure Research*, **1** (1), 45–60.

Rouwendal, J. and E. Verhoef (2006), 'Basic economic principles of road pricing from theory to applications', *Transport Policy*, **13** (2), 106–14.

Spinedi, M. (2006), 'La City Logistics in Italia – esperienze a confronto', 2nd Convegno Nazionale City Logistics Association, Rome, 16 March.

Stefan, W. (2009), 'Cityporto Padova – La mobilità sostenibile delle merci nelle aree urbane', Mobilitytech, Milan, 5 October.

Vaghi, C. (2006), 'Successful city logistics experimentations in Italy: results evaluation and perspectives', BESTUFS II 5th Workshop, Vienna, 20 September.

Vaghi, C. (2008), 'La city logistics dagli approfondimenti metodologici agli aspetti operativi', in M. Spinedi (ed.), *Primo quaderno della logistica urbana*, Regione Emilia Romagna: Edizioni Studio Lavia.

Vaghi, C. and M. Pastanella (2006), 'Valutazione ex post dei benefici sociali e ambientali di una sperimentazione di city logistics', VIII Riunione Scientifica Società Italiana degli Economisti dei Trasporti, Trieste, 30 June.

Verhoef, E., P. Nijkamp and P. Rietveld (1997), 'Tradable permits: their potential in the regulation of road transport externalities', *Environment and Planning B: Planning and Design*, **24**, 527–48.

8. Transport of goods to and from the center of Brussels: using the port to improve sustainability

Tom van Lier and Cathy Macharis

INTRODUCTION

This chapter examines the role inland ports can play in increasing the sustainability of city distribution. By analyzing the external costs linked to incoming and outgoing good flows by barge for a particular inland city port, namely the port of Brussels, and comparing these costs with the external costs linked to road transport, one is able to calculate the societal gain that can be achieved by using barge instead of road transport when transporting goods in and out of cities.

The inland port of Brussels, equipped with 12 km of quays and 14 km of waterways, can accommodate ships up to 4500 tons, making it accessible for short sea shipping. Sailing time to the main port of Antwerp is five hours. Since the port of Brussels is located close to the center of the city, it creates the opportunity to open up Brussels for the transport of goods via inland waterways and enables city distribution from the port. The port can thus contribute to a more sustainable mobility since transporting these goods by barges represents a reduction in the number of trucks on the road. On the other hand, being located so close to the center of the Belgian capital also creates pressure on the port and its industrial and logistic activities from various societal groups and real-estate developers. These stakeholders oppose the development of logistic activities in an urban environment for various reasons. Calculating exactly how much more sustainable this mobility by barge traffic is compared to truck transport seemed a valuable contribution on this topic.

The research goal was therefore to quantify the external costs that would be imposed on society and its individuals if road transport had been used instead of barge traffic. This calculation was carried out for the goods that were loaded and unloaded in the port of Brussels in the year 2007. The focus was solely on the transport aspect, since it was assumed that the current industrial activity in the port area (e.g. concrete factories providing materials for construction sites in Brussels) would remain located in this urban area, regardless of the scenario considered. By comparing the external costs of this hypothetical situation of truck transport with the external costs of the real situation of barge transport, the yearly external cost saving generated by using the port of Brussels could be established, both on a Belgian and a European level.

However, before calculating these figures, it is important to define clearly the relevant external costs and determine appropriate key figures that can be used in a specific case study of this kind. Therefore the chapter will start with a short theoretical background on external costs. Also a brief explanation of the policy relevance of external costs within the EU will be provided. Finally this first section will conclude with a selection of relevant key figures for the different external cost categories that can be used in our research context. In the second section the results for both scenarios are calculated and discussed. In the third section we draw conclusions.

EXTERNAL COSTS: THEORETICAL BACKGROUND, RELEVANCE AND KEY FIGURES

Theoretical Background of External Costs

Externalities are changes in welfare caused by economic activities but not reflected in market prices (Weinreich et al., 1998). In the field of transport these externalities arise when transport consumers/producers impose additional costs on society and its individuals without having to bear these costs themselves. External costs are externalities expressed in monetary terms.

In the literature a distinction is made between the following external costs of transport (Schreyer et al., 2004):

- accidents
- noise
- air pollution
- climate change
- congestion
- nature (disturbance of ecosystems) and landscape (visual infringements)
- additional costs in urban areas (space availability and separation effects)
- up- and downstream processes.

Regarding the external costs of road transport, an important distinction is made between 'intra-sectoral externalities' and 'inter-sectoral externalities' (Verhoef, 2000). Intra-sectoral externalities are, like (most of) congestion and part of the external accident costs, imposed upon each other by road users. Inter-sectoral externalities are, like environmental externalities, noise nuisance and another part of the external accident costs, imposed upon society at large. It is sometimes argued that intra-sectoral externalities such as congestion are not an externality since it is almost entirely internal to the road transport sector.[1] As Verhoef (2000) states however, for a correct welfare analysis, the relevant level of disaggregation is the individual level, so that at least from a welfare-economic point of view both intra-sectoral and inter-sectoral externalities are Pareto-relevant. Given the specific case of the port of Brussels and its urban location, combined with the relatively high degree of congestion on the road network in Belgium in general, marginal congestion costs are thus most relevant in our comparison of barge traffic and road transport. Congestion will therefore be included in the analysis, but in order to avoid simply adding intra- and inter-sectoral externalities together, results will be presented both with and without external congestion costs.

Concerning environmental costs (air pollution, climate change, noise, nature), two aspects are involved: measurement of the environmental effects and monetarization of these effects. Measurement of environmental effects belongs to the domain of environmental technology (e.g. through dose–response functions), while the conversion to monetary values belongs to the field of economics. Regarding monetarization of external costs in the field of environmental effects, four evaluation methods can be identified: stated preference, revealed preference, shadow prices, and productivity effects (Blauwens et al., 2001).

Calculation of the relevant external costs in this case study is based on the best practices in the field of marginal external cost assessment currently available in the scientific literature. Note that we calculate the impact of additional units of transported goods via road or inland waterway, which means that we are interested in marginal rather than average external costs. Although there is growing consensus on the main methodological issues (Maibach et al., 2008), there remain many uncertainties when performing such an external cost assessment in practice.[2] Numerous studies have shown that marginal external costs of transport activities depend strongly on parameters such as fuel type, location (urban, inter-urban, rural), driving conditions (peak, off-peak, night) and vehicle characteristics (Euro standards) (Panis and Mayeres, 2006). As a result, the external cost of one truck-kilometer in urban areas during peak traffic can be up to five times higher than the cost of an off-peak inter-urban kilometer of the same vehicle

(Maibach et al., 2008). For this specific case, differentiation was made at the road type and congestion level. For reasons of consistency and to avoid double-counting, appropriate values of the same study for all the external cost categories were selected, since externalities are sometimes linked to other causes and/or effects in different studies and, moreover, sometimes other assumptions are made. Given the desire to work with values expressed in ton-kilometers in order to be able to take into account the origins/destinations of the good flows, the update study of INFRAS/IWW from 2004 (Schreyer et al., 2004) was chosen. Here, for the different cost categories, marginal external costs are expressed in ton-kilometers, and for road transport a distinction is made per road type where this is relevant (e.g. accidents, congestion). Table 8.1 gives an overview of the external costs being considered, as listed in the INFRAS/IWW study, indicating for each category the type of effects, the cost components, the method used for monetarization, the leverage points and variability, and the type of externality. The different categories of external costs are described in a later section.

A distinction is also made between short- and long-run marginal costs. Short-run marginal costs are related to an additional vehicle entering the (existing) system and consider only variable costs (i.e. costs depending on traffic volume), neglecting fixed costs to run the system or additional costs for possible network improvements in the longer run. Long-run marginal costs consider future system enlargements due to increased traffic volume (Maibach et al., 2008). The focus in this study is on short-run marginal costs, excluding long-run externalities such as the long-run part of separation and space scarcity in urban areas and of up- and downstream processes, since adjustments to the transport infrastructure are not considered here.

Relevance

Although it is relevant from a societal point of view to calculate the amount of potential external cost savings from barge transport compared to road transport, these calculations are also important from a transport policy perspective. The importance of external costs and the ever-growing attention they receive in the transport sector is explained by the fact that non-internalization of external costs gives wrong market signals and thus leads to significant overconsumption and inefficiencies such as congestion, security problems and environmental nuisances. In order to develop more sustainable transport solutions, an internalization of external costs towards fair and efficient prices between transport means is considered essential. When these external effects are internalized, they are made part of the decision-making process of transport users, leading to a more efficient use of transport infrastructure. The European Commission has recommended this

Table 8.1   Overview of external cost categories and characteristics

Type of effect	Cost components	Method	Leverage points and variability	Type of Externality
Accidents	Additional costs of • medical care • economic production • losses • suffering and grief	The value of human life is estimated using studies for willingness to pay (WTP) to reduce accident risks	Depending on different factors (partly on vkm)	Partly external (part which is not covered by individual insurance), especially opportunity cost and suffering and grief
Noise	Damages (opportunity costs of land value) and human health	WTP approach for disturbed persons, medical costs and risk value due to transport noise	Depending on traffic volume and environmental performance	Fully external
Air pollution	Damages (opportunity costs) of • human health • material/buildings • crop losses	PM_{10} dose–response functions are the basis for the repair and damage costs	Depending on vkm, energy consumption and environmental performance	Fully external
Climate change	Damages (opportunity costs) of global warming	Avoidance costs (2 scenarios) to reach Kyoto targets per country or to reach long-term reduction targets	Depending on consumption of fossil fuels	Fully external
Nature and landscape, ground sealing	Additional cost to repair damages, compensation costs	Costs are based on unit types of repair measures, based on space indicators	Fixed costs	Fully external
Additional costs in urban areas (separation and space scarcity)	• Separation: time losses of pedestrians • Space scarcity: space compensation for bicycles	Cost calculation based on random sample evaluation for different cities in Europe	Depending on traffic volume	Fully external

Table 8.1   (continued)

Type of effect	Cost components	Method	Leverage points and variability	Type of Externality
Up- and down-stream processes	Additional environmental costs (climate change, air pollution and nuclear risks)	Calculation of the impact of additional emissions contributing to air pollution and climate change based on life cycle analysis data	Fixed costs (grey energy of infra-structure and rolling stock)	Fully external
Congestion	External additional time and operating costs	Time costs and additional operating costs of road users due to congestion	Depending on traffic amount (number of vehicles)	Average costs are internal to the users. Differences between marginal and average costs are external costs

Note: vkm = vehicle-kilometer.

Source: Schreyer et al. (2004).

policy of internalization in several strategy papers such as the Green Paper on fair and efficient pricing (1995), the White Paper on the overall transport strategy (2001), its mid-term review (2006), the Greening transport package (2008) and most recently the new 2011 Transport White Paper, published in April 2011. The European Commission proposes a stepwise strategy for the internalization of external costs in all transport modes, which contemplates, among other measures, the inclusion of aviation in the EU emission trading scheme from 2012 and the introduction of internalization charges for heavy goods vehicles. To some extent the introduction of market-based instruments for internalization of external costs has already been substantiated in EU directives, most particular the Eurovignette Directive on road charges, which is under review at the time of writing.

External Cost Categories and Key Figures

In this section the different external cost categories are described. This is followed by the development of necessary scenarios for road types and congestion levels, in order to come to recommended marginal external cost key figures per category.

Accidents

External accident costs are the social costs of traffic accidents not covered by risk-oriented insurance premiums and consist of material damages, administrative costs, medical costs, production losses and the so-called risk value. This risk value is a proxy to estimate pain, grief and suffering caused by traffic accidents in monetary values. Mostly this risk value is not covered properly by the private insurance systems. This risk value for fatalities and injuries can be estimated on the basis of a risk-elasticity approach, using values of statistical life (van Lier, 2007).

It is important to note that the knowledge of marginal accident costs is quite poor. Reviewing the literature on accident costs, there are many studies and conventions available on total (social) accident costs, but not many studies have focused on marginal external accident costs (Maibach et al., 2008). Marginal accident costs are those costs induced by an additional vehicle using the road network, and this might cause positive or negative effects. On the one hand, drivers can be disturbed by the growing traffic, so that the number of accidents increases more than proportionally. On the other hand, it is conceivable that average speed slows down with increasing traffic, so that the number of accidents increases more slowly than traffic volumes. Also a shift from severe to slight accidents is possible with slower traffic speeds on congested roads (Banfi et al., 2000). Studies show very diverging results for marginal accident costs on motorways, country roads and urban roads and, on each of these road types, marginal accident costs differ for low and high traffic flows. Due to the inconclusive results concerning lower or higher marginal accident costs in low and high traffic flows, the values presented in the INFRAS/IWW update study of 2004 (Schreyer et al., 2004) used here are only differentiated by road network type (motorways, inter-urban and urban roads).

Noise

Transport noise costs consist of costs for undesired social disturbances (annoyance) and physical and psychological health damages. The annoyance costs are usually economically based on preferences of individuals (by stated- or revealed-preference methods) whereas health costs (especially due to increased risk of heart attacks) are based on dose–response figures (Maibach et al., 2008). Noise is an extremely local phenomenon, making receptor density a determining factor in assessing the marginal cost of a single additional vehicle. Notable for marginal noise costs is that they decrease with increasing traffic volumes, making the definition and measurement of these costs quite crucial and differentiated.

Air pollution

Air pollution costs are caused by the emission of air pollutants such as particulate matter (PM), nitrogen oxides (NO_x), sulphur dioxide (SO_2) and volatile organic compounds (VOC), and consist of impacts on human health, impacts on materials and buildings, agricultural crop losses and costs for further damages for the ecosystem (biosphere, soil, water, forest). Health costs (mainly caused by PM, from exhaust emissions or transformation of other pollutants) are by far the most important air pollution cost category (Maibach et al., 2008). The state of research on these costs is much more advanced than for the other components, since estimations are carried out using the impact pathway approach (developed within the EU-funded ExternE program), which is able to estimate air pollution and climate change damages based on the most important dose-response functions, making the validity for the estimation of health costs quite high and very significant (European Commission, 2005).

Climate change

Climate change or global warming impacts of transport are mainly caused by emissions of the greenhouse gases carbon dioxide (CO_2), nitrous oxide (N_2O) and methane (CH_4), and to a smaller extent emission of refrigerants (hydrofluorocarbons) from mobile air conditioners (MAC). The estimation of the costs of climate change poses a high level of complexity due to the fact that the effects are long term and global, and risk patterns are very difficult to anticipate (Maibach et al., 2008). Therefore a differentiated approach is necessary, using both the damage cost approach, which uses the impact pathway approach (very limited in this context, however, since long-term climate change risks on a global scale are very difficult to estimate) and avoidance cost approaches, based on specific (political or scientific) reduction aims.

Nature and landscape

External effects of transport on nature and landscape include on the one hand effects caused by the provision of the infrastructure (roads, bridges, canals) such as spatial separation effects/barrier effect, reduction of quality of landscapes and loss of natural land area (loss of biotopes), and on the other hand effects caused by the utilization of the infrastructure such as pollution of soils and surface/groundwater systems and pollution caused by accidents (Banfi et al., 2000). It is important to note that these effects are largely related to transport infrastructure and do not in general depend on the level of use, and are thus only of limited relevance for the social marginal cost approach. The determination of these effects, including pollution of soil and groundwater due to transport, is based on either the repair and compensation cost approach or the prevention cost approach, but remains difficult in practice.

Additional costs in urban areas
Three major effects can be distinguished when analyzing higher specific external costs of transport in urban areas: time losses due to separation effects for pedestrians, scarcity problems expressed as the loss of space availability for bicycles, and urban visual intrusion due to transport volume and infrastructure.[3] The legitimization of these costs is based on a fairness principle, since road transport leads to space scarcity in cities, which causes additional costs, especially for non-motorized transport (Banfi et al., 2000). Only the separation effects are linked to traffic volumes, and are relevant for short-run marginal costs.

Up- and downstream processes
Indirect effects of transport such as energy production (pre-combustion processes), vehicle production and maintenance, and infrastructure construction and maintenance might cause additional external effects. These effects refer to nuisances already considered in other categories such as air pollution and climate change, but are traditionally treated separately in order to increase transparency. Only the pre-combustion processes are directly dependent on vehicle-kilometers and thus relevant for short-run marginal costs.

Congestion
Congestion arises when, due to a growing density of traffic, vehicles start to disturb each other, causing travel speeds to decrease, so that time and operating costs of all users within the transport system will increase. Since individuals only take into account their private cost function and do not consider the additional costs they impose on others in their travel decisions, there are unconsidered effects, namely marginal external congestion costs. Thus, from a welfare-economic view, 'external' congestion costs arise when additional transport users impose extra costs on other transport users (additional time losses, increased fuel consumption, reduced comfort). Marginal external congestion costs per vehicle-kilometer are thus defined as the difference between the marginal social cost the user imposes on the whole system and the private cost perceived by him. Congestion costs consist primarily of time costs and are calculated on the basis of speed–flow relationships (in the case of the delay of a traffic flow)

or queuing analysis (in the case of the build-up of a queue) (Blauwens et al., 2001). Where marginal congestion costs are close to zero under relaxed traffic conditions, these figures might rise up to several euros per vehicle-kilometer under dense and congested traffic conditions.[4] Since congestion effects also differ greatly depending on the road type, there is a great diversity of marginal social congestion costs regarding different traffic situations and road types.

Due to the chosen welfare-economic approach, which concentrates on the individual point of view, congestion costs by definition appear only for transport modes where single users decide on the use they make of infrastructure. Consequently means of transport where the allocation of infrastructure is planned centrally are free of congestion (Banfi et al., 2000). This means that external congestion costs based on a welfare-theoretical definition are only computed for road transport.[5]

Scenarios and recommended marginal external costs per category
To determine the external costs, use is made of the marginal cost figures expressed in €/1000 ton-kilometer published in the INFRAS/IWW update study of 2004 (Schreyer et al., 2004). In this study a distinction is made between different vehicle categories, countries and traffic situations, making it possible to differentiate the marginal external costs of road transport by road type and congestion level.

Since it was beyond the scope of this study to split every potential road trajectory up according to network type (percentages of motorways, inter-urban roads and urban roads) to all origins and destinations, three scenarios for road transport (A, B and C) were developed, with each scenario having a different proportion of rural, inter-urban and urban road sections, coupled with different congestion levels. Due to a lack of detailed congestion figures (both on a Belgian and on a European level), scenarios for congestion also had to be developed. It was assumed that a higher proportion of urban roads is linked to a higher congestion level. Recently this assumption was confirmed on the Belgian level (Maerivoet and Yperman, 2008).[6] Another indication of higher congestion in urban networks was provided by the percentage of lost hours in road freight traffic in 2006 for the Flanders and Brussels region, namely 3.80 percent and 8.2 percent respectively (Steunpunt Goederenvervoer, 2008). The combinations of different road and congestion scenarios are represented in Table 8.2. For example, road scenario B assumes that 60 percent of the roads that would be used are motorways, 30 percent are inter-urban roads and 10 percent are urban roads. In the moderate congestion scenario related to road scenario B, 25 percent of the time traffic is slightly congested and 5 percent of the time traffic is more severely congested, with related marginal

Table 8.2   Moderate and strong congestion scenarios for road scenarios A, B and C

Road	Thin	Dense	Dense
	A (Low)	B (Mean)	C (High)
% motorways	75	60	40
% inter-urban roads	20	30	40
% urban roads	5	10	20
Total	100	100	100
Congestion: MODERATE	**Thin**	**Dense**	**Dense**
% low	25	25	25
% mean	0	5	5
% high	0	0	5
Total	25	30	35
Congestion: STRONG	**Thin**	**Dense**	**Dense**
% low	95	85	75
% mean	0	10	15
% high	5	5	10
Total	100	100	100

Source: VUB MOSI-T, 2008.

congestion costs (so for 70 percent of the time there is free-flowing traffic, resulting in no marginal congestion costs). In the strong congestion scenario there is, for road scenario B, 85 percent of the time slightly congested traffic, 10 percent of the time more severely congested traffic and 5 percent of the time strongly congested traffic, with related marginal costs for each traffic flow category on each road type.

Since congestion costs are an intra-sectoral external cost category that is best analyzed separately, calculations were made of external costs excluding congestion costs to determine the inter-sectoral external costs of transport for society as a whole. It is important to note that since marginal noise costs are decreasing with increasing traffic volumes, a distinction also has to be made as to whether traffic on a specific road section is thin or dense. For reasons of simplicity we therefore assume that traffic in scenario A is thin, while for scenarios B and C it is assumed dense.

The motivation for using the different congestion scenarios is to calculate in first instance the impact of moderate congestion, where most of the time free-flowing and relaxed traffic conditions occur and dense and congested traffic is non-existent (road A) or rare (roads B and C). In the second instance, the impact of more severe congestion scenarios, where there is at least mild congestion most of the time and severe congestion occurs frequently, is calculated. Table 8.3 gives an overview of the key figures that were used for the external cost calculations for road transport for the port of Brussels case for the moderate and more severe congestion scenarios, together with the values for barge transport and rail (in euros per 1000 ton-kilometer).

Immediately notable in Table 8.3 is, apart from the higher values for road compared to inland waterway and rail, the significant impact of congestion costs in the total of the external costs for road transport. Looking at total external costs without congestion for road transport, it becomes clear that the impact of changing the proportion of road types has only a small effect, ranging from €44.19/1000 ton-kilometers for road scenario A (less urban roads) to €50.45/1000 ton-kilometers for road scenario C (more urban roads), with €46.01/1000 ton-kilometers for reference scenario B. However, when congestion is included, the total external costs range from €46.35/1000 ton-kilometers for (very) moderate congestion in road scenario A to no less than €315.32/1000 ton-kilometers for strong congestion in road scenario C.

Thus for reference road scenario B, external congestion costs compose 52 percent of total marginal external costs in the moderate congestion scenario and 77.4 percent in the strong congestion scenario.

Since the external costs of road transport depend highly on the location, time and vehicle type, there are significant country-related differences. Given the magnitude of our calculated external congestion costs, it was considered useful to compare these congestion figures with specific external cost figures for road transport to be found in the literature to see if the order of magnitude of these congestion costs was confirmed. De Ceuster's study (2004) is particularly interesting in this respect for four main reasons:

- it calculates values on a Belgian level (more specifically the Flemish part of Belgium);
- it takes into account the five most important short-term marginal external cost categories: air pollution, climate change, accidents, noise and congestion.[7] In addition, the short-term marginal external cost of damage to the road caused by additional trucks on the road is taken into account (MEC road in Figure 8.3);
- it differentiates between different vehicle types, giving figures for diesel trucks;
- it takes into account the effects of taxation of road transport (including duties and VAT on fuel, traffic taxes, taxes on insurance premiums and on maintenance of vehicles, Eurovignette, vehicle purchase taxes and registration taxes) in order to determine which part of the external costs is already internalized.[8]

Table 8.3 Recommended marginal external costs per category (moderate and strong road congestion)

INFRAS 2004 €/1000 ton-km	Motorways			Inter-urban roads			Urban roads			Total				
	Low	Mean	High	Low	Mean	High	Low	Mean	High	Road A	Road B	Road C	Water-borne	Rail
Accidents	1.2	2.4	2.9	6.4	7.3	9	11.2	11.6	11.9	2.74	4.79	7.14	0	0
	Thin		Dense	Thin		Dense	Thin		Dense					
Noise	0.24		0.11	2.07		0.74	32.1		13.24	2.20	1.61	2.99	0	0.53
Air pollution	33.5	33.5	33.5	33.5	33.5	33.5	33.5	33.5	33.5	33.5	33.5	33.5	8.8	7.4
Climate change	1.8	1.8	1.8	1.8	1.8	1.8	1.8	1.8	1.8	1.8	1.8	1.8	0.6	0.6
Urban							7.1	7.1	7.1	0.36	0.71	1.42	0	0
Up & downstream	3.6	3.6	3.6	3.6	3.6	3.6	3.6	3.6	3.6	3.60	3.60	3.60	0.75	0.25
Congestion	Relaxed	Dense	Congested	Relaxed	Dense	Congested	Relaxed	Dense	Congested					
Moderate	5.5	1017.8	1045.9	19.2	645.2	1004.1	13.3	1394	1593.6	2.16	49.78	107.27	0	0
Strong	5.5	1017.8	1045.9	19.2	645.2	1004.1	13.3	1394	1593.6	61.44	157.60	264.87	0	0
Total														
Total excl. congestion										44.19	46.01	50.45	10.15	8.788
Moderate congestion										46.35	95.79	157.72	10.15	8.78
Strong congestion										105.64	203.61	315.32	10.15	8.78

Source: VUB MOSI-T, 2008 using data from Schreyer et al. (2004).

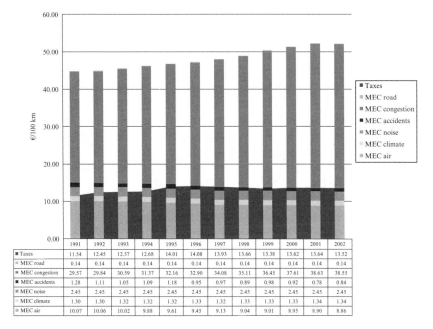

	1991	1992	1993	1994	1995	1996	1997	1998	1999	2000	2001	2002
■ Taxes	11.54	12.45	12.57	12.68	14.01	14.08	13.93	13.66	13.38	13.62	13.64	13.52
▨ MEC road	0.14	0.14	0.14	0.14	0.14	0.14	0.14	0.14	0.14	0.14	0.14	0.14
▨ MEC congestion	29.57	29.84	30.59	31.37	32.16	32.90	34.08	35.11	36.45	37.61	38.63	38.55
■ MEC accidents	1.28	1.11	1.05	1.09	1.18	0.95	0.97	0.89	0.98	0.92	0.78	0.84
▨ MEC noise	2.45	2.45	2.45	2.45	2.45	2.45	2.45	2.45	2.45	2.45	2.45	2.45
▨ MEC climate	1.30	1.30	1.32	1.32	1.32	1.33	1.32	1.33	1.33	1.33	1.34	1.34
▨ MEC air	10.07	10.06	10.02	9.88	9.61	9.45	9.13	9.04	9.01	8.95	8.90	8.86

Note: MEC = marginal external costs.

Source: Based on De Ceuster (2004).

Figure 8.1   *Marginal external costs versus taxes – heavy-duty diesel truck, Flanders, 1991–2002, 2002 prices*

Figure 8.1 shows the values for the marginal external costs and taxes for a heavy-duty diesel truck in Flanders over the period 1991–2002. In 2002 total marginal external costs amounted to €52.18/100 ton/km, with a high and increasing proportion of congestion costs over the years, accounting for 73.87 percent of total short-term marginal external costs in 2002, which is in line with the strong congestion scenario. Therefore it is concluded that the marginal congestion values calculated in the case of the Port of Brussels are in line with other Belgian findings. It is also interesting to note that the other external cost categories in Figure 8.1 remained stable or gradually reduced between 1991 and 2002.[9]

In a recent publication of the Federal Planning Office, Hertveldt et al. (2009) calculated the proportion of congestion costs in the total of congestion and direct environmental external costs for Belgium for 2005 and 2030. The result is shown in Figure 8.2, indicating that during peak traffic the proportion of congestion is well above 80 percent, whereas it

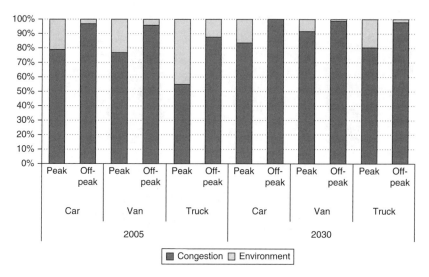

Figure 8.2   The proportion of congestion and environmental costs in the direct marginal external costs per vehicle-km in Belgium (2005 and 2030)

is still more than 50 percent during off-peak hours, but since important external cost categories such as accidents and noise are not considered in Hertverldt et al., comparison with results from our calculations is less straightforward.

Table 8.4 compares key figures for the different marginal external costs of transport for three transport modes, provided by three different studies (from Vito, EC and Planco). The differences between the three studies show that there is no such thing as standard key figures for this type of costs. This is explained by the fact that, as mentioned before, marginal external costs of transport activities depend strongly on parameters such as fuel type, location, driving conditions and vehicle characteristics. Especially for road transport, parameters such as network type and driving conditions can vary strongly and are therefore differentiated in our calculations. However, as can be seen in Table 8.4, marginal external costs for trucks are consistently and significantly higher than for the other two modes. For air pollution and climate change, marginal external costs of barge and train are comparable; for the other categories barge has lower marginal external costs than train (for infrastructure the data are inconclusive). Table 8.4 also shows that other (European)

Table 8.4   Marginal average external costs per transport mode from various sources

€/100 km Externalities	Truck			Barge			Train		
	Vito	EC	Planco	Vito	EC	Planco	Vito	EC	Planco
Accidents	22.8	5.4	37.8	0.01	0.0	0.3	1.6	1.5	2.3
Noise	4.4	2.1	7.4	<0.1	0.0	0.0	2.8	3.5	12.7
Air	6.8	7.9	29.1	4.8	3.0	4.2	0.0–8.2	3.8	3.5
Climate	2.3	0.8	0.0	0.6	neg.	0.0	0.4–1.26	0.5	0.0
Congestion	5.4	5.5	1.2		neg.	0.0	neg.	0.2	0.0
Infrastructure	1.9	2.5	0.0	0.7	1.0	0.0	0.2	2.9	0.0
Space availability			1.3	–		0.0	–		0.4
Soil and water pollution	–		8.6	–		0.0	–		0.0
Total	**43.5**	**24.1**	**85.4**	**6.1**	**5.0**	**4.5**	**7.1**	**12.3**	**19.0**
Difference with truck	–	–	–	**37.4**	**19.1**	**80.8**	**36.4**	**11.8**	**66.3**

Note: neg. = negligible.

Source: Based on De Vlieger et al. (2004).

studies often find much smaller congestion values than those mentioned in Table 8.3 and Figure 8.1, but this might be an indication that congestion levels for Belgium are much higher than European averages, due to, among other things, a higher-than-average degree of urbanization.

RESULTS

Introduction

In a first phase we calculated the number of trucks that would be added on the road if barge traffic to the port of Brussels were not possible. In a second phase we compared the external costs of two scenarios: on the one hand the existing situation where goods are transported by barge to and from the port, and on the other hand a hypothetical situation where the same goods are transported by trucks from the same origins and destinations to and from the port. In this manner it is possible to calculate the external costs that are avoided by using barge transport compared to road transport. As mentioned in the previous sections, specific attention is given

Table 8.5   Number of loaded trucks needed to replace barge traffic

(A) Loaded trucks / port-related traffic (no transit) (2007)

Product category (NSTR)	Tonnage (t)	Average truck load (t)	# trucks
Minerals and building materials (6)	2 291 000	18.42	124 376
Petroleum products (3)	1 036 000	17.12	60 514
Agriculture products (0)	370 000	15.33	24 136
Foodstuffs (1)	261 000	14.09	18 524
Miscellaneous – containers (9)	152 000	9.11	16 685
Ores and iron steel waste (4)	133 000	18.59	7 154
Metal products (5)	73 000	17.57	4 55
Total			**255 543**

(B) All trucks (empty & loaded) / port-related traffic and transit (2007)

	Total tonnage (t)	Average truck load (t)	# trucks
Port-related traffic	4 345 897	10.8	**402 398**
Transit	3 090 723	10.8	**286 178**
Total	7 436 620	10.8	**688 576**

Source: VUB MOSI-T, 2008.

to the impact of congestion. Also, the fact that barge transport might require road transport to bridge the last mile to final destination or from initial origin is taken into consideration.

Number of Trucks Avoided

Taking into account the proportion of different goods categories and the related average truck load (Steunpunt Goederenvervoer, 2008), calculations showed that more than 255 000 loaded trucks would be needed to replace the port-related barge traffic to and from the port of Brussels, based on 2007 figures (Table 8.5). When also taking empty trucks and transit barge traffic into account, the number of avoided trucks increased to more than 688 000. One can debate the relevance of this exercise from a Brussels perspective since it can be argued that goods transported by barge to or from the port of Brussels require pre- and post-road transport to bridge the first mile from the initial origin and the last mile to the final destination so that for the Brussels region the number of trucks would not be greatly affected. Two remarks can be made in this respect. First, the largest product category is minerals and building materials, mainly due to the presence of several concrete plants in the port area. In this case there is no last- or first-mile truck transport for the barge transport to these facilities. Second, even if the number of avoided trucks can be debated from the Brussels perspective, on a larger Belgian and European scale this effect of pre- and post-transport in Brussels is relatively short compared to the total length of the trajectories. However, this additional pre- and post-transport connected to the barge traffic in port of Brussels is taken into consideration when comparing the external costs of both scenarios.

External Costs of Barge Transport versus Road Transport

Methodology
The goal is to compare the external costs of, on the one hand, the current situation where goods are transported by barge to and from the port, and, on the other hand, the hypothetical situation where the same goods would be transported by trucks from the same origins and destinations. To calculate the total external costs of road transport including congestion, the values based on the moderate congestion scenarios were used first. In a second phase the values based on the strong congestion scenarios were considered. Road scenario B, which is representative for road transport between the ports of Antwerp and Brussels, is considered in both cases to be the reference scenario, with scenarios A and C serving as sensitivity analyses to measure the impact of changes in assumptions with regard to the proportion of road sections. The tonnages are the amounts of goods loaded and unloaded in the port of Brussels in the year 2007. Since we are focusing on the external costs linked to the port of Brussels, transit through the port was not taken into account.[10] Because the external costs are calculated based on the amount of ton-kilometers, clusters were formed based on the origins/destinations of the good flows. In this manner 98.5 percent of the goods flows were assigned to a specific origin/destination.[11] For these flows the distance was calculated separately for transport via waterway and via road in order to calculate the ton-kilometers for every transport mode, using an ArcGIS application. Concerning the international flows, transport coming via short sea shipping was taken into consideration. The remaining 1.5 percent consists of smaller inland goods flows, where an average distance was calculated based on the main Belgian origins/destinations. The calculation of the external costs was performed on a European and on a Belgian level. In the latter case only the Belgian part of the international trajectories by barge or truck is taken into account.

Table 8.6   Overview of external costs for road scenario B (year 2007)

Situation 2007	Belgian level	Road scenario B				
Inland waterway	+ extra pre-/post road transport			Road transport		
	Without congestion	Moderate cong.	Strong congestion	Without congestion	Moderate cong.	Strong congestion
3 253 583	7 252 852	11 579 496	20 951 119	14 749 151	30 705 653	65 267 844

Difference	Congestion		
Road transport	None	Moderate	Strong
w.r.t. inland navigation	11 495 567	27 452 070	62 014 261
w.r.t. inland navigation + extra pre-/post road	7 496 299	19 126 157	44 316 725

Source: VUB MOSI-T, 2008.

Results for 2007

Table 8.6 gives an overview of the main results for road scenario B for the three congestion scenarios (no congestion, moderate congestion and strong congestion), with an indication of the difference between the external costs of barge transport versus road transport, based on the traffic figures for 2007. Based on the linking of the goods flows to specific origin and destination regions, it was calculated that of a total of 4.3 million tons of goods loaded and unloaded in the port of Brussels in 2007, 1.4 million tons had a Belgian and 3 million tons had a foreign origin or destination.

The results show that if these 4.3 million tons had been transported via trucks on the road network in reference scenario B, this would have generated, on a Belgian level (so only looking at the part of the goods flows on Belgian territory) without taking congestion into account, a total external cost of €14.8 million. In contrast, the transport of the same 4.3 million tons via inland waterway generates an external cost of only €3.3 million (€1 million is caused by Belgian inland flows, €2.3 million is due to the Belgian component of international flows). The external cost saving of barge transport compared to truck transport in this scenario thus equals €11.5 million. Taking into account that goods leaving or arriving by barge in the port of Brussels potentially require a pre- or post-road transport of 20 km to or from the port, the total external cost of this combined transport amounts to €7.3 million (if we assume road scenario B without congestion for the road transport part). This is still only half compared with unimodal road transport. So even in this minimum scenario the external cost savings are significant (€7.5 million).

If the congestion costs are also taken into account, the difference between road and barge transport (with or without pre- and post-transport) becomes even more obvious. Looking first at the moderate congestion scenarios, reference scenario B (with 25 percent relaxed and 5 percent dense traffic congestion conditions) results in a total external cost of €30.7 million for road transport. Taking into account the more severe congestion scenarios, the external costs of road transport increase significantly. In reference scenario B (with a share of 5 percent highly congested traffic conditions), the total external cost of road transport amounts to €65.3 million. Also considering congestion in the pre- and post-transport for barge traffic to and from the port of Brussels increases the total external costs for combined transport in scenario B to €11.6 million for a moderate congestion scenario and to €21.0 million for a strong congestion scenario.[12]

Including the international component of the goods flows to and from the port of Brussels obviously increases the share of the external costs of these international flows. For inland waterways the total external cost in that case amounts to €9.7 million. Taking into account a pre- and post-transport of 20 km (based on road scenario B) the external cost increases to €13.7 million without congestion and €18.0 million and €27.4 million respectively in a moderate and a strong congestion scenario. However, if this transport had been executed entirely by truck transport, the external costs would have been €44.0 million in scenario B without congestion. Including congestion costs, the total external costs of road transport arrive at significantly higher levels: between €91.5 million (for scenario B with moderate congestion) and €194.5 million (for scenario B with strong congestion).

It becomes very clear from these calculations that the congestion levels have an enormous impact on the difference between the external costs of inland navigation compared to road transport. Using the port of Brussels saved €11.5 million of external costs in reference scenario B on a Belgian level in 2007, not taking congestion into account. Taking congestion into account, the cost saved as much as amounts to €27.5 million in a moderate congestion scenario and €62.0 million in a strong congestion scenario. Taking into account the potential pre- and post-road transport when considering inland waterway transport reduces these figures somewhat but the external cost savings remain substantially high: €7.5 million without congestion, €19.1 million with moderate congestion and €44.3 million with strong congestion.

Including the international part of trajectories, the savings further increase to, respectively, on average €34.3 million (without congestion), €81.8 million (with moderate congestion) and €184.8 million (with strong congestion). Taking into account the potential pre- and post-transport again reduces these figures somewhat, but the external cost savings remain substantially high.

CONCLUSIONS

The unique location of the port of Brussels close to the center of the city makes it possible to open up the city for freight transport by inland waterway. Due to this barge transport to and from the port of Brussels, some 255 000 loaded trucks were avoided on the road in 2007 (and even 688 000 trucks when empty trucks and transit flows are also taken into account). In this chapter the size of the external costs currently avoided by using the port were calculated. Based on loading and unloading in the port of Brussels for the year 2007, it was calculated that the avoided external cost on a Belgian level of using barge transport compared to road transport equals €11.5 million without taking into account congestion. Since congestion is an intra-sectoral externality, it was added separately to the analysis. If moderate congestion is assumed, the external cost saving increases to €27.5 million. Taking into account an average pre- or post-road transport of 20 km in the case of barge traffic, the external cost saving is still €7.5 million (without congestion) and €19.1 million (with moderate congestion). When also adding the international part of the trajectories, the external cost savings increased further.

Looking at total external costs excluding congestion, the impact of changing the proportion of road types (motorways, inter-urban roads and urban roads) had only a small effect on total external costs. But when congestion was added to the analysis, the proportion of road types had a large impact on results. Given the sensitivity of the results for the assumed congestion levels and proportion of network types, congestion data gathering on a European and Belgian level should be enhanced in order to make it possible to calculate marginal external congestion costs more exactly. The magnitude of congestion costs, 51.5 percent in the moderate congestion scenario and 77.1 percent in the severe congestion scenario, seemed, however, to be supported with other findings in literature.

NOTES

1.   Effects of congestion that are also imposed on the rest of society (and thus not only on transport users) include increased noise effects (due to more accelerating and braking), increased emissions (less efficient fuel consumption) and increased up- and downstream effects (higher wear and tear). On the relation between congestion and accidents, the results in the literature are mixed: probably the number of accidents increases with higher congestion, but the severity is often lower (Maibach et al., 2008). Accidents can, mostly in urban areas, also involve other members of society such as pedestrians and cyclists.

2.   For an overview on the assessment of external costs, see, among others, INFRAS/ IWW (Banfi et al., 2000 and Schreyer et al., 2004), ExternE, EC (2005), Forkenbrock (2001), Witboek, EC (2001) and revision EC (2006), Mauch et al. (1995), Maddison et al. (1996), Kreutzberger et al. (2006), Macharis and Van Mierlo (2006). For a recent summary of the different external cost categories, the most relevant studies in a European context and recently recommended key figures as proposed by the European Commission, see Maibach et al. (2008).

3.   The last element is very difficult to measure and no reliable estimates exist, so usually only the first two effects are taken into account.

4.   In the INFRAS/IWW studies (2000 and 2004), traffic situations are categorized by 'free flow' (up to 500 PCU/h/lane) 'relaxed' (500–800 PCU/h/lane), 'dense' (up to 1000 PCU/h/lane) and 'congested' (above 1000 PCU/h/lane) (with PCU = passenger car units).

5.   An economic measure of external costs due to traffic delays embracing all modes can be provided by scarcity costs (Banfi et al., 2000). Scarcity costs are the production losses of the economy due to the increased binding of material and human resources in transport. Due to a lack of delay data in barge transport, the focus in this study is on congestion costs from a welfare-economic point of view.

6.   In their analysis of traffic congestion in Belgium, Maerivoet and Yperman (2008) concluded that 'time lost' (defined as the average travel time compared to the travel time in an uncongested network with free-flowing traffic) was higher on the underlying road network (regional and urban roads) compared to the main road network (motorways). For example, in the Flanders region, 'time lost' was 3.5 sec./km on motorways, 9.1 sec./ km on regional roads and 15.5 sec./km on urban roads. In the Brussels region, 'time lost' was higher on the main network compared to the underlying network (8.6 sec./km on motorways, 6.3 sec./km on regional roads and 5.9 sec./km on urban roads), but time lost on urban roads in Brussels was still higher than time lost on motorways in the rest of Belgium.

7.   In De Ceuster (2004), the short-term component of up- and downstream processes, which consists mainly of pre-combustion processes (= external costs due to energy production), is not taken into account as a short-run marginal external transport cost.

8.   We abstract from the fact that, ideally, transport users that cause higher external costs should be taxed more heavily in order to give the correct price signal to transport users. Therefore taxes should vary according to place (urban, non-urban), time (peak, off-peak) and vehicle characteristics (Euro norm). This differentiation, however, is achieved only very partially in current legislation.

9.   As can also be seen from Figure 8.1, the existing taxation system on heavy diesel trucks compensated for 25.91 percent of short-term marginal external costs in Flanders in 2002, leaving 74.09 percent of external costs non-internalized. This almost equals the proportion of congestion costs, so it could be said that this taxation system internalizes all the external cost categories, except the largest category, namely congestion. Since congestion is very time and location dependent, this implies that a full internalization of external costs requires the introduction of some form of differentiated congestion charging.

10. Without the presence of the port these transit flows would still pass along the canal, assuming the working of the locks and bridges would not be affected.
11. For the Belgian locations, exact origins and destinations were used. For the port of Antwerp, goods flows were considered on an aggregate basis (coming from a central point in the port). For the Netherlands, the flows were considered to originate mainly from the port of Rotterdam. For the other foreign flows, points of origin/destination were selected based on information provided by the port of Brussels.
12. It is important to stress that in these scenarios, based on INFRAS/IWW values, inland waterway traffic is assumed completely free of congestion (see also above).

REFERENCES

Banfi, S., C. Doll, M. Maibach, W. Rothengatter, P. Schenkel, N. Sieber and J. Zuber (INFRAS/IWW) (2000), *External Costs of Transport: Accident, Environmental and Congestions Costs in Western Europe*, Karlsruhe/Zürich/Paris: The International Union of Railways (UIC).
Blauwens, G., P. De Baere and E. Van de Voorde (2001) *Vervoerseconomie*, Antwerpen: Standaard Uitgeverij.
De Ceuster, G. (2004), *Internalisering van externe kosten van wegverkeer in Vlaanderen*, study performed for Vlaamse Milieumaatschappij, MIRA, MIRA/2004/4, Transport & Mobility Leuven.
De Vlieger, I., E. Cornelis, H. Joul and L.I. Panis (2004), *Milieuprestaties van de binnenvaart in Vlaanderen; Eindrapport*, study performed for Promotie Binnenvaart Vlaanderen, Vito.
European Commission (1995), *Green Paper: Fair and Efficient Pricing in Transport*, Brussels.
European Commission (2001), *White Paper: European Transport Policy for 2010: Time to Decide*, Brussels.
European Commission (2005), *ExternE: Methodology 2005 update Report*, 2nd edn, Brussels.
European Commission (2006), *Keep Europe Moving. Mid-term review of the European Commission's 2001 transport White Paper*, Brussels.
European Commission (2008), *Greening Transport Package*, Brussels.
European Commission (2009), *A Sustainable Future For Transport*, DG Energy & Transport, Luxembourg.
European Commission (2011), *White Paper: Roadmap to a Single European Transport Area – towards a competitive and resource efficient transport system*, Brussels.
Forkenbrock, D.J. (2001), 'Comparison of external costs of rail and truck freight transportation', *Transportation Research Part A: Logistics and Transportation Review*, **35**, 321–37.
HEATCO (2005), *Developing Harmonised European Approaches for Transport Costing and Project Assessment (HEATCO), Deliverable 2: State-of-the-art in project assessment*, Stuttgart.
Hertveldt, B., B. Hoornaert and I. Mayeres (2009), 'Langetermijnvooruitzichten voor transport in België: referentiescenario', Federaal Planbureau, Planning Paper 107.
Kreutzberger, E., C. Macharis and J. Woxenius (2006), 'Intermodal versus unimodal road freight transport – a review of comparisons of the external costs',

in B. Jourquin, P. Rietveld and K. Westin (eds), *Transportation Economics: Towards Better Performance Systems*, Abingdon, UK: Routledge, pp. 17–42.

Macharis, C. and J. Van Mierlo (2006), 'Intermodaal vervoer: Milieuvriendelijker ook in de toekomst?', *Tijdschrift Vervoerswetenschap*, **42** (1), 8–11.

Maddison, D., D. Pearce, O. Johansson, E. Calthrop, T. Litman and E. Verhoef (1996), *Blueprint 5: The True Costs of Road Transport*, London: Earthscan.

Maerivoet, S. and I. Yperman (2008), *Analyse van de Verkeerscongestie in België*, Transport & Mobility Leuven, Rapport 07.15, Leuven.

Maibach, M., C. Schreyer, D. Sutter (INFRAS), H. P. Van Essen, B. H. Boon, R. Smokers, A. Schroten (CE Delft), C. Doll (Fraunhofer Gesellschaft-ISI), B. Pawlowska and M. Bak (University of Gdansk) (2008), *Handbook on Estimation of External Cost in the Transport Sector. Internalisation Measures and Policies for All external Cost of Transport (IMPACT)*, Version 1.1., European Commission DG TREN, Delft, CE, the Netherlands.

Mauch, S.P., S. Banfi and W. Rothengatter (1995) *External Effects of Transport*, Paris: International Union of Railways.

Panis, L.I. and I. Mayeres (2006), 'Externe kosten van personenvervoer', in M. Despontin and C. Macharis (eds), *Mobiliteit en (groot)stedenbeleid. 27ste Vlaams Wetenschappelijk Economisch congres*, 19 and 20 October, Brussels, pp. 417–46.

Schreyer, C., C. Schneider, M. Maibach, W. Rothengatter, C. Doll and D. Schmedding (INFRAS/IWW) (2004), *External Costs of Transport: Update Study*, Karlsruhe/Zürich/Paris: The International Union of Railways (UIC).

Steunpunt Goederenvervoer (2008), *Indicatorenboek Duurzaam Goederenvervoer Vlaanderen 2007*, Universiteit Antwerpen, Antwerpen.

van Lier, T. (2007), *De Economische Waardebepaling van een Mensenleven*, thesis, Vrije Universiteit Brussel, Brussels.

Verhoef, E.T. (2000), 'The implementation of marginal external cost pricing in road transport. Long run vs short run and first best vs second best', *Papers in Regional Science*, **79** (3), 307–32.

Weinreich, S., K. Rennings, C. Geßner, B. Schlomann and T. Engel (1998), 'External costs of road, rail and air transport – a bottom-up approach', paper presented at the 8th WCTR, Antwerp.

9. Optimization of urban deliveries: evaluating a courier, express and parcel services pilot project in Berlin

Julius Menge and Paul Hebes

INTRODUCTION

Urban freight transport ensures that consumers and business establishments have the right goods, in the right place, at the right time and in perfect condition. This is an essential ingredient for the vitality and prosperity of our cities (Anderson et al., 2005). Courier, express and parcel services (CEP) play a particularly important role in our ever-increasing 24-hour society.

This chapter deals with the German research and implementation project 'SmartTruck'. To successfully implement new technologies and logistic concepts for urban CEP businesses at a large scale, an analytical base for evaluating and monitoring the effectiveness of the intended inventions was necessary. We focused on monitoring and evaluating the developments at the DHL Express Depot in Germany's capital Berlin, and the drivers' and couriers' attitudes to the developments.

After providing a short insight into the project, we discuss several constraints affecting the intended optimization process. The chosen evaluation method and procedure as well as selected indicators will later be presented. Finally we provide an insight into some aspects of drivers' acceptance of the system.

BACKGROUND

Urban areas are facing an increasing demand for frequent and just-in-time delivery. The ongoing structural change in the urban economic structure and stock reductions, particularly within the retail sector, led to significant growth rates of urban goods traffic. Today up to 35 per cent of this urban goods traffic is generated by CEP (courier, express and parcel) services (Kuchenbecker, 2009, p. 2). The first and last mile (pick-up and delivery), run with much smaller vehicles than on the long haul, is the part of the value chain with the biggest share of overall process costs for CEP services. Hence focusing on improvements in the last mile is a promising approach, not only for the company or the private sector. In order to increase efficiency and at the same time reduce negative impacts of CEP services, providers are willing to cooperate. Especially for urban areas this entrepreneurial commitment offers a wide variety of measures to reduce urban energy consumption and emissions (CO_2, NO_X, PM_{10}, noise). This gains importance if one looks at the main activity space of CEP: these service providers are in particular linked to dense areas (e.g. city centres) because of customer density and the consequent output of pick-up and delivery (PUD) processes. Additionally CEP processes are often fixed to certain service times (e.g. delivery before 9 p.m.) – a constraint that makes it more difficult to optimize and regulate this field of urban goods movement (Sanchez-Rodrigues et al., 2007).

The utilization of ICT is promoted as one basic technological strategy to reduce negative effects by relieving the road network capacity, in particular in those dense metropolitan areas. However, it is hard to identify and evaluate the direct impact of ICT.

Facing these challenges and constraints, a consortium led by the corporate DHL Technology & Innovation Management (TIM) developed intelligent vehicles equipped with several telematic solutions. Besides monitoring consignments by RFID (radio-frequency identification), a real-time dynamic route planning has been implemented (based on FCD – floating car data). The dynamic optimization of tour planning, route selection and vehicle capacities allows flexible and reliable customer relationships while lowering resource consumption and transport costs.

SMARTTRUCK – A BRIEF PROJECT INTRODUCTION

One of the main challenges for the daily business of CEP service providers is that PUD processes and tours are planned based on static information. Dynamic regional data of traffic situations or traffic-network-impeding events (accidents, construction sites) are not a standardized parameter for tour planning.

The project SmartTruck worked on developing and testing new technological concepts for a dynamic optimization of PUD tours for DHL Express. The project started in January 2008 and included a three-month pilot phase in PUD processes. This field test was conducted in 2009 in Berlin.

But dynamic (and thus more flexible) tour planning was just one of several technological systems and solutions; for example, the optimization of route planning integrated real-time traffic data provided by floating car data (FCD). Furthermore, every consignment was RFID labelled and therefore monitored throughout the whole process. Those developments enabled DHL to develop a reliable rendezvous management whereby consignments between two couriers were exchanged during a tour so that they would arrive at their destination as swiftly and efficiently as possible. So the aim of the project was not only to optimize the PUD tours, but also to improve the performance of the tours and routes by using the vehicle's capacities more efficiently.

Nevertheless the top priority has always been the customer. The SmartTruck system therefore assured that all assignments were picked up or delivered according to the customer's needs and the related product features while providing greater flexibility for all actors (suppliers, couriers and customers) and lower resource consumption.

During the pilot phase two fully equipped vehicles were tested under real-life conditions in Berlin to prove the operational capabilities of the solution.

As a project partner, the DLR – Institute of Transport Research (DLR–IVF) – accompanied the one-year implementation of the 'intelligent' vehicles in Berlin. DLR–IVF's responsibility within the project was the evaluation of the status quo (*ex ante*) and field test results (*ex post*) from an economic and transport perspective.

Therefore a broad methodological approach was applied to establish performance indicators as benchmarks and to reveal the influence of systemic improvements on economic performance as well as on urban transport.

Besides hard facts, the results of the evaluation process demonstrate the challenges in achieving drivers' acceptance of the implemented solutions, especially dynamic routing.

An essential question was which effects the implementation of the different technologies would have on the traffic-related key performance indicators (micro and macro level). Although some projects (e.g. OVID, NESTOR) offer preliminary estimates, substantiated knowledge and quantifiable cause-and-effect structures are missing until today. Therefore the evaluation process within SmartTruck considered those aspects in detail.

CONSTRAINTS

This chapter presents the multiple constraints that influence the different aspects of optimization for the daily process of DHL Express, the

Table 9.1   DHL: prices for different services

	Standard delivery (no time limit)	**DHL Express (no time limit)**	**DHL Express (before 12 p.m.)**	**DHL Express (before 9 a.m.)**
Service	Standard	**Premium**		
Type		Parcel		
Size		40 × 25 × 15 cm		
Weight		Up to 5 kg		
Hand in		At service point		
Delivery time	1–2 days	**1 day**	**1 day**	**1 day**
Price	€5.90	**€35**	**€37.50**	**€48**

Source: www.dhl.com.

premium segment of Deutsche Post DHL. Due to their high share of daily urban transport, CEP services account for many emissions (e.g. CO_2, PM_{10} and noise). This is particularly true for very dense urban areas with thousands of inhabitants per km^2. Hence a reduction of these emissions is essential. To achieve this goal an optimization of PUD processes is necessary. This means that the time needed for a delivery or a pick-up should be reduced. Moreover, the distance driven on a tour should also be reduced. Therefore an optimization process can address customers by improving the service quality. It might also deal with CEP hardware, for example by using alternative fuel for CEP vehicles to reduce environmental impacts. But nevertheless, the turnover of both, the CEP firm and the courier, should be enhanced within the process of optimization.

So it is not primarily the environmental aspect that implies optimization. The economic endeavours of CEP firms and of the couriers, many of whom are freelancers, also encourage optimization. Therefore the different parties with differing interests may or may not choose the same approach to optimize CEP services. These distinct opinions of how to improve the processes can constrain and thus complicate the success of optimization. Besides the dissimilar parties involved, many more constraints arise in day-to-day business.

The more time-sensitive a delivery is, the more a client has to pay (see Table 9.1). Associated with the higher costs, the client on the one hand expects a high-quality service; that is, the consignment is delivered on time and without any damage. On the other hand, this means that the service provider increases his turnover but loses temporal flexibility because of the predefined time slots, and he faces higher productions costs. Hence optimization is constrained by high customer expectations.

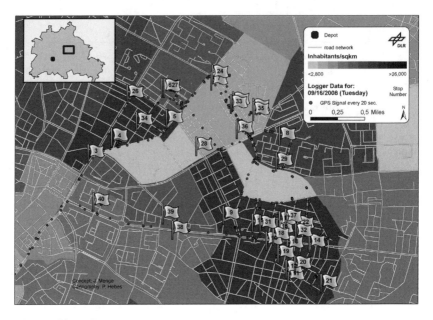

Source: The authors.

Figure 9.1   Tour pattern of a SmartTruck on an appointed date

In detail this means that a consignment that has to be delivered before 9 a.m. forces the CEP service provider to adjust his tour and route accordingly. Whereas it might be meaningful to deliver the parcel at the end of the day to optimize the route ecologically (i.e. reduce the daily distance driven), the driver has to stop and deliver the consignment in the morning. That way the firm optimizes the client's satisfaction and ensures a high profit (see Table 9.1).

Figure 9.1 shows the travel pattern of SmartTruck on an appointed date. The flags indicate the delivery and pick-up points. The numbers within the flags represent the stop sequence. These numbers show that the pattern is determined by temporal constraints. The driver has to return several times within his service area to the same coordinates due to the strict time frames (see Browne et al., 2007). Even with an active SmartTruck system the constraints would still force the SmartTruck to adhere to the delivery times requested by the customer or offered by the CEP service provider. Hence an optimization is feasible but mainly for timeless express logistics, that is, to optimize the stop sequence of deliveries with no time limit (see Table 9.1). None the less, this optimization would help greatly to achieve more sustainable CEP transport in dense urban areas due to the fact that

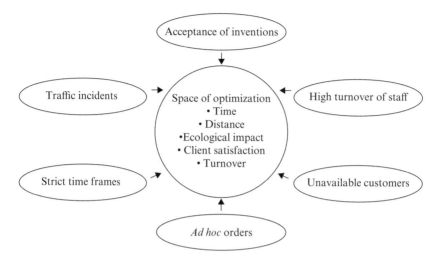

Figure 9.2   Factors constraining CEP service optimization

optimization within a particular service area would relieve many inhabitants (see Figure 9.1).

Beside the strict time frames, there are some more constraints that affect the optimization. The most important constraints are depicted in Figure 9.2. While some of them have a general meaning, others depend on the particular CEP service provider.

One of the most constraining factors is the *ad hoc* order, which is unforeseeable and thus challenges optimal tour and route planning. If a customer wants a consignment to be picked up immediately, almost everything is done to fulfil the customer's needs. The worst case – from both an ecological and an economic perspective – is that a new vehicle has to be sent out. So *ad hoc* orders have a high impact and constrain time, distance and ecological optimization approaches (see Figure 9.2). In a similar way, the unavailability of customers accounts for a higher daily distance travelled. The route has to be re-run.

Closely related to unavailable customers and *ad hoc* orders is the driver's quest for high earnings. Because the courier is often paid for the number of deliveries and pick-ups he makes, he seldom rejects an *ad hoc* order or a re-run of a delivery. The courier's optimization approach departs from an ecological one. Primarily the CEP courier tries to make as many stops as possible to earn the most money, and eventually chooses a stop sequence that departs from the ecological optimum. He does not necessarily focus on an ecological route or driving behaviour (e.g. acceleration, speed limits). Thus the courier's endeavours to optimize his own turnover can constrain the ecological optimization process. So evidently the courier is one of the key actors if inventions like SmartTruck are to be successful. This becomes even more obvious if the question of acceptance is considered. Acceptance of the inventions, in this specific case by the courier, is a further constraint on optimization (see Franken and Lenz, 2005). However, in general it is a management task to ensure service quality and the couriers' compliance with new optimization processes. For success, it is vital that all components of SmartTruck go hand in hand.

SmartTruck aims at improvements in the courier's information level to ease the necessary decision-making process (e.g. for the optimal stop sequence). However, information provision is a significant challenge. As long as detailed and on-time information is missing, couriers will have to rely on their experience. According to the rational-choice approach, access to relevant real-time information like that provided by the SmartTruck system leads to more rational decisions as regards the route choice bearing in mind the congestion level. The rational consideration of cost and utility would lead to an optimal route choice.

At least in the field of passenger transport this assumption is contrasted by reality. Even when they are provided with information, people still act as they did in a similar situation (habitual behaviour). A comparable discussion considers routines in travel behaviour. Routines are understood here as the outcome of a sequence of actions that end up with a satisfying result, so that the way the action is performed becomes 'automated' (Harms, 2004). Yet routines are not an automatic reflex, but are based on 'strategic' behaviour (Bargh et al., 2001). So at least there was once a decision-making process about how to perform an activity. The major reason for not modifying routines afterwards is the lack of information supporting a behavioural change.

What does that discussion about habitual behaviour or routines mean for the application of a real-time, dynamic system like the SmartTruck? Change of transport mode is unrealistic for the given project context. Nevertheless habitualized travel behaviour might be influenced by providing information for the courier. Additional benefits can be expected as the system includes detailed information about congestion and integrates *ad hoc* pick-ups optimal (algorithm based) into the PUD process.

Therefore, besides various economic aspects, the acceptance of the SmartTruck has to be evaluated for its discernible usefulness. And, like any innovation, the SmartTruck will be labelled as particularly 'useful' if the couriers can use it profitably in their everyday business context. The system itself and its configuration in the vehicle must fulfil the specific requirements of the couriers in respect of operability and functionality.

Much effort was invested during the evaluation to assess the 'usefulness'

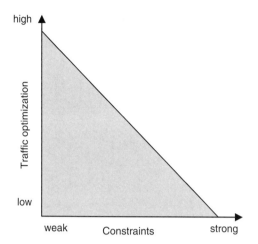

Figure 9.3   Relationship between optimization and constraints

of the system for the courier. One main research question was how habitualized behaviour – not only travel behaviour but also 'PUD-process behaviour' – is influenced by new information sources and advanced technical devices.

Finally, some general traffic constraints can occur in urban areas and hinder an optimization, such as traffic incidents, construction sites and demonstrations.

The more constraints interact during a day, and thus the stronger they are, the less potential for optimization exists. This is particularly true for traffic and thus ecological optimization. Integrating the different SmartTruck components into one coherent system leads to management and operational improvements anyway. However, Figure 9.3 depicts a simple linear interdependence between traffic optimization and the affecting constraints. In real terms, at least some of the constraints will always be affecting business at the same time.

This leads to a shrinking 'space of optimization' in the daily business at tour level (see Figure 9.4). Without any constraints, one can imagine a theoretical space with potential x. Under the influence of the manifold constraints the space shrinks to a smaller size y and hence the prospects of optimization diminish accordingly. This complicates many approaches of ecological and sustainable urban transport.

However, the remaining space of optimization gives the CEP service provider the chance to contribute to sustainable and at the same time profitable development. To use this potential SmartTruck system seems to be most applicable.

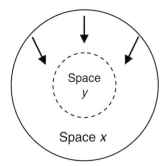

Figure 9.4   Shrinking space of optimization

EVALUATION

As SmartTruck was funded by the 'Intelligent Logistics' initiative of the German Federal Ministry of Economics and Technology (BMWi), the evaluation had to make sure that statements concerning the following key parameters were valid and scientifically sound:

1. Reduction of vehicle-kilometres travelled (VKT):
   SmartTruck approach: reduction of the VKT through an optimized dynamic tour and route planning
2. Increased use of vehicle's capacity:
   SmartTruck approach: increased use of vehicle's capacity by introducing intelligent, IT-based planning tools, rendezvous management
3. Acceleration of the PUD processes:
   SmartTruck approach: realization of advantages by introducing new infrastructure within the depot and the vehicle itself, supporting the couriers with advanced mobile devices, providing necessary real time traffic and process information

The chosen *ex ante – ex post* design for the evaluation included the dispatchers at the DHL Express terminal and the couriers of one selected service partner. It was based on a business process analysis, a detailed requirements definition and supported by frequent on-site interviews with the staff at the DHL Express terminal in Berlin.

The set of general indicators and key performance indicators (KPI) included several operational as well as traffic-related aspects (qualitative and quantitative values) to ensure a robust assessment of SmartTruck (see DfT, 2006; Leonardi and Browne, 2009):

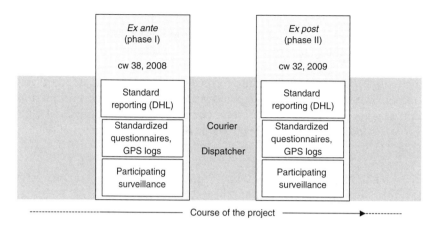

Note: CW = calendar week.

Figure 9.5   SmartTruck evaluation structure

1. Basic data about the DHL Express terminal/tour area (overall number of tours, consignments, drop-offs and pick-ups etc.)
2. Basic data about the vehicle/tour (reported daily)
3. PUD process-related indicators
4. Use of vehicle's capacity
5. KPI (e.g. time per stop, km per stop).

Overall, a set of more than 50 indicators and characteristics was included. In close collaboration, DHL Technology & Innovation Management (TIM), DHL Express Germany and the DLR – Institute of Transport Research – identified the most reliable sources for the chosen indicators and therefore defined an appropriate empirical design. The result was a broad methodological approach to use existing data and minimize the 'respondents' burden' (see Allen and Browne, 2008).

Within the first phase (*ex ante*, about one year before the execution of the field test), the actual conditions of the couriers and vehicles in the PUD process, as well as the workload of the dispatchers, were surveyed (see Figure 9.5). In this chapter the focus is strictly on the couriers.

The first evaluation steps aimed at the collection of the following characteristics:

1. road performance of the vehicles (especially VKT), number of loading/ unloading, use of vehicle's capacity, tour duration, fuel consumption etc.;

2. use of ICT/ITS during the PUD process; and
3. sources and intensity of traffic information use before starting as well as during the PUD process.

The couriers of the service partner formed the sample for the standardized questioning. All couriers participated and provided detailed information and insights into their daily business. Therefore the paper-based and GPS surveys conducted in September 2008 in Berlin derived high-quality data from:

1. *standardized questionnaires*: all 17 drivers, each participant reported for 5 resp. 6 work days within the selected week,
2. *participating surveillance*: two different vehicles for 2 work days; and
3. *GPS logs* for all 17 vehicles for 5 resp. 6 work days within a week.

The selected couriers involved in the field test were interviewed again in phase II (*ex post*) in order to identify changes of working processes. Two of the drivers were equipped with the SmartTruck prototypes – vehicles with all intended systems running. Furthermore, two additional tours were included, intended as a possible extension of the field test. Thus 16 questionnaires were valid for the evaluation:

1. *standardized questionnaires*: four drivers, each participant reported for four work days within the selected week;
2. *participating surveillance*: two different vehicles for 2 work days and
3. *GPS logs* for four vehicles for four work days within the week.

The data – as those in the first phase – were completed by the evaluation of standard DHL data (see Figure 9.5).

The described conglomerate of data formed the basis for the general evaluation of the performance indicators. It also revealed the influence of systemic improvements by the SmartTruck system on economic performance (to provide estimates for a large-scale transferability of SmartTruck) as well as on urban transport.

Relating to the complex technical and process-related changes through SmartTruck, it was not sufficient to stick strictly to quantitative statistics or standardized data collection. To answer the questions relating to 'routines' and 'habitualized behaviour' in particular, it was necessary to get a differentiated view on the 'lived practice' – beyond expert interviews. Becoming a part of daily practice allowed statements to be made about the acceptance of integrated systems and/or the performance of the vehicles and systems during the PUD process.

Exactly this is the methodological strength of the participating surveillance: during the two field research phases in each case two vehicles (*ex ante*: intended SmartTruck tours; *ex post*: realized SmartTruck tours) were accompanied by an observer on two selected days. This 'shadowing' of the couriers allowed statements on the research questions outlined. The selected method further offers the advantage that with direct observation of the courier's behaviour there is no 'social desirability' problem. Results of the participating surveillance were eight observation protocols that gave a profound basis for interpretation with a high degree of detail.

SELECTED RESULTS

The *ex ante* evaluation recorded an average distance driven per day between 147 and 190 km (see Table 9.2). The clear differences in the VKT per day result from the unequal characteristics of the tour areas. While several tours were strictly city tours (dense area, high stop frequency, short distances between stops, high impact), other tours served the surrounding countryside (long distance to the tour area, long distances between stops, low population, comparatively low environmental impact).

So the diverging tour profiles (dense areas versus areas of low density) were not only reflected in the road performance; the number of stops also differed significantly. The intended SmartTruck tours (extremely dense area in the city centre of Berlin) showed a constantly high stop frequency in a small neighbouring area. Hence the field test for the dynamic systems of the SmartTruck exactly fulfilled the needs of the project.

The *ex ante – ex post* comparison showed clear modifications of various indicators during the PUD process, for example regarding the VKT and the tour duration.[1] The introduction of SmartTruck resulted in more compact tours and routes, characterized by significantly fewer kilometres per tour and stop while increasing the use of the vehicle's capacity. This

Table 9.2 VKT per day

		MON	TUE	WED	THU	FRI	SAT
Daily km driven (calculated)	**Minimum**	63.0	51.0	56.0	57.0	52.0	52.0
	Mean	189.8	178.3	190.0	172.8	170.1	147.6
	Maximum	442.0	410.0	479.0	489.0	468.0	362.0
	Valid *n*	13.0	17.0	16.0	16.0	14.0	5.0

Source: *Ex ante* survey.

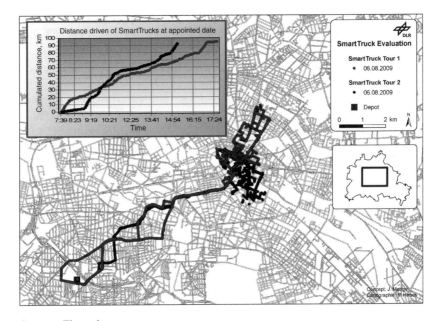

Source: The authors.

Figure 9.6   SmartTruck system evaluation based upon GPS logs

accounted for reduced fuel consumption and therefore also greenhouse-gas emissions. The SmartTruck system caused economic improvements as well as improvements in overall urban goods traffic in the area of investigation (see Figure 9.6).

However, the evaluation process is restricted by the drivers' adherence to the SmartTruck system. Since drivers partly intervened in the optimized stop sequence, the final assessment of SmartTruck is limited to these specific circumstances. None the less, the SmartTruck system has proved its success in a wide set of current problems within the field of dispatching. Since more extensive data (position of the vehicle, loading condition) have been provided by SmartTruck to the dispatcher, the allocation of couriers to *ad hoc* pick-ups become easier.

At the same time the SmartTruck dispatch system (named DRADA) allowed us to calculate in advance whether the driver can cope with planned time restrictions. Thus the system created the possibility of passing this information on to the customers. Hence the dispatcher could decide to accept the order or to decline it. Moreover, DRADA enabled the CEP service provider to inform the customer of the estimated arrival time of its transmission and thereby increase accessibility and customer satisfaction. An important source of interference in the daily business was identified by the dispatchers. They stated (*ex ante*) that most of the time there is no back-up for experienced drivers and their tours in cases of illness or holidays. SmartTruck enables inexperienced drivers to do their job in the unknown service areas by providing them with an optimized stop sequence and an appropriate route. Thus in the future it will be possible to recruit less skilled or experienced drivers but to guarantee a high degree of service quality at the same time.

During the field phase (*ex post* and *ex ante*) the SmartTruck technical applications and systems competed with drivers who act in a 'multi-criteria optimizing' way, who possess experience in the process of PUD and their service area. Among other things, this became obvious when the address and the actual entrance to the customer's premises vary. A prominent example is the 'The Red City Hall' of Berlin, seat of Berlin's mayor. While the official address of the city hall is 'Rathausstraße, 10178 Berlin', deliveries should be made at 'Jüdenstr. 1'. The experienced drivers modify the delivery point 'automatically' – a clear advantage in relation to a system that uses the address of the shipment according to target selection algorithms. In this context a set of cases was pointed out during the evaluation that show the necessity for a future implementation of the drivers' tacit knowledge in the SmartTruck system. Because the drivers used this implicit knowledge for their work and to judge special situations, the SmartTruck sometimes seemed to be less efficient in the field phase.

Regardless of these 'disadvantages', the drivers acknowledged clear improvements in SmartTruck performance (reliability and speed of the on-board system) in the process of the three-month field test.

Detailed results of the defined indicators, characteristics and measures cannot be presented here due to confidentiality, but are available to the coordinator of the research project and form a basis for future developments and planned expansions.

METHODOLOGICAL OUTLOOK AND CONCLUSIONS

Most of the results presented are of a qualitative nature. To assess the ICT impact in a quantitative way is still a practical challenge. Hence in future we shall try to evaluate the SmartTruck potential using a 'fishnet' approach (see Figure 9.7). To give a first impression we put a rectangle grid (fishnet cells 200×200 m²) above the service area to measure the returns into one cell by one SmartTruck. The approach follows the assumption that the more returns measured in one cell, the less optimized the tours.

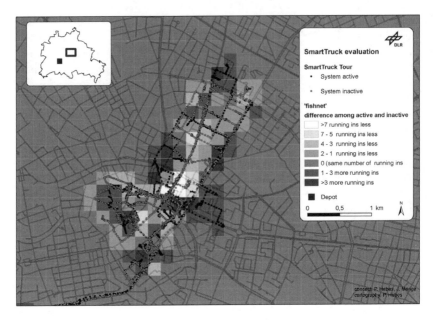

Source: The authors.

Figure 9.7   Fishnet approach applied to the SmartTruck area of investigation

Figure 9.7 shows a first outcome of this approach when we compared two days of the field test, one day with an active SmartTruck system and one day with an inactive system. The white and bright grey fields indicate that with an activated SmartTruck system there are fewer running-ins; darker fields mean that there are more returns into one cell. Hence, bright grey and white colour would indicate a positive effect of using ICT within SmartTruck.

Because this is only a two day example, the results are not reliable and thus are not interpreted here. It is advisable to enhance this approach to a long time period to suppress short-term effects such as different customers at different locations and day-specific aspects. None the less, this might be a chance to quantify the use of ICT and the direct impact of CEP services on urban life. It is especially interesting to measure the impact in special locations such as residential areas or areas around schools and kindergartens. To protect these areas from emissions is crucial for further sustainable urban development. SmartTruck not only supported skilled and experienced drivers, but even ensured the designated level of service with inexperienced drivers. In future the system will be an ideal support for novice or inexperienced couriers or back-up drivers (e.g. in case the usual driver is ill). It might also support drivers as well as dispatchers if tour patterns are changed on a large scale. Thus the system enables us to calculate in advance whether time restrictions can be fulfilled and shortcomings can be avoided in the PUD process. The evaluation process showed clearly that the success of implemented new technical solutions relies not only on the system itself. It was proved once more how important it is to gain the acceptance of the courier. Couriers willing to overcome their habitual behaviour enable an evolutionary process of the technical solution by providing detailed information about strengths and weaknesses of the system.

One future challenge will be to combine the optimization interests of the CEP service providers and the drivers/couriers. Especially if they are freelancers, drivers clearly focus on the maximization of their own benefits. Environmental awareness is rarely assessable for the couriers, which contrasts with the general DHL attempt to reduce greenhouse-gas emissions. If the future SmartTruck system can gain the full acceptance of drivers, the system might establish equilibrium between those interests.

Within the first pilot phase only two vehicles were deployed in Berlin and therefore investigated within the evaluation. It is planned to enlarge the field test and to equip the whole fleet of the participating service partner in the near future (16 SmartTrucks). This enlarged field test will include more diverse tour profiles – from dense areas up to less populated areas around Berlin. But it will take time to complete that development.

It will be an interesting task to apply the set of developed indicators and the methodology again in the future and to compare those 'early-stage' results with detailed long-term results when the large-scale implementation has been completed.

NOTE

1. Because some of the results are confidential, we cannot present quantitative results in detail.

REFERENCES

Allen, J. and M. Browne (2008), 'Review of survey techniques used in urban freight studies', Report produced as part of the Green Logistics Project: Work Module 9 (Urban Freight Transport).
Anderson, S., J. Allen and M. Browne (2005), 'Urban logistics – how can it meet policy makers' sustainability objectives?', *Journal of Transport Geography*, **13**, 71–81.

Bargh, J.A., P.M. Gollwitzer, A.Y. Lee-Chai, K. Barndollar and R. Troetschel (2001), 'The automated will: nonconscious activation and pursuit of behavioral goals', *Journal of Personality and Social Psychology*, **81**, 1014–27.

Browne, M., M. Piotrowska, A. Woodburn and J. Allen (2007), 'Part I – urban freight transport, literature review', WM9 Report, carried out as part of Work Module 1 Green Logistics Project.

DfT – UK Department for Transport (2006), 'Key performance indicators for the next-day parcel delivery sector' (=Freight Best Practice).

Franken, V. and B. Lenz (2005), 'Influence of mobility information services on travel behavior', Research Symposium on Societies and Cities in the Age of Instant Access, Salt Lake City, USA.

Harms, S. (2004), 'Besitzen oder Teilen. Sozialwissenschaftliche Analyse des Car Sharings', Zürich, Switzerland.

Kuchenbecker, M. (2009), 'Handlungsfeld City-Logistik/e-Mobility-Integration', Presentation at Dialogworkshop der Modellregion Berlin-Potsdam, 27 August.

Leonardi, J. and M. Browne (2009), 'Data management and data collection techniques for sustainable distribution. Data needs and data review for Green Logistics research', WM3 Report.

Sanchez-Rodrigues, V., A. Potter and M. Naim (2007), 'Determine the uncertainties hindering sustainability in the UK freight transport sector', Logistics Research Network – Conference Paper.

10. The use of rail transport as part of the supply chain in an urban logistics context

Jochen Maes and Thierry Vanelslander

INTRODUCTION

In Western Europe, the rail freight industry has been liberalized during recent years. The number of actors multiplies, the network connections of railroad and intermodal logistics companies grow, and new actors enter the market. European rail freight has been liberalized mainly on the initiative of the European Commission by Directive 91/440. This directive called for separated accounting structures between network provider and operational activities. The right to operate first international and later national freight trains came afterwards. However, different market structures were implemented as national member states of the European Union were responsible for the implementation of the new legal framework. As a result, some countries had anticipated the liberalization; others delayed as long as possible. The liberalization had a major impact on the former state-owned monopolistic rail companies (the incumbents) and logistics actors using them. New market possibilities arose, but more actors now need to collaborate. This chapter explores new logistics concepts involving rail transport in Western Europe now in the trial – or investigation – phase (Lewis et al., 2002; Maes et al., 2008).

This chapter will deal with the use of rail transport as part of the supply chain in an urban logistics context. The link will be made between two research subjects: the economic and ecological viability of rail or intermodal transport, and the logistics capacity problems in an urban context, the latter of which is a growing research stream. A part of this chapter will build on research conducted, among others, by Deketele et al. (2008).

First we give a brief overview of the European railway market. The difference between the European short-distance rail freight organization and US short-haul services will be described. Second, the concept of a new smart supply chain involving rail, developed by Deketele et al., will be elaborated. The theory of the concept was put into practice in Belgium by the fast moving consumer goods (FMCG) producer Procter and Gamble. This will be highlighted shortly. Afterwards, the concept of the modern supply chain involving rail will be compared with the actual supply chain of the French retail group Monoprix. The Monoprix supply chain will be discussed in the framework developed by Deketele et al. The French logistics bottlenecks, modal split, important legislation and outcomes will be described, and results of the Monoprix supply chain will be given. Finally, conclusions will be drawn.

THE EUROPEAN CONTEXT OF RAIL TRANSPORT

In the last 30 years, Europe's transport sector has experienced important growth, but freight growth can principally be attributed to road and sea transport. Both modes displayed large increases of respectively 38 per cent and 35 per cent from 1995 to 2005 (in millions of tonne-km). According to the European Commission's 2001 White Paper, the dominating trend for the long-term future is a continued growth of maritime and road transport. Rail transport and inland waterways will show considerably less growth according to this forecast (European Commission, 2001).

The high share of road transport is posing serious problems regarding the environment, congestion and road safety. The European transport sector is responsible for 24 per cent of Europe's CO_2 emissions. Within total transport emissions, road traffic accounted for the single largest share of 71 per cent. Rail transport accounts for only 0.8 per cent (European Communities, 2009, p. 210). See Table 10.1.

As a result, unless major new measures for a more rational use of each transport mode are taken, by 2010 heavy goods vehicle traffic in the EU

Table 10.1   Freight transport by rail (billion tonne-km)

	1990	1995	2000	2005	2006	2007	% change 06–07
EU-27	526.3	386.1	403.7	414.1	440.2	452.2	2.7
EU-15	256.5	222.7	257.1	262.9	285.9	296.2	3.6
EU-12	269.8	163.4	146.6	151.3	154.3	156.0	1.1
Belgium	8.37	7.30	7.67	8.13	8.57	8.24	−3.9
France	52.24	48.27	57.73	40.7	40.95	42.62	4.1

Source: European Communities (2009).

will increase by nearly 50 per cent over the 1998 level. This means that more congestion is likely (European Commission, 2001).

The evolution in European rail transport has been varied, but is marked by a constant decline in market share. Among the member states, different market situations obtain. Until the 1990s, national markets, forming the European market, were dominated by state-owned monopolistic companies taking care of national rail transport as well as of infrastructure management. These companies were not working efficiently, showed hardly any market thinking and were regularly misled by political influences. As a result, debts grew enormously and, as shown in Figure 10.1, rail as a transport mode lost market share year after year. The total traffic of rail freight grew a little (European Communities, 2009).

A reaction of the European Commission followed, mainly inspired by the concerns regarding growing road congestion and increasing lack of sustainability of the general European transport sector. Looking at Figure 10.1, we can see that the market share of rail dropped to 10.7 per cent (EU-25 performance by mode measured in tonnes-km). Intermodal traffic accounts for 5 per cent of all freight traffic carried by land modes (measured in tonnes-km). Two-thirds of the traffic is international. The development of intermodal traffic has also been a major European policy goal for a number of years (Debrie and Gouvernal, 2006; European Communities, 2009).

The European Commission chose to liberalize the European railway market. Competition was the answer to the bad condition of the rail transport sector. Economists such as Baumol (1977) suggested in economic theories (e.g. the theory of contestability) that the threat of new entrants was sufficient to ensure competition. However, opening up the industry to more competition has been difficult due to the integrated nature of the sector (Debrie and Gouvernal, 2006).

The process of liberalization took decades. It all started in 1957 when the Treaty of Rome founded the European Economic Community. However, the first big step was splitting up the incumbents in 1991. Separated companies arose to control the network and to perform operational activities. Infrastructure managers needed separate budgets and accounts. Different models were implicated, but transparency is a necessity. The second step was to hand out licences to newcomers. New companies, when complying with European and national rules, can obtain a licence to operate rail freight activities. In 2003 and 2006, the market for international European rail freight traffic was liberalized; the national market was liberalized in 2007. International passenger transport opened for competition in January 2010. For national passenger transport, agreement is yet to be reached (Corthouts, 2007; Maes et al., 2008).

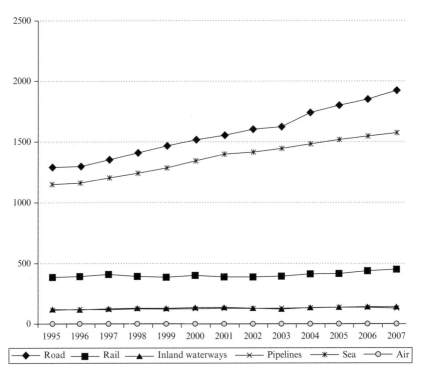

Source: European Communities (2009).

Figure 10.1   Freight traffic EU-25 per mode (in billions tonnes-km)

The actors occupying key positions in rail freight movements are dispersed. In fewer than 20 years, the total sector organization changed. The first level is now the rail track provider. In each national member state, the track provider is a separate company. The degree of separation differs. The second level comprises the railway companies providing traction. However, as indicated above, the principle criterion is the provision of traction. In 2009 large state-owned companies still dominated the market. Some private companies increased their market share rapidly. The third level, according to Debrie and Gouvernal (2006), is the intermodal transport operators. This brings together many different types of actors, many with the status of forwarding agents. These buy traction services from the railway companies (Debrie and Gouvernal, 2006). To start up a new service, several parties need to work together closely.

In order to improve their financial performance, most European incumbents have been undergoing major reorganizations over the past 20 years. Often reorganizations bring reductions or disappearance of railway services. At the same time society is largely looking at railway transport as a solution for increasing fossil-fuel consumption and climate change (Dablanc, 2009a).

Dablanc (2009b) highlights these contradictory influences concerning regional and short-distance rail freight links. One the one hand, this segment of the market is under pressure due to the relatively high costs and low margins. In contrast, these links are seen, certainly by local governments, as a necessary solution to shift freight traffic to rail. To understand this matter, a brief link towards the US context has to be made. Dablanc (2009a) compared the European, US and Canadian meaning of 'shortlines'. Shortlines in a North American context are, according to the US surface transport board, seen as Class III railway companies, with operating revenue of less than US$28 million, operating independently to provide freight traffic to a major railway company (Class I). In a European context, shortlines are mostly new private railway companies competing with the incumbents on specific, high-margin parts of the market. There is no integration. Only the German incumbent DB Schenker, with a long history of regional rail operators, has a dozen local companies providing traffic to the major carrier. Posner (2009) recently argued that the main feature of the French railway freight situation is a lack of local rail entrepreneurship. Since deregulation, eight operators have obtained French licences and safety certificates. As they bid for traffic, they hardly cooperate or innovate. On the other hand, newcomers on the French market (mainly European incumbents) compete heavily with the incumbent SNCF, and have gained a 10 per cent share of the market (figure for 2008). The decreasing relative competitiveness of road transport, mainly due to road congestion and increasing fuel prices, means that many traditional trucking markets are becoming rail sensitive (Dablanc, 2009b; Betke, 2006).

A NEW SMART SUPPLY CHAIN CONCEPT INVOLVING RAIL

Deketele et al. (2008) describe the use of intermodal transport in the context of a new smart supply chain. This concept is built on the rational use of competing transport modes. This chapter takes the view of the European framework of co-modality, that is the efficient use of different modes on their own and in combination, which results in an

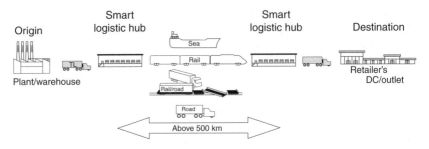

Source: Deketele et al. (2008).

*Figure 10.2   Future state of an FMCG company supply chain: including
           smart logistic hubs and spokes*

optimal and sustainable utilization of resources (European Commission, 2006).

The specific advantage of each individual mode is evaluated. A network of smart logistic hubs should be based on geographical factors such as existing transport infrastructures and future opportunities, but also on economic factors such as trade flow analysis of prospected major users of these hubs (see Figure 10.2). Per hub, at least two means of transport are available to reach other hubs. This enables a company to anticipate crisis situations or reliability issues in transport lanes. These hubs should ideally be operated by one or a few (FMCG) companies and/or retailers with sufficiently large volumes or more probably by an independent logistics provider that can combine flows. When flows are consolidated, the economic viability of non-road transportation increases and, therefore, large constant volumes of goods can be shipped. Peak transport capacity or occasional express shipments can still be carried by truck. Additionally, when possible, short- to medium-range outbound traffic should be combined with several suppliers of a retailer distribution centre. This set-up may allow goods to be transported by rail or barge, or at least to load a full truck. Where sufficient volume is consolidated, shared truck transports could go directly to retailer outlets, bypassing the retailer DC (Deketele et al., 2008).

The key idea in the paper by Deketele et al. (2008) is bundling of transport flows via a hub-and-spoke network. Bundling flows delivers economies of scale by using low-cost transhipment points. Therefore the nodes between modes, the smart logistics hubs, are obliged to operate cost-efficiently and -effectively. These smart logistic hubs can be similar to the concept of new-generation (NG) terminals described in Kreuzberger

(1999). Kreuzberger, performing research in the field of smart logistics rail networks, looked at complex bundling concepts. The main reason to be competitive is to have qualitative terminals. Performance requirements are fulfilled when working with new-generation terminals. These are intelligent and compact, and create synergetic operations for transhipment, storage and internal transport. As such, quality-to-cost ratios go up. Similarities can be seen between the smart logistics hubs and new-generation terminals. The nodes in Deketele et al. (2008) can be seen as a smaller version of/or part of new-generation terminals. Both are cost-efficient and fast (Kreuzberger, 1999; Deketele et al., 2008; Trip and Bontekoning, 2002).

A NEW SMART SUPPLY CHAIN CONCEPT INVOLVING RAIL, AS USED BY PROCTER AND GAMBLE

As a result of this first study by Deketele et al., the concept in Figure 10.3 is used in Belgium by the FMCG company Procter and Gamble (P&G). The supply chain involving rail is as in Figure 10.3.

P&G ships batteries, chips and washing products produced in Mechelen (Belgium) partially by train to the UK. This way, 5000 truckloads a year are kept from the roads and CO_2 emissions are lowered by 350 tonnes per year (Debacker and Verbeeck, 2009).

This company first transports the freight from the production plant in Mechelen to a nearby railroad terminal in Muizen, which is only 5 km by truck. From there the transhipment to the train is made. The goods are unloaded again at the port of Zeebrugge, which is 120 km from Muizen terminal. There the goods are loaded in a vessel bound for the UK. The extra handling cost in the port is lower compared to the fees that have to be paid to use the Eurotunnel.

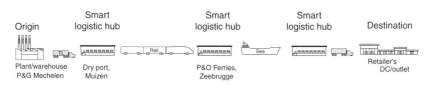

Source: Based on Deketele et al. (2008)

Figure 10.3   An FMCG company supply chain: from P&G Mechelen towards the UK

A NEW SMART SUPPLY CHAIN CONCEPT INVOLVING RAIL, AS USED BY MONOPRIX

Starting from the smart logistics hub-and-spoke concept by Deketele et al. (2008), the concept is broadened. The possibilities of integrating rail transport in the modern supply chain are described. Specifically, we look at urban transport.

The use of rail transport for a relatively short distance is possible, as stated by P&G. This chapter analyses the possibility of expanding the concept elaborated above. Monoprix, an innovative French retail group owning 300 shops with an annual turnover of €3575 million in 2007, has been using rail freight in an urban distribution context since December 2007. An innovative concept, rarely seen before in a European context, is used. Therefore the research for this chapter was mainly based on the Monoprix case. Specifically, Monoprix ships by rail to a downtown logistics centre over a very short distance (30 km). Hence road congestion now hardly influences the supply chain, in contrast to the former supply chain organization. From the Paris transhipment centre, more than 80 shops located in downtown Paris are connected. From a sustainable point of view, the last mile is done by natural-gas-powered vehicles. Furthermore, these are equipped with noise-reducing techniques. To summarize: the trains use the tracks of the public transport lines (Paris RER); 30 per cent of the total supply chain at Monoprix Paris is oriented to this concept (120 000 tonnes or 210 000 pallets per year); and the total emissions of CO_2 are lowered by 337 tonnes per year. On the other hand, only non-alcoholic beverages and heavy goods were selected. These goods take up a great deal of storage space and are heavy (Samson, 2009). The concept is shown in Figure 10.4.

This concept of the Monoprix supply chain can be linked to the framework described by Deketele et al. (2008), as some conditions are fulfilled. The new smart supply chain of Deketele et al. (2008) can be summarized by 'the use of each individual mode where most advantageous'. Monoprix

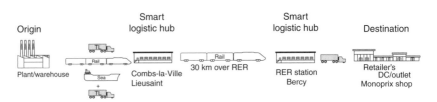

Source: Based on Deketele et al. (2008).

Figure 10.4   Concept of supply chain used by Monoprix in France

has not totally cancelled road freight, but the supply chain is focused on other modes. Trucks will be used as little as possible. Research by Monoprix took into account the geographical and economic factors. At the nodes (Combs-la-Ville/Lieusaint and Bercy) transhipment is made as fast as and at the lowest possible cost. The flows coming to Combs-la-Ville/Lieusaint also have a multimodal nature. At Lieusaint, six or seven rail wagons arrive per day (mainly bottled drinks). The rest arrives via truck. Some goods arrive in France by barge, and are then loaded on to trucks for the warehouses. From the warehouses, goods go to Paris by rail (30 per cent of the flows); the rest goes by truck. Other French shops are also supplied from the warehouses. In that case, only trucks are used.

From the node in Bercy, goods are transported by low-noise and low-emission gas-powered trucks. The supply chain is controlled by the 100 per cent subsidiary of Monoprix, Samada. Transport-related activities were outsourced to, among others, Geodis or GT location. Combining transport activities with other suppliers is not advantageous, as the flows are big enough. Monoprix, as a 50 per cent subsidiary of Casino and 50 per cent of Groupe Galleries Lafayette (two French retail groups), is working on negotiations with suppliers, but not at an operational or logistics level. The concept is proved to be efficient and also flexible. In summertime, for example, demand for non-alcoholic beverages can be very high. In that case, the rail link is used to the maximum and three or even four inner-city delivery rounds can be done by the delivery trucks (Samson, 2009).

History of the Concept

In 2004, Monoprix participated in a research project launched by several local governments and the French railway infrastructure manager (RFF). The objective of this project was to start an experiment in 2007. The research and economic analysis was done in 2004–05. In May 2006, a public tender was launched, which resulted in the selection of Fret SNCF by December 2006. A year later, the first train left the Monoprix logistics centre in Combs-la-Ville/Lieusaint. The implementation was done in three steps. In November 2007, 27 shops were included. By January 2008, eight new shops were selected. Another 20 followed in February, and 16 in April and 14 in June, which amounts to almost 90 shops now (Samson, 2009; Monoprix, 2007).

The motivation to set up a totally new concept for supplying Paris-based shops lies in the growing road congestion problems in and around Paris (see Table 10.2). When looking at French congestion data, a stabilizing trend can be seen. A combination of a slight increase in traffic, and an elimination of certain bottlenecks gave a constant number of lost hours. Although road

Table 10.2   Road congestion in France (in thousands of hour-kilometres)

	95	96	97	98	99	00	01	02	03	04	05
Paris region national network	420	396	479	533	492	557	586	607	568	593	497
Paris ring motorway	262	220	262	268	225	273	308	302	298	254	243
Total Paris region	682	616	742	802	717	830	894	909	865	848	740
National network, provinces	123	134	121	76	94	99	147	153	170	154	183
Whole of France	805	750	863	878	811	929	1,041	1,062	1,036	1,002	923
of which Paris ring motorway	33%	29%	30%	31%	28%	29%	30%	28%	29%	25%	26%
of which greater Paris region + Paris ring motorway	85%	82%	86%	91%	88%	89%	86%	86%	84%	85%	80%

Source: Union Routière de France (2006).

congestion stabilized during recent years, a continuous increase can be seen since the 1990s. Commercial vehicles drove 25 billion vehicle-kilometres in 1969. This amounted to 120 billion by 2005. The growth in total traffic comes mainly from passenger cars (going from 125 to 400 billion vehicle-kilometres in 40 years' time) (Union Routière de France, 2006).

A closer look at the Paris city centre logistics problems is necessary. According to a study by Cuenca (2008), a total of 32 million tonnes of freight is transported within the Paris inner city region. Trucks are dominant with 28.5 million tonnes; 2.5 million tonnes are transported by barge. The rest, only 1 million tonnes (less than 4 per cent) is transported by rail. The freight vehicles within Paris represent only between 9 and 15 per cent of the total traffic. In contrast, the occupation or road-lane capacity by freight vehicles accounts for 25 per cent. In the historical centre, occupation of road lanes reaches as much as 62 per cent. Longer stops and double parking problems create bottlenecks on the road network. As a result, the number of accidents involving a freight vehicle increased by 25 per cent, and even by 50 per cent for heavy freight traffic. City logistics in France accounts for 40 per cent of the total French greenhouse-gas emissions from transport operations. A last negative influence of increasing freight traffic is an increase in noise emissions. As people living in the city centre are also (potential) customers for retailers, this issue gets increasing attention (Cuenca, 2008; Peignard, 2007a).

City logistics is a case of conflicts of interests. Inhabitants have other needs than commuters and inner-city-located companies or offices. Inhabitants are at one moment willing to buy commodities but tend to forget when standing in a traffic jam that shops need to be supplied in order to make that possible. The inner-city supply chain influences five different variables. These are of an environmental, functional, economic, urban and social nature. Local governments are responsible for limitations concerning noise pollution and emissions. City centres need to be dynamic with respect for open spaces and need to cope with a new retail and logistics environment. Three different kinds of actor need to cooperate to make a city a liveable environment: the transport company, the shipper and the local inhabitants. The circle starts at the consumer. Consumers these days, especially in vibrant international cities, have a different way of consuming. Thus smaller within-city shops are becoming more popular. On the other hand, e-commerce is the source of new logistics problems, as the number of trucks and small vans entering city centres increases drastically (Peignard, 2007a).

As legislation concerning urban logistics is not present or not adapted to the current situation, the mayor of Paris took the initiative to set up a charter to reduce urban logistics problems. The process took several years to complete. France has an innovative strategy concerning urban logistics. In 1993, 'Le programme national Marchandises en Ville' was created by ADEME (the French Environment and Energy Management Agency), EDF, GART and Prédit. This group is facilitating research in urban distribution and is operating as a knowledge base. The programme was also the basis of several innovative experiments. In 2005, 'L'Association Centre Ville en Mouvement' was created by different partners, from local and federal governments to researchers (Ministère de l'Écologie, de l'Energie, du Développement durable et de la Mer, 2007). The most practical result, as introduced above, was the 'charte de bonnes pratiques des transports et livraison de merchandise dans Paris'. It was signed on 28 June by the mayor of Paris and 46 professional partners and institutions, and set official targets. By complying with the rules stipulated in the contract, the logistics companies involved are allowed to use specially designed unloading areas in Paris city centre. The charter treats the incoming and outgoing flows as well as the waste and reverse logistics. Legislation regarding urban logistics was simplified. Low-emission vehicles can stay longer in the city centre and can enjoy wider time windows. Vehicles equipped with electricity, gas, hybrid or engines, and complying with the latest Euro[1] legislation, can deliver 24 hours per day (Peignard, 2007a).

Some other targets were also set. The French president Sarkozy fixed some ambitious policy goals. By 2012, a 25 per cent increase from non-road modes is expected. The 2004 Paris climate plan also wants to limit greenhouse-gas emissions in the Paris region by 25 per cent by 2020. The region Île-de-France in Paris, with more than 11 million inhabitants, supports these strategies (Monoprix, 2007).

The French Railway Market

A short description of the French railway market is necessary to understand the current situation. The French railway infrastructure is managed by the RFF (Réseau Ferré de France). SNCF, the incumbent, was formed as a separated body. SNCF is mainly a passenger and freight rail operator. SNCF Fret is the division for freight traffic. TGV, Thalys, Eurostar, TER, Transilien and other brands are used for (high-speed) passenger transport. Other participations in transport-related sectors are held. As RFF does not have the skilled personnel or experience to maintain the national rail network, the majority of tasks are outsourced to SNCF. As such, questions arise about the non-discriminatory nature of RFF. Complaints concerning this issue usually come from the new entrants competing with SNCF on the rail freight market. Aside from SNCF, eight other companies have a French licence: Veolia Cargo, Rail4Chem, Euro Cargo Rail, B-Cargo, CFL Cargo, Colas Rail, Europorte 2 and VFLI (a 100 per cent private subsidiary of SNCF Group). Fret SNCF is following the integration example of German competitor DB Schenker. SNCF is investing in rail operations as well as in logistics side activities. Beginning in September 2009, SCNF acquired the non-French activities of Veolia Cargo. The French activities were bought by Europorte 2, being groupe Eurotunnel. The year 2009 saw a loss of almost €1 billion (Dablanc, 2009a; Massy-Beresford, 2009).

The Supply Chain in Detail

As briefly discussed above, Monoprix uses a rail link in the modern supply chain. The first train was loaded on 28 November 2007. The warehouse, located in Combs-la-Ville/Lieusaint, 40 km out of Paris's city centre, is supplied by truck and rail. In this logistics centre, pallets are prepared for the shops located in downtown Paris between 6 a.m. and 4 p.m. The rail track siding the warehouse allows direct transhipment to the rail wagons. These are charged between 1 p.m. and 6.30 p.m. The train leaves every weekday at 8 p.m., and arrives one hour later at the city-located warehouse (Bercy). The transhipment is made to gas-powered trucks. The next day, the trucks deliver to 90 Paris-located shops in a minimum of two roundtrips. Less is supplied at the weekend. As the total volume is not big enough, this is still done by truck.

Results

The results of Monoprix are promising. With 12 000 trucks not entering Paris city centre, 70 000 litres of fuel have been saved, which results in a decline of 340 000 tonnes of CO_2 and 25 tonnes of NO_x (validated by ADEME and supervised by consultants of Lyon Interface Transport). The most problematic issues concerning freight traffic in the Paris region, more specifically within Paris, are dealt with (Samson, 2009; Monoprix, 2007).

First, there is a reduction in vehicle-kilometres. This lowers traffic congestion problems on the road network surrounding Paris. Second, this concept lowers greenhouse-gas emissions considerably. As stated above, a significant decrease of CO_2 and NO_x emissions is a fact. Third, the last-mile issue is dealt with as the last part of the supply chain is rethought. The trucks involved in the Paris last-mile traffic are, like liquid-gas-powered engines, equipped with noise reduction measures. Automatic gearboxes were chosen. Trucks are, according to Paris's limitations, take up less than 29 m² on the ground. This limitation has a positive impact on safety issues and turning circle problems in the narrow streets of the historic centre. On the other hand, one must take into account that smaller vehicles create a need for more roundtrips to transport the same volume of goods.

The results show a clear profit for society. Noise, emissions and congestion are reduced. Looking at the Monoprix case, questions can be asked about the internal costs of the project. Is logistics profiting from these results? An interview was organized with Claude Samson, Samada logistics CEO (logistics subsidiary of Monoprix).

From a company point of view, positive implications can be recognized. In the past, when the supply chain was mainly focused on road transport, congestion had a major impact on scheduling truck rides. Time was lost, efficiency went down, costs rose. This concept, now in use for 30 per cent of the Monoprix Paris supply chain, has positive impacts on this issue. In contrast to SNCF Fret's reputation, during almost two years no train was delayed. Even in periods of rail strikes, the daily train left on time. This can be almost totally attributed to SNCF's operational organization. SNCF's subsidiary VFLI is responsible for the Monoprix train. VFLI, a 100 per cent subsidiary of SNCF, works by different private sector contracts. This resulted in a more flexible, customer-oriented and price-competitive company. As these issues were critical for Monoprix to set up a rail connection, SNCF was chosen as operator. Concerning rail freight wagons, a compromise was made. A total of 25 wagons was awarded to the Monoprix group by the SNCF group. Thus capacity problems will not arise. As a last step, very progressive for an incumbent, penalties were

Table 10.3   Comparison of 100% road supply chain and new concept involving rail

	EUR	€/pallet
SNCF traction	1 770 000	8.43
Warehouse Bercy	459 000	2.19
Total SNCF	2 229 000	10.61
Distribution city centre	1 470 000	7.00
Total RAIL	3 699 000	17.61
100 % ROAD	2 782 500	13.25

Source: Samson (2009).

written into the contract. If quality problems arise, compensation can be claimed (Samson, 2009; Peignard, 2007b; Rencontres de l'eco mobilité, 2009).

As shown in Table 10.3, when looking only at the logistics cost per pallet, the supply chain involving rail is slightly more expensive. The rail part increases the total cost from €13.25 per pallet to €17.61 per pallet. Samson (2009) indicated that Samada and Monoprix see this cost increase as a rather short-term disadvantage. Looking to the future, taking into account variables such as fuel prices and road pricing, the balance can change quite fast. Recently, the French law concerning 'éco-redevance sur les poids lourds' (road pricing for heavy-loaded trucks) was adopted. A fixed price or date was not agreed. But according to this French regulation, starting from 2011, road pricing can be implemented. France is now charging a third of all freight vehicle-kilometres; however, an increase of 30 per cent of charged vehicle kilometres is expected (Samson, 2009; Peyrache, 2008). For the time being, the rail connection can be used as a marketing tool.

Looking at the positive effects, the trial phase is now over. Monoprix uses the supply chain on a daily basis. An increase of the use of non-road modes is expected. As far as the rail connection between Combs-la-Ville/Lieusaint and Bercy is concerned, Samson (2009) even regrets having chosen the smallest part of the Bercy-located warehouse. Monoprix/Samada chose to rent 3700 m^2 of the 10 000 m^2 warehouse, which is now proving rather small. The transhipment quay can be used for the full 200 m length, as the company occupying the other part is not using rail transport (Samson, 2009; Naaman, 2009; Rencontres de l'eco mobilité, 2009).

CONCLUSION

To conclude, the concept of a smart logistics supply chain, used in the first part of this chapter, was expanded. Since the Monoprix case proves to deliver positive results, the conclusion can be drawn that the use of rail transport for city distribution purposes should be possible. Nevertheless, the context is of large importance. The current supply chains, now dominated by road transport, will have to be rethought and reorganized.

As discussed above, positive results emerging from the Monoprix test case highlight the most important variables involved in setting up a rail connection. From a society point of view, a reduction in vehicle-kilometres can limit road congestion. The road network surrounding Paris is congested, and this concept is one of the solutions. Second, by lowering greenhouse-gas emissions, the supply chain is more sustainable. Also noise is taken into account as an emission, which can increase the attractiveness of the city centres. From a logistics company point of view, these reductions in emissions and congestion can influence the supply chain. Planning deliveries becomes easier and more efficient. As diesel prices are likely to increase, the cost of transport per pallet will go up if road transport is not reduced. The current cost–benefit balance for Monoprix is negative, expressed in euros. But the increasing supply chain efficiency should be taken into account. Keeping in mind a possible road charging scheme in France (and Europe), increasing limitations to urban logistics, increasing fuel prices, ever-increasing road congestion, and Europe's policy on co-modality, the concept could be profitable in the near future. Monoprix in this case is counting on the first-mover advantage. By becoming competitive, knowledge is created and set-up problems are resolved.

In Europe, rail transport is rarely used in supply chains nowadays. The mode share of rail transport in Europe has declined in recent decades to less than 15 per cent. The authors think that the results of this project, highlighting best practices, can change the thinking pattern of supply chain executives. In a European context, rail transport can be a solution to current road transport problems. In theory, this is proved. However, awareness of practical and organizational problems in the railway sector exists.

Further research is possible. As highlighted shortly, Procter and Gamble is using rail transport as a part of the supply chain. A reasonable amount of emissions has been reduced. Further research could look at the broader context of shipping goods by rail. A link between the Procter and Gamble supply chain, using rail, and the Monoprix warehouses (connected to the rail network) can be made. As such, the increase in road congestion can be limited and sustainability of the total supply chain can be increased. It would also be worthwhile quantifying this first introduction of rail freight in an urban logistics context.

Finally, a comparison of American or Canadian shortlines and European short-distance rail transport can be made. Best practices of cooperation between shortlines and long-distance operators are likely to be an example for European market organization problems.

NOTE

1. Euro (European emission standards) define the acceptable limits for exhaust emissions of new vehicles sold in EU member states.

REFERENCES

Baumol, W. (1977), 'On the proper cost tests for natural monopoly in a multi-product industry', *American Economic Review*, **67** (5), 809–22.

Betke, G. (2006), 'Let's be in it for the "short-haul" too', *Railway Age*, October, p. 44.

Corthouts, J. (2007), 'NMBS behoudt monopolie op binnenlands spoorverkeer', *De Morgen*, 19 January.

Cuenca, L.-R. 'Le problème du dernier kilomètre à Paris intra-muros. Introduction du paramètre environnemental dans la réservation d'aires de livraison', Escola Tècnica Superior, d'Enginyers de Camins, Canals I Ports de Barcelona, Universitat Politècnica de Catalunya.

Dablanc, L. (2009a), *Quel fret ferroviaire local? Réalités françaises, éclairages allemands*, Paris: La documentation française.

Dablanc, L. (2009b), 'Regional policy issues for rail freight services', *Transport Policy*, **16**, 163–72.

Debacker, I. and M. Verbeeck (2009), 'Gebruik spoorlijn Muizen-Zeebrugge vermindert verkeersdrukte met 5000 vrachtwagens en doet CO_2-uitstoot met 350 ton dalen', Press Release B-Cargo Group, online at http://www.bcargogroup. be/nl/News/P-G2.html.

Debrie, J. and E. Gouvernal (2006), 'Intermodal rail in Western Europe: actors and services in a new regulatory environment', *Growth and Change*, **37** (3), 444–59.

Deketele, L., P. Coelho M. Grosso and A.-R. Lynce (2008), 'Moving from 80% road to 80% non road – implementing modal shift in a fast moving consumer goods supply chain', TransportNET project.

European Commission (2001), White paper, *European transport policy for 2010: time to decide*, COM(2001) 370 final, Brussels.

European Commission (2006), Communication from the Commission to the council and the European Parliament, *Keep Europe moving – Sustainable mobility for our continent*, Mid-term review of the European Commission's 2001 Transport White Paper (SEC (2006) 768).

European Communities (2009), 'EU energy and transport in figures', *Statistical Pocketbook*, Brussels.

Kreuzberger, E. (1999), 'Promising innovative intermodal networks with new-generation terminals', TERMINET D7, OTB, Delft.

Lewis, I., J. Semeijn and D. Vellenga (2002), 'Issues and initiatives surrounding rail freight transportation in Europe', *Transportation Journal*, **41** (3), 23–31.

Maes, J., T. Vanelslander and T. Notteboom (2008), 'De liberalisering van de goederenvervoermarkt per spoor: De Belgische stand van zaken', Master's thesis, Faculty of Applied Economics, University of Antwerp, June.

Massy-Beresford, H. (2009), 'SNCF, Eurotunnel buy Veolia's rail cargo business', Reuters, online at http://www.reuters.com/article/rbssIndustryMaterialsUtilitiesNews/idUSB11338420090902.

Ministère de l'Écologie, de l'Energie, du Développement durable et de la Mer (2007), 'Zoom sur les marchandises en ville', online at http://www.transports.equipement.gouv.fr/article.php3?id_article=8073.

Monoprix (2007), 'Notre rapport d'activités pour un développement durable 2007', online at http://www.monoprix.fr/Includes/Pdfs/Monoprix_RDD_2007.pdf.

Naaman, R. (2009), 'Monoprix plébiscite le fret', online at http://lachaineverte.fr.msn.com/dossiers/transport/article.aspx?cp-documentid=14405733.

Peignard, K. (2007a), 'Acteurs de la logistique et du transport, CCI Du Loiret', online at http://logistique.loiret.cci.fr.

Peignard, K. (2007b), 'Ca gaze entre Monoprix et la SNCF, CCI Du Loiret', online at http://logistique.loiret.cci.fr.

Peyrache, C. (2008), '"L'éco-relevance" sur les poids lourds adoptée', *Le Figaro*, 16 October.

Posner, H. (2009), 'Le potential pour des short lines en France, une question de transposition', presentation at the conference Fret Ferrovière Local, Inrets, Paris, 11 March.

Rencontres de l'eco mobilité (2009), 'Actes de rencontres de l'éco-mobilité 2009 – Transports et Logistique, SciencesPo, SNCF, 4 February, Assemblée Nationale, Paris.

Samson, C. (2009), Interview with Claude Samson by Jochen Maes and Thierry Vanelslander, CEO Samada, 25 August, 4 Rue du Courson, 94320 Thiais.

Trip, J.-J. and Y. Bontekoning (2002), 'Integration of small freight flows in the intermodal transport system', *Journal of Transport Geography*, **10**, 221–29.

Union Routière de France (2006), 'Physical data on transport: road traffic', online at http://www.urf.asso.fr/index.php?id=1039#physical data.

11. Evaluation of urban goods distribution initiatives: an empirical overview in the Portuguese context

Sandra Melo

INTRODUCTION

The topic of urban goods distribution (UGD), as well as the closely related subject of freight traffic, has been underestimated by researchers and planners. It has been treated as a marginal issue of passenger traffic and usually studied in an inappropriate geographical scale, not taking into account the specificities of freight.

Throughout the last decade, increasing concern with key concepts such as mobility and sustainability has, however, contributed to an increase in research on UGD. Research is now taking its first steps concerning this issue and, as has happened in the past with other recent themes, the first tendency has been to look at solutions adopted by other well-known perspectives (like that of the passenger) and apply them to the new specific context (that of freight).

This chapter, which results from more extensive research into the topic of UGD, tries to steer clear of that tendency, applying a tailor-made methodology to the study of this subject. The next section presents mobility and sustainability criteria as the two main pillars to validate alternative solutions to UGD as 'good practices'. To put those evaluation criteria into practice, a set of indicators is adopted, developed and validated for the particular study of UGD (Melo, 2010). The set reflects the stakeholders' main interests in urban freight (public and private objectives) as briefly described in the section. I then present the case study that was carried out in Porto, which explicitly shows how to consider mobility and sustainability criteria on the evaluation of alternative practices in UGD, highlighting the impacts on the main stakeholders and the respective geographical effect of the initiatives. The methodology adopted for the case study evaluates 'good practices' through the use of modelling tools, from both passenger and freight perspectives, considering the specificities of the topic and the local intrinsic characteristics of implementation. The base conditions of the area are presented in a further section, and support the simulation of scenarios described in the following section. The simulation exercise is carried out through a systemic model specifically developed to the city of Porto and using the microscopic traffic simulator AIMSUN. This software calculates each of the output indicators adopted to measure mobility and sustainability under public and private objectives. The quantification of three scenarios is then presented and compared with a *laissez-faire* scenario. Finally, conclusions on the empirical evaluation are presented. This analysis allows us to assert in advance whether the initiative can be considered good practice in terms of mobility and sustainability to supply the study area and consequently whether it could or should be implemented.

'SUSTAINABILITY' AND 'MOBILITY' CRITERIA IN RELATION TO STAKEHOLDER INTERESTS

Each city is unique and its development is affected by numerous decisions made by people and enterprises within it. Thus there is no single model or reference of cities; each has a distinctive culture, shape and organization, which defy generalization (Melo, 2010). Despite the intrinsic discrepancies, cities also exhibit a certain number of common problems and worries, and share a great number of common expectations (Mega, 1996). One of these expectations is that cities want to attract more people and capital and, at the same time, achieve a sustainable development. To achieve this expectation, some targets are established to maintain an internal balance between economic activity, population growth, infrastructure and services, pollution, waste, noise and so on in such a way that the urban system and its dynamics evolve in harmony, internally limiting (as much as possible) impacts on the natural environment (Barredo and Demicheli, 2003). In this sense, 'sustainability' and 'mobility' have become the guiding vision for many cities and, consequently, for its users.

The literature review on 'sustainability' and 'mobility' reveals a recent common use of the concept relating to freight as a policy target. To overcome the usual vagueness of the implementation of both concepts and to make them operational and measurable, a set of indicators is defined for the study. The set of indicators may serve as a framework for the assessment of the performance of goods distribution initiatives and for the analysis and comparisons of policy scenarios/strategies to mitigate negative impacts that result from delivery activities.

Indicators reflect society's values and goals, and are key tools to measure the performance of a system, the evolution of a process or to evaluate the results of a particular action within a complex system. Thus indicators are a useful tool for policy-making and for assessing policy implementation (Mega and Pedersen, 1998). The set was developed considering stakeholders interests as follows.

Regarding the organization of the goods distribution system, sustainability and mobility may have a different meaning and content for each group of stakeholders, which may depend on their short- and long-term objectives and preferences. The main group of stakeholders to be considered in UGD includes suppliers, residents/users (community), receivers/ shopkeepers and (local) administrators, all with different and complex transportation and consumption needs.

A common distinction made through the analysis of stakeholders' positions is based on their public or private objectives. Public objectives are often related to the well-being of all stakeholders in a specific area, such as quality of life (accidents, noise, emissions, nuisance etc.), economic vitality and mobility. Public interests reflect administrators, companies, residents and users' (visitors', tourists', employees') concerns about promoting the public good. Private objectives are often related to turnover levels, such as sales levels, customer levels, cost levels, service levels and competition. Private interests reflect suppliers and transport industry's worries about improving the efficiency and profits of their service.

The best way to get the support of both public and private stakeholders is to (a) understand and care for their needs and concerns, and (b) get them involved throughout the whole process: problem analysis, objectives definition, and selection of solution, implementation and evaluation (STRATEC, 2005). To achieve this, it is essential to make their different positions and expectations transparent. If all the interested parties can predict the (public and private) effects of a specific initiative, the negotiation process is more transparent and can lead to an integrated strategy, which will in principle lead to better results. In this way, the quantification of the impacts of promoting mobility and sustainability through the use of tailor-made indicators and of microscopic traffic simulation exercises (like the one described in the following section) are useful tools to support negotiation between public and private stakeholders and to promote more friendly and, simultaneously, operationally effective UGD practices.

Based on a review of literature and on results from participation in meetings, discussions devoted to this topic and empirical evidence and once-proposed indicators have gone through an initial round of scrutiny, it was considered that the following set of selected indicators was valid to be used on the case study on the evaluation of initiatives on UGD:

- Delivery times
- Supplier operational costs
- Deliveries/day
- Energy intensity (fuel consumption in litres by vehicle type)
- Emissions g per area or km by vehicle type (e.g. NO_x, VOC_s, PM)
- CO_2 emissions (g per area or km)
- Average speed (excluding stops to make deliveries – km/hour)
- Average vehicle journey time on the area
- Travel time (sec./km)
- Delay time (sec./km)
- Distance travelled by HGV, LGV, car, bus and taxi (vehicle-km)
- Use of load capacity
- Proportion of goods vehicles in total traffic
- Density (vehicle/km)

The input indicators are mainly used to describe the distribution patterns of the area and to select plausible initiatives to be evaluated; the output indicators were obtained through microsimulation exercises.

CASE STUDY

Overview of the Area

The chosen area for the study was Marquês, located in Porto (Portugal). Figure 11.1 shows the Marquês area and its respective streets and landscape. At its core is the important Marquês square, surrounded by streets with high traffic pressure caused by freight vehicles (on parking and delivering operations – dark grey stretches).

Marquês is mostly a residential area with traditional commercial stores, which has faced since the dawn of the decade the phenomenon of an ageing population. During recent years, a new dynamism came about due to an increase of the younger population (mainly from Brazilian and Eastern European immigrant communities), which has led to a new vitality and diversity for the commercial activities located in the area. The pattern of location of commercial activities together with the respective distribution profile determine the characteristics of the input variables to be used in the model and the potential solutions to be considered in the simulation of scenarios. The Marquês area is currently one of the areas in the city characterized by higher density of commercial activities, with a small diversity of commercial branches. Figure 11.2 illustrates the pattern of location of activities in the area.

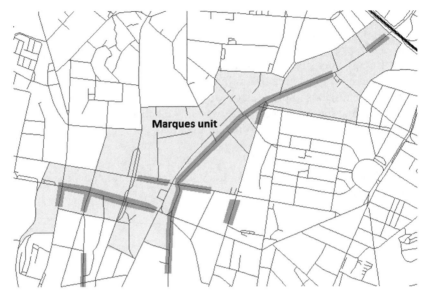

Source: Melo (2010).

Figure 11.1   The case study area

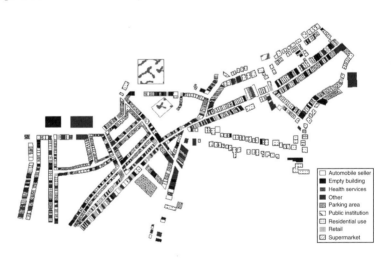

Source: Melo (2010).

Figure 11.2   Distribution of commercial activities in the area

The dominance of residential use in a close interaction with commercial use is obvious. The average height of buildings in the area is three floors, of which the ground floor is reserved for commercial activities and the others for residential use. From the commercial activities represented in Figure 11.2, there is a clear dominance of fashion, followed by food-related stores. This physical dominance in terms of land use is not proportionally related to the share of deliveries to the area nor to the impacts caused by their respective distribution flows. There are indeed commercial activities that due to their specific and intrinsic demand needs, cause higher impacts than others. To better characterize the demand needs of the Marquês area, the next subsection describes the respective goods distribution patterns.

Goods Distribution Pattern

The distribution profile of the area was obtained through a local survey. The data collection of the survey included the following indicators: traffic count by direction and type of vehicle (bicycle, motorbike, car, van, coach, bus and truck), parking time/delivery, frequency of deliveries according to the branch of activity, type of freight vehicle (truck, lorries, vans, car), traffic freight flows, use of capacity of the vehicle (full, 50 percent, less than 50 percent) and the share of cars and vans in freight traffic.

A total of 121 commercial stores with an average of 14 deliveries/day, mainly belonging to the food and fashion sectors, was included in the survey. Altogether, 44 percent of the stores located there refer to the fashion sector (shoes, clothes and other accessories) and 16 percent are restaurants and coffee shops.

The survey revealed that the average parking time in the area is 10 minutes per delivery, with the fashion sector having the lowest average parking time (4 minutes per delivery) and the largest one registered by the food sector (27 minutes per delivery). The food sector also registers the highest share of deliveries to the area (64 percent). Goods vehicles account for 12 percent of all movements between 7:30 and 19:30 in the area, split by 3 percent of HGV and 9 percent of LGV.

The division between the three categories of freight vehicle is constituted by light vans (71 percent), trucks (23 percent) and cars, with a share of less than 1 percent of in freight traffic. About 75 percent of these freight vehicles that supply the area have a load factor of less than 50 percent. Other data were collected, such as which store received the goods, the exact place where the supplier stopped the vehicle and the parking solution adopted (bus lane, ramps, double lane, pavement). This information was used to characterize in detail the area's delivery patterns.

The demanding distribution profile of the area, together with the wide-spread transgressions of traffic rules by freight vehicles, lead to major impacts in the Marquês area. Furthermore, the existence of buildings of high architectural quality prevents physical changes in the infrastructure layout that could potentially reduce the impact of UGD activities. Therefore, and bearing in mind the strong restrictions on altering the infrastructure layout, UGD initiatives related to traffic management in the specific context of the study area were selected as potential better delivery practices with regard to mobility and sustainability. The following section examines three selected practices.

SIMULATION OF SCENARIOS

In recent years, several initiatives have been proposed to achieve sustainable targets, and some have even been seen as 'good practices', according to their theoretical or practical results at the economic, environmental or social levels (sustainability dimensions). Stemming from these good practices, and considering the distribution profile of the area as well as its land use, three initiatives were selected for evaluation: cooperative systems; collaborative systems; and enforcement. The evaluation was conducted through the simulation of the impacts of each of the initiatives implemented separately, as the characteristics of the area and respective supply pattern do not require a complex solution involving the harmonization of two or more initiatives. This quantification was obtained with AIMSUN software incorporating the input indicators listed above and calculating the output indicators in the case study area. The impacts of the three initiatives were then compared in order to choose the one that might produce more benefits for the study area.

Besides providing a better understanding of the Portuguese reality regarding UGD, this chapter aims to contribute to the use of microscopic traffic simulation to support UGD management decisions.

It was established that the objective of the microsimulation exercise was to evaluate the micro-behaviour of stakeholders, and also the changes produced at different spatial scales. Thus the impact was analysed at three geographical levels: the overall system (inside the VCI – Via de Cintura Interna, the inner Porto highway); the unit of study illustrated in Figure 11.1 (the Marquês area); and the street level (where the initiative was to be implemented). Such analysis reflects the behaviour at different spatial scales and allows one to have a broader view on the geographical coverage of each initiative. To complement this perspective, effects were also analysed at a disaggregated level by stakeholder interest group. A

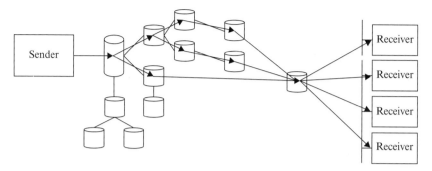

Figure 11.3   Cooperative delivery system scheme

major categorization was made at the micro-behaviour analysis stage, distinguishing between public and private objectives. To incorporate both categories in the microsimulation exercise, stakeholders are assigned to their main objective. Stakeholders whose main objective is public include (motorized) citizens and city users, public transport (city buses, intercity buses and taxis, and the whole of the motorized society). Suppliers by LGVs and by HGVs reflect stakeholders whose main objective is private.

Throughout the simulation process, priority is first given to the evaluation of the initiative bearing in mind the main criteria of the public objective. If the initiative reveals itself to be good practice for that purpose and respective set of indicators, a more detailed analysis follows to confirm that it also fulfils the private objective criterion (see below). Such an approach attempts to make the different stakeholders' interests more transparent, thus optimizing the decision-making process.

Scenario 1: Cooperative Distribution Systems

The street's physical limitations to sustain delivery operations, as well as the fact that 75 percent of the freight vehicles supplying the area have a load factor of less than 50 percent, lead to the consideration of cooperative delivery systems. These are systems in which loads are consolidated and a reduced number of trucks is used for collecting or delivering the same amount of goods (Taniguchi and van der Heijden, 2000). See Figure 11.3.

Scenario 1 represents a prediction of the effects of cooperative distribution systems. It assumes that freight vehicles that supply the area aggregate the deliveries with an arrival time difference no greater than 30 minutes. Such a condition implies that about 30 percent of direct supply trips would be reduced, but each delivery and respective parking times on the street would take longer.

Such systems are reproduced on AIMSUN, acting on the traffic incidents feature. In a first phase, following the delivery pattern observed during the survey on which the modeling exercise was based, all the incidents are shown: the lane (or lanes) where it occurred, the 'position' (distance from the beginning of the section) and the 'length' of the incident (distance from the beginning of the incident until the end) are simulated on the network. In a second phase, to simulate the effects of cooperative distribution systems and given that the majority of suppliers park illegally, incidents that would start within a 30-minute period to supply that branch were aggregated. Such a condition implies that a new incident v will be created to replace the respective aggregated incidents n. The incident v will occur at a random position between those at which the respective n incidents were occurring. The extent of the incident v corresponds to the sum of duration of the respective n incidents (sum of the n delivery parking times, as suppliers park illegally in double lanes). The length of the incident v is the average space occupied by the sample of incidents n (depending of the type of vehicle used).

The simulation exercise assumed that the initiative would be in force 7 hours per day, 5 days per week, covering the daily peak of deliveries in the area (7:00–14:00). The initiative applies to all light and heavy goods vehicles supplying the unit. The flow unit relates to vehicles, not to passengers or cargo. The delivery patterns applied in the exercise are those gathered by the survey. The parking time of trips delivering aggregate loads is the sum of parking times if such loads had been delivered separately. The consolidation of loads is carried out in a micro-platform located outside the unit. Finally, the outputs of the simulation exercise refer to the hourly average of the period in question.

The results reveal that within the overall system (city coverage), the effects of the implementation of cooperative systems in the area are negative. Such impacts seem to derive from the additional flows generated by the need to consolidate; yet there is no clear evidence to support this statement.

The results by stakeholder group within the overall system reveal that the initiative is negative for both private and public stakeholders. The range of total effects is low (−7–7 percent), with total delays increasing 7 percent. The general increase of delays and travel times (5 percent), together with a decrease of the average speed (<1 percent), indicates worse mobility in the overall system. Vehicles in the system travel a lower distance (−6 percent) due to congestion and therefore consume less fuel (−4 percent). CO_2 emissions vary with the amount of fossil fuel use and its mix, which leads to lower values (−4 percent). CO, which is a result of incomplete combustion in traffic engines, increases due to congestion (+4 percent). NO_x also presents a general slight increase of 3 percent. Within the overall system, cooperative distribution systems are an inappropriate measure of increasing mobility and sustainability.

At a lower geographical level, namely the Marquês area, results are also negative in general, although a higher range of effects on the total (−3–14 percent) was observed. The decrease of the number of delivery trips with the implementation of cooperative distribution systems leads to an increase of delays (5 percent) and travel times (2 percent). Such an increase in congestion, followed by a slight decrease in the average speed (−2 percent), leads to a very slight increase in fuel consumption (−3 percent) and CO_2 emissions (−3 percent). Such reductions due to congestion are also visible in the increase of CO by 14 percent and NO_x by 13 percent respectively.

The negative effects felt at the unit level affect public stakeholders and suppliers by HGVs. Suppliers by LGVs have a positive, despite low, impact. Suppliers by LGVs would experience a decrease of travel times by −7 percent respectively, and delays would be reduced by −14 percent. Such an improvement in mobility would lead to an increase in speed (+4 percent). Faster suppliers and less distance travelled (−3 percent) due to cooperative distribution systems contribute to a reduction in energy consumption and in pollutants emitted (−1 percent). Despite the fact that at the unit spatial level results show some positive potential, this low range of effects on a particular group of stakeholders is not enough to consider the measure as a 'good practice' for the Marquês area.

Moreover, the implementation of cooperative systems implies a reduction in the number of vans (higher share of goods vehicles distribution) to move the same amount of goods. Thus the change of the fleet can influence the indicators' variations to suppliers by LGVs (in a modeling perspective).

Finally, at the micro (street) level, the initiative has a negative impact on most of the stakeholders, as illustrated in Figure 11.4. The reduction in the number of delivery trips with the implementation of cooperative distribution systems, leads to worse mobility and (environmental) sustainability. As the (cooperative) supplier has to make more than one delivery to the street in question, it takes more time to supply, which implies longer periods for parking and consequently a greater impediment to circulation. Such behaviour affects all stakeholders in a significant and negative way. In total, delays increase by 56 percent, travel times by 36 percent and the average speed is reduced by 10 percent. Such signs of increasing congestion are confirmed by a reduction in distance travelled and consequent reduction of fuel consumption levels and CO_2 emissions.

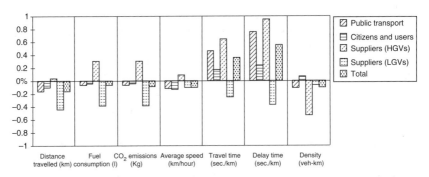

Figure 11.4   Cooperative systems at street level

The reduction in the number of vans used to move the same amount of goods implies that the fleet is different. The analysis of the variations in terms of suppliers by LGVs should take this change into account. Concerning all other stakeholders, the general tendency is an increase in travel times and delays, as well as a decrease in distance travelled due to congestion and consequent reduction of fuel consumption vehicles and CO_2 emissions.

The results illustrated in Figure 11.4 in terms of traffic analysis are counterintuitive. It would be expected that a measure forcing suppliers to consolidate in order to privilege the other road users of the city would be more beneficial to society in general. The results obtained from modeling show that it affects public transport (STCP and intercity buses) negatively, as well as citizens and users, due to longer parking times for the purpose of delivery. Furthermore, it negatively affects suppliers by HGVs due to the additional distance they have to travel and it benefits suppliers by LGVs. Suppliers by LGVs have a share of 75 percent of the freight traffic and thus the reduction of delivery trips obtained with cooperative systems is mainly achieved through their loads.

The analysis of cooperative distribution systems revealed that the initiative can be positive for suppliers by LGVs, but with clear negative effects on the other stakeholders. The estimated impacts of cooperative distribution systems have also revealed that it is not good practice at any of the spatial levels considered in this study. Moreover, the implementation of this initiative would not minimize the problems of circulation in the area, despite the reduction in the number of delivery trips. On the contrary, it would aggravate the existing problems due to longer periods of illegal parking. Furthermore, in the present study it was assumed that once the platform was in place, no additional operational costs would occur, which is an optimistic assumption.

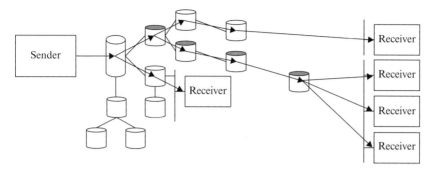

Figure 11.5   Collaborative delivery system scheme

The previous facts, combined with the fact that only a small number of carriers are (predictably) willing to take part in such a system, indicate few benefits within the overall system. Considering such effects, cooperative systems cannot be deemed a better initiative to supply the area according to mobility and sustainability criteria, and taking into account public and private objectives.

Scenario 2: Collaborative Delivery Systems

The strong dominance of the fashion sector, representing 44 percent of the stores located in the area, as well as the fact that 75 percent of the freight vehicles supplying the area have a load factor of less than 50 percent, lead to consideration of collaborative delivery systems. These are promoted by shops in the same business segment and by shops that sell products with similar physical and marketing characteristics, located within close proximity of each other (Melo and Costa, 2007). Figure 11.5 illustrates suppliers that integrate collaborative delivery systems within a typical supply chain network.

Scenario 2 represents a prediction of the effects of collaborative systems. It assumes that freight vehicles that supply the fashion sector would aggregate their deliveries with an arrival time not over 60 minutes. Such a condition would imply that about 40 percent of supply trips would be reduced. Such systems are reproduced on AIMSUN, acting on the traffic incidents feature. In a first phase, following the delivery pattern observed during the survey, which was the basis for the modeling exercise, all the incidents were shown. In a second phase, to simulate the effects of collaborative distribution systems and given that the majority of suppliers park illegally, incidents n that would start within a 60-minute period to supply that area are aggregated. Such a condition implies that a new incident v will be created to replace the respective aggregated incidents n. The incident v will occur at a random position between those at which the respective n incidents occurred. The extent of the incident v corresponds to the total of duration of the respective n incidents (sum of the n delivery parking times).

The simulation exercise assumed that the initiative would be in force 7 hours per day, 5 days per week, during the morning period (7:00–14:00). It covered the daily peak of deliveries in the area. The initiative applies to all light and heavy goods vehicles supplying the unit. The flow unit consists of vehicles, not passengers or cargo. The delivery patterns adopted in the exercise are those obtained during the survey. The consolidation of loads is carried out on a micro platform located outside the unit. Finally, outputs of the simulation exercise relate to the hourly average of the period in question.

The results of the simulation reveal that the impact of collaborative systems in the overall system is negative. Although the overall relative effects are very low (−3 percent; +3 percent), they are consistent enough to indicate a negative tendency. Increasing travel times (3 percent), delays (3 percent) and density (2 percent) show a decrease of mobility patterns caused by congestion. Such unease of movement leads to a decrease of distance travelled (−3 percent) by cars inside the study area and because they are idling during that time, lower fuel consumption (−2 percent) is registered, as well as lower CO_2 emissions (−2 percent). CO and NOx also increase by 4 percent and 3 percent, respectively due to decreasing mobility.

These low and negative effects are not homogeneous for all stakeholders. Public stakeholders and one of the private stakeholders (suppliers by LGVs) would experience a negative effect. The other private stakeholders – suppliers by HGVs – would have minor but positive results, achieving a reduction by 1 percent of delays and by 1 percent of travel times. Such a small variation, added to the fact it happens within the overall system, makes this heterogeneity irrelevant.

Within the overall system, collaborative systems are a negative measure in respect of mobility and sustainability. In the Marquês area, results are already positive, contradicting the yielding tendency observed in the overall system. The effects are still low in relative terms, yet they indicate a positive direction towards an increase of mobility and sustainability. The general effects vary between −5 and 11 percent, which is quite similar to the range of effects of scenario 1 at this level of analysis. Both public stakeholders and private stakeholders benefit from it.

The decrease of the number of delivery trips with the implementation of collaborative distribution systems leads to a decrease in delays (−5 percent) and of travel times (−4 percent). Such a decrease of congestion, followed by a slight increase of the average speed (2 percent), leads to a very slight decrease of fuel consumption (−5 percent) and CO_2 emissions (−5 percent). Such improvements in the quality of the urban environment are also visible in the decrease of CO by 3 percent and NOx by 4 percent, respectively.

The effects for suppliers by HGVs are significant for most of the indicators: delays (−16 percent), travel times (−8 percent), average speed (3 percent), fuel consumption (−5 percent), CO_2 emissions (−5 percent), CO (−2 percent) and NO_x (−6 percent).

Despite the low (but positive) dimension of the effects, their homogeneity for all groups of stakeholders indicates that collaborative systems are a potential good delivery practice for the area.

At the street level, results confirm the previous analyses, but with a higher range of impacts – from 37 percent to 10 percent. Total general delays are reduced by −18 percent and travel times by −11 percent. These two indicators, combined with higher speed (10 percent), indicate better mobility, which can be explained by the reduction in delivery trips and consequent reduction in obstacles to road circulation. The improvement of mobility leads also to an improvement in sustainability through the decrease of the energy consumed (−37 percent) and of the CO_2 emissions (−38 percent). Suppliers by HGVs are those who benefit most from collaborative delivery systems, achieving an impressive reduction of −74 percent for delays, −49 percent for travel times, −55 percent for fuel consumption and an increase of average speed by 49 percent. The analysis of collaborative delivery systems made clear that the initiative has more potential at the street and unit levels than at the level of city coverage. It is expected to be more beneficial for private stakeholders, although its implementation would also require more from them than from the other actors. Determinant requirements like the existence of a specific commercial software program to make the deliveries, a particular depot to consolidate or the acceptance of shopkeepers to be included in such a scheme make the estimated positive effects insignificant when it comes to persuading public and private stakeholders to implement collaborative systems. In relation to costs, a particular focus on platform feasibility is required. In the present study it was assumed that as the platform already existed, no additional operational costs would arise, which is not true in most cases.

Regarding the stakeholders involved, a more exhaustive analysis is necessary. Collaborative systems require an extraordinary goal alignment that can only be achieved by finding critical goals that stakeholders can agree on. An initiative of this nature has more potential benefits for some branches than for others. Therefore a special effort to satisfy expectations of the main partners is needed.

The previous facts, in combination with the insufficient number of actors that can join such a system, amounts to low benefits in the overall system. Considering such effects, scenario 2 cannot be deemed a better initiative to supply the area according to mobility and sustainability criteria and considering public and private objectives.

Scenario 3: Enforcement

In contrast to the previous scenarios, which are strongly dependent on organizational requirements, it was decided to quantify the effects of strict enforcement. Parking enforcement significantly improves traffic flow, reduces congestion and contributes to the quality of life in the community. In London, figures show that the implementation of this measure reduced illegal parking by 35 percent, from 2638 vehicles in February 2006 to 1708 in February 2007 (TfL, 2007).

Scenario 3 establishes that freight vehicles are not allowed to park illegally to make deliveries in the area. All vehicles would be forced to park legally in the nearest available and valid parking place in relation to the store to be supplied. According with the delivery pattern of the unit, such a scenario would affect 100 percent of the freight vehicles supplying the area.

The simulation exercise assumed that the initiative would be implemented effectively 7 hours per day, 5 days per week, covering the morning peak period of the bus lane and the daily peak of deliveries in the area (7:00–14:00). Suppliers are expected to park legally and behave responsibly, which implies not parking in a place that will obstruct normal road circulation. The enforcement is put into practice only with human resources, without the use of additional automated technology. Outputs of the simulation exercise refer to the morning average hour.

The analysis of results by area of impacts reveals that strict enforcement applied in the area would not have a significant impact on the overall system.

The range of effects within the overall system would be low (−11–3 percent), as was also observed in the previous scenarios. The effects of the enforcement in the overall system would be negative, leading to a decrease in mobility and sustainability. The general effects in terms of density, travel times, delay times and average speed would be lower than 3 percent. The remaining indicators would be slightly higher in absolute terms, but still not significant.

An analysis of results by stakeholders group reveals that at the city level, enforcement would be slightly negative for public stakeholders (public transport, citizens and users), but positive for private stakeholders, which is quite a surprising result. It can be explained by the positive effects that suppliers of the total system feel from a system with less congestion, although the variation is too low to be easily explained by a direct cause–effect relationship.

At the unit level, in the Marquês area, the results are less positive when it comes to improving mobility. The range of effects is lower than at street level, varying between (−2 and 8 percent) (not including the CO and NO_x variation). The decrease of delays (−2 percent) and travel times (−1 percent) seems to indicate lower congestion in the unit. This lower congestion, combined with a higher speed average (1 percent), reveals ease of movement – one of the measures of mobility. The distance travelled in the area increases 2 percent (due to the search for legal parking places). Fuel consumption and CO_2 emissions decrease by −3 percent, suggesting an improvement of the sustainability of the unit.

At the street level, the results are even more obvious and the range of effects clearly higher (−44–19 percent) than at the previous spatial analysis. Delay times in total decrease by 44 percent, which corresponds to 29 seconds throughout the street, and travel times by 28 percent, which in turn corresponds to 31 seconds. Such impressive results, together with an increase of the average speed of 5 km/h to 36 km/h, confirm a higher mobility rate throughout the street. Also, in terms of sustainability, the results are quite positive, with average reductions of fuel consumption levels by 24 percent and of CO_2 emissions by 19 percent. Only the 'distance travelled' indicator does not follow this remarkable positive tendency. The indicator shows a slight increase of 5 percent, mainly due to the need to search for an available legal parking place. As expected, the results are significantly positive for all stakeholders. Public transport endures the lowest effects, which is explained by the fact that in one of the directions there is an exclusive bus lane, where the effects are negligible. Intercity buses circulating in the other direction experience a low effect. Citizens and users experience the effects of the enforcement in a significant way, because incidents occur in the road direction in which they circulate. Suppliers have more benefits in terms of mobility but they also have to travel more extensively (distance travelled) due to enforcement.

In terms of mobility, the positive results observed throughout the street are ascribed mainly to the opposite direction of the bus lane, where the incidents occurred before the implementation of the measure.

The reduction of delays in the opposite direction of the bus lane is of about 80 percent and corresponds to 30 seconds throughout the street, which is quite high. Furthermore, the increase of 11 km/h to 43 km/h and the decrease of travel times by 30 seconds confirm the impressive results in this direction.

Along the bus lane, the effects are more evident in terms of sustainability,

Table 11.1   Cost effects of enforcement at street level in the Unit

	Costa Cabral Street	
	Operational costs/day (%)	Environmental externalities/day (%)
Total	−21	5
Bus	−19	7
Car	−17	8
Taxi	−12	4
Truck	−37	4
Van	23	38

with a reduction of distance travelled, energy consumed and the CO_2 emissions. The effects throughout this direction are clearly minor due to the fact that the bus lane is not significantly affected by the disappearance of illegal parking; as was the other direction.

Private objective and public interests compatibility
Due to the positive results of enforcement in a first analysis at all geographical coverage levels, and according to the criteria of mobility and sustainability – the public objective – a more detailed analysis followed to confirm that it also fulfils the private objective criteria. Given the indicators used in the previous analysis and the translation of those values into economic terms, the financial/operational impacts of enforcement are encouraging.

The fixed and the variable costs were quantified by stakeholders group. The fixed costs included vehicle and parking taxes. The variable costs included operation and maintenance, amortization, travel time, delays and environmental externalities. The values (€/km) of each of these costs were gathered from the scientific literature (Small and Verhoef, 2007).

At the street level, the sum of the total operational costs with the implementation of enforcement would lead to a benefit throughout Costa Cabral Street by 21 percent (Table 11.1). Throughout this street, these relative variations correspond to an average decrease of total costs by €58/day for all road users. Suppliers by LGVs are the only group with higher operational costs due to enforcement, mostly due to the a greater distance travelled (+38 percent) in search of legal parking, as can also be confirmed by the much higher variation of environmental externalities for this group (38 percent).

The general estimated costs would be slightly lower if environmental externalities were added to the calculation.

Table 11.2 Summary of initiatives' effects towards increasing mobility and sustainability

	Public transport	Citizens and city users	Suppliers HGVs	Suppliers LGVs	Society (total)
Cooperative systems					
System	–	–	–	–	–
Unit	–	–	–	+	–
Street	–	–	–	+	–
Collaborative systems					
System	–	+	+	–	–
Unit	+	+	+	+	+
Street	+	+	+	+	+
Enforcement					
System	–	–	+	+	n.c.
Unit	+	+	+	+	+
Street	+	+	+	+	+

Note: Negative; n.c. Not conclusive; + Positive.

At the unit level, enforcement would lead to a general reduction of distance travelled, as well as of travel times and congestion. Therefore, at this level of analysis, enforcement would lead to a reduction of operational costs by 10 percent and of environmental externalities by 2 percent. At the system level, the total effects are irrelevant in terms of operational costs (less than 1 percent), and in terms of environmental externalities the predicted reduction is of −2 percent. The effects of the enforcement are significant at the micro and meso level within the city, both in geographical coverage and in terms of consistent effects for stakeholders. For the unit and street levels, it is positive and clearly easier and cheaper to implement than other measures. These effects raise some doubts about whether goods distribution in Porto really needs to have innovative good practices implemented or simply stricter enforcement.

Comparison of Results of all Policy Measures

Table 11.2 summarizes the contribution of the three initiatives towards increasing mobility and sustainability levels. Cooperative delivery systems are the least beneficial measure to supply the area, whereas the best one is enforcement.

Measures that are considered 'good practices' by the scientific community and that were simulated in this chapter in terms of the specific context of Porto were shown to have quite visible benefits at street level but not so evident at the meso and macro level. The results in the overall system are rather disappointing and the cause–effect relationship is not obvious enough to provide an explanation. The results at the street level are quite significant and easily readable and understandable.

Two of them are in fact 'good practices' at a micro-geographical level (street) and unit level, although neither has the same status at the city level. This raises the question of which stakeholders and priorities should be considered. Would it make sense to benefit stakeholders and the street level but to the disadvantage of the remaining actors of the system?

Stakeholders that collect more benefits from mobility and sustainability are the suppliers, followed in general by citizens and users. Public transport (buses and taxis) is usually affected in a less positive way according to the chosen indicators.

EMPIRICAL CONCLUSIONS AND THEORETICAL CONTRIBUTION

The evaluation of three scenarios simulated in an area with specific characteristics and commercial patterns corresponds to three initiatives, recently labelled as 'best practices' by the scientific community in diverse geographical, economical and cultural contexts. The area selected to be studied has similarities and differences between the various geographical levels of analysis (street, unit, system). The noticeable similarities are the problems all of them have in relation to UGD: (a) the layout restrictions to changing the infrastructure; (b) the lack of proper unloading facilities to accommodate delivery operations; (c) the common cultural context that justifies a flexible attitude from other road users towards suppliers; and (d) the disturbance suppliers cause to the normal road circulation. The discrepancies are mostly (a) the commercial activities pattern of location, (b) the supply patterns, directly dependent on (a), (c) the land-use pattern, (d) the infrastructure layout and (e) the low rotation of parking places, promoting illegal parking.

The results demonstrate the types of initiatives that are likely to give positive results and therefore merit further study. However, theoretical, methodological and data limitations mean that some care is required in their interpretation and dissemination. Despite these reservations, the fact that most of the results point in the same direction for each initiative, irrespective of the differences between the geographical level of analysis, is understandable and confirms the validity of the underlying theoretical considerations. Also the fact that most of the effects reveal such homogeneity validates the adequacy of those specific initiatives in areas with common problems to the ones observed on the street, unit and system in this case study.

One of the common points revealed in the case study is that the benefits of each measure are rather visible at street level and decrease at a meso and macro level (see Annex 11.1). The results at the street level are quite significant and easily readable and understandable. Those at the overall system level are rather disappointing, and the cause–effect relation is not obvious. This fact seems to indicate the context in which UGD should be considered: the local level. The implications of this are that local administrators, supported by planners and consulting the main stakeholders involved, can significantly contribute to the achievement of good practice in UGD. This does not imply that it should merely become a municipal issue. UGD measures taken at city level should be integrated as much as possible with neighbouring municipalities. The intermunicipality integration and cooperation can contribute to the creation of the needed economies of scale, determinant for the success of the implementation of some measures. Initiatives requiring the use of adequate logistics infrastructure are good examples of which feasibility can be more easily assured in a context of intermunicipal cooperation. Furthermore, collaboration between neighboring municipalities can promote the establishment of integrated strategies, like the regulation of access based on time. This integration, and in some situations homogeneity, can also contribute to a better acceptance by suppliers.

The evaluation at a disaggregated level by stakeholder interest group (Annex 11.1) revealed that stakeholders having more benefits in respect of mobility and sustainability are the suppliers, followed (in general) by citizens and users. Public transport (buses and taxis) are usually affected in a less positive way. Such a conclusion can be due to the fact that the 16 scenarios refer to initiatives that were labeled 'best practices'. This label stems from the ability to solve a specific problem on UGD, affecting suppliers or citizens (society in general). Thus public transport was probably not considered when promoting such reactive policies, and thus it is not positively affected by its implementation.

To get all actors involved (including public transport), some changes to the approach that has been followed must be made. Suppliers, and other stakeholders, have been given limited opportunity in the past to influence the drafting of mobility and sustainability strategies. Added to this is the fact that administrators haven't tried to involve them in these discussions, and the freight industry and the public transport sector do not speak with one voice. However, there is consensus on some policy issues, and some policies appear to be commonly negatively perceived by certain sectors. The challenge is to find that common level of acceptance by all stakeholders involved in the negotiation. That level will not be the best level each group would individually aspire to, but it is the one that maximizes the consideration of all the interests involved.

As regards the possible contestation that might arise, microscopic traffic simulation might be a useful tool to predict the effects of a specific initiative on all the interested parties. If the effects are estimated and the stakeholders are aware of the benefits of a specific measure, the negotiation process is more transparent and can easily lead to an integrated strategy. Therefore the simulation can lead to a better acceptance by the interested stakeholders.

Mobility and sustainability were established as the main targets to be achieved in a public-good perspective. Operational costs were established as the main target in a private interests' perspective. Regarding these different targets, some difficulties might arise in attaining a flexible attitude from such different and almost conflicting perspectives. It is recognized that suppliers will not by themselves be able to achieve adequate system-wide improvements in urban freight efficiency. In some instances there may be a lack of concern with distribution costs since these costs may be only a small proportion of total service costs. In some cases there may be reluctant agreement by the suppliers to reduce current levels of congestion, since there is no competitive advantage to any one supplier from a lower congestion level. In this context some compensation should be offered to suppliers who accept to be part of a solution promoting the public good.

The most surprising facts revealed by the case study in relation to mobility and sustainability targets seem to contradict what appear to be accepted propositions. First, initiatives that imply significant reductions of supply trips to the city do not have a relevant (or necessarily positive) effect on mobility and sustainability. This raises the question whether urban planners want to promote the reduction of the number of movements to the city or the regulation of the periods in which those movements would preferably occur. The results of the case study indicate the choice of the second option, with obvious advantages.

Second, recent initiatives labeled 'best practices' do not necessarily promote both mobility and sustainability and are simultaneously economically feasible. This raises doubt as to whether goods distribution in Porto really needs to implement the so-called innovative 'best practices' or just to implement common solutions such as strict enforcement and regulation. Moreover, these results highlight the power of the context and the fallacy of the concept of 'best practices' pointing towards 'tailor-made' solutions, which raises the question of which stakeholders and priorities should be considered.

ACKNOWLEDGEMENTS

This chapter is based on the Ph.D. thesis of Sandra Melo, developed with financial support from Fundação para a Ciência e a Tecnologia (FCT). The grant SFRH/BD/18025 provided by FCT is gratefully acknowledged by the author.

REFERENCES

Barredo, J. and L. Demicheli (2003), 'Urban sustainability in developing countries' megacities: modeling and predicting future urban growth in Lagos', *Cities*, **20**, 297–310.
Mega, V (1996), 'Our city, our future: towards sustainable development in European cities', *Environment and Urbanization*, **8**, 133–54.
Mega, V. and J. Pedersen (1998), 'Urban sustainability indicators', Report for the European Foundation for the Improvement of Living and Working Conditions.
Melo, S. (2010), 'Evaluation of urban goods distribution initiatives towards mobility and sustainability: indicators, stakeholders and assessment tools', Ph.D. thesis, Faculdade de Engenharia da Universidade do Porto, Porto, Portugal.
Melo, S. and A. Costa (2007), 'Effects of collaborative systems on urban goods distribution', Proceedings of the 11th World Conference on Transport Research (CD), Berkeley, EUA, June.
Small, K. and E. Verhoef (2007), *Economics of Urban Transport*, London: Routledge.
STRATEC (2005), CITY FREIGHT: Inter- and Intra-City Freight Distribution Networks, Project funded by the European Commission on the 5th RTD Framework Programme.
Taniguchi, E. and R. van der Heijden (2000), 'An evaluation methodology for city logistics', *Transport Reviews*, **20** (1), 65–90.
TfL (2007), *Traffic Enforcement Impact Analysis – Second Annual Report*, Transport Policing and Enforcement Directorate, Transport for London.

ANNEX 11.1 COMPARATIVE BENEFITS OF MEASURES AT DIFFERENT LEVELS (IN PERCENTAGES)

	Cooperative distribution systems – street level								
	Distance trav.	Fuel cons	CO	NOx	CO_2 emissions	Average speed	Travel time	Delay time	Density
Total motorized society	−16	−7			−8	−10	36	56	−10
Public transport	−16	−6			−6	−11	46	76	−11
Citizens and users	−10	−4			−4	−13	17	24	−7
Suppliers (HGVs)	−4	−31			−31	−9	65	94	−53
Suppliers (LGVs)	−44	−38			−38	−10	−25	−37	−6

	Cooperative distribution systems – unit level – Marquês								
	Distance trav.	Fuel cons	CO	NOx	CO_2 emissions	Average speed	Travel time	Delay time	Density
Total motorized society	0	−3	14	−13	−3	−2	2	5	−10
Public transport	−5	0	8	−10	0	−2	10	17	−32
Citizens and users	1	−4	15	−13	−4	−2	2	6	−8
Suppliers (HGVs)	−4	0	13	−19	0	0	6	13	−67
Suppliers (LGVs)	−3	−1	9	−14	−1	4	−7	−14	4

ANNEX 11.1 (continued)

	Cooperative distribution systems – overall systems								
	Dis-tance trav.	Fuel cons	CO	NO_x	CO_2 emi-ssions	Ave-rage speed	Travel time	Delay time	Den-sity
Total moto-rized society	−6	−4	4	3	−4	0	5	7	4
Public transport	−10	−10	−10	−15	−10	−4	1	2	9
Citizens and users	−6	−3	6	4	−3	−2	6	8	4
Suppliers (HGVs)	−5	−10	−3	−17	−10	−4	3	3	32
Suppliers (LGVs)	−3	0	2	2	0	−1	0	0	40

	Cooperative distribution systems – street level								
	Dis-tance trav.	Fuel cons	CO	NO_x	CO_2 emi-ssions	Ave-rage speed	Travel time	Delay time	Den-sity
Total moto-rized society	−22	−37			−38	10	−11	−18	3
Public transport	−23	−35			−35	6	−6	−9	3
Citizens and users	−32	−42			−42	4	−27	−36	3
Suppliers (HGVs)	−8	−55			−55	49	−49	−74	11
Suppliers (LGVs)	−6	−34			−34	21	−29	−44	13

ANNEX 11.1 (continued)

	Cooperative distribution systems – unit level – Marquês								
	Dis-tance trav.	Fuel cons	CO	NO$_x$	CO$_2$ emi-ssions	Ave-rage speed	Travel time	Delay time	Den-sity
Total motorized society	−5	−5	−3	−4	−5	2	−4	−5	11
Public transport	−7	−7	−2	−4	−7	1	−2	−4	26
Citizens and users	−5	−5	−3	−3	−5	2	−2	−5	11
Suppliers (HGVs)	−6	−5	−2	−6	−5	3	−8	−16	20
Suppliers (LGVs)	−9	−9	−16	−29	−9	5	−5	−11	14

	Cooperative distribution systems – overall system								
	Dis-tance trav.	Fuel cons	CO	NO$_x$	CO$_2$ emi-ssions	Ave-rage speed	Travel time	Delay time	Den-sity
Total motorized society	−3	−2	4	3	−2	−2	3	3	2
Public transport	−5	−6	−10	−15	−6	−2	0	0	−10
Citizens and users	−2	−1	6	4	−1	0	3	5	2
Suppliers (HGVs)	−6	−9	−3	−17	−9	−2	−1	−1	16
Suppliers (LGVs)	−1	−5	2	2	−5	0	1	1	13

ANNEX 11.1 (continued)

	Enforcement – street level								
	Dis-tance trav.	Fuel cons	CO	NO$_x$	CO$_2$ emi-ssions	Ave-rage speed	Travel time	Delay time	Den-sity
Total moto-rized society	5	−24			−19	19	−28	−44	0
Public transport	7	−18			−18	12	−25	−40	0
Citizens and users	8	−11			−11	17	−34	−47	0
Suppliers (HGVs)	4	−65			−65	84	−59	−87	0
Suppliers (LGVs)	38	−14			−14	45	−55	−82	0

	Enforcement – unit level – Marquês								
	Dis-tance trav.	Fuel cons	CO	NO$_x$	CO$_2$ emis-sions	Ave-rage speed	Travel time	Delay time	Den-sity
Total moto-rized society	−2	−3	−17	21	−3	1	−1	−2	4
Public transport	−3	−4	−34	25	−4	2	−3	−4	19
Citizens and users	−2	−3	−16	17	−3	1	−1	−2	4
Suppliers (HGVs)	−2	−2	−42	31	−2	1	−6	−13	0
Suppliers (LGVs)	−3	−3	−22	29	−3	2	−3	−7	7

ANNEX 11.1   (continued)

	Enforcement – overall system								
	Dis-tance trav.	Fuel cons	CO	NO$_x$	CO$_2$ emi-ssions	Ave-rage speed	Travel time	Delay time	Den-sity
Total moto-rized society	−11	−8			−8	0	2	2	3
Public transport	−13	−13			−13	−3	4	5	−4
Citizens and users	−10	−7			−7	−2	2	2	−3
Suppliers (HGVs)	−14	−11			−11	−6	0	−1	18
Suppliers (LGVs)	−10	−7			−7	0	−3	−3	7

Index